Mastering PhoneGap Mobile Application Development

Take your PhoneGap experience to the next level and create engaging real-world applications

Kerri Shotts

[PACKT] open source ✳
PUBLISHING   community experience distilled

BIRMINGHAM - MUMBAI

Mastering PhoneGap Mobile Application Development

First published: February 2016

Production reference: 1190216

Published by Packt Publishing Ltd.
Livery Place
35 Livery Street
Birmingham B3 2PB, UK.

ISBN 978-1-78328-843-4

www.packtpub.com

Credits

Author
Kerri Shotts

Reviewers
Michael Brooks
Rory Standley
Eddy Verbruggen

Commissioning Editor
Akram Hussain

Acquisition Editors
Reshma Raman
Owen Roberts

Content Development Editor
Dharmesh Parmar

Technical Editors
Chinmay S. Puranik
Jayesh Sonawane

Copy Editor
Akshata Lobo

Project Coordinator
Nidhi Joshi

Proofreader
Safis Editing

Indexer
Tejal Daruwale Soni

Production Coordinator
Arvindkumar Gupta

Cover Work
Arvindkumar Gupta

About the Author

Kerri Shotts has worked with computers for nearly 25 years. Her love for technology and programming started when she was introduced to her first computer: a Commodore 64. She obtained a degree in computer science while at college, and moved on to become a software test engineer. Afterward, she became an Oracle Database Administrator for several years. Now, she works as a technology consultant, creating, implementing, and maintaining custom applications (both desktop and mobile), websites, graphics and logos, and more for her clients. You can find her blog posts on her website (http://www.photokandy.com/) and she is active on the Google Groups for PhoneGap. When she isn't working, she enjoys photography, music, and fish keeping. She is the author of several books published by Packt Publishing.

Thanks first to my family for their incredible support, even with the late night clacking of the keyboard. Thanks also to those who have made PhoneGap and Cordova such an awesome tool and also to those who support it on the forums. Thanks especially to the technical reviewers for this book—you're all amazing! Finally, thank you to Packt Publishing and your editorial staff for making sure everything came out just right.

About the Reviewers

Rory Standley is a senior web developer from Staffordshire in the UK, who builds enterprise apps for clients by day and works on fun stuff (`http://www.rstandley.co.uk`) for the rest of us in his spare time.

Rory started working with PhoneGap way back in version 1, creating an e-commerce application on iOS and Android, and has loved watching PhoneGap grow into what it has become today.

Eddy Verbruggen is the author of many PhoneGap plugins. Over the past few years, he created popular plugins such as SocialSharing, Calendar, and Toast. What started as an open source hobby resulted in him teaming up with Telerik with the goal to increase the quality of the Cordova plugin ecosystem. These days, Eddy is the maintainer of the Telerik Verified Plugins Marketplace at `http://plugins.telerik.com`.

In the recent past, Eddy worked on several PhoneGap apps. The most ambitious one was the online banking app of a medium-sized Dutch bank. With way over a million monthly sessions on three different platforms this app proofs PhoneGap can be a serious tool for creating apps with great performance and user experience.

When Eddy is not hacking Cordova or NativeScript plugins, he is working as a cofounder of Combidesk, a Dutch start-up that aims at making connecting cloud API's so easy your mom could do it.

www.PacktPub.com

Support files, eBooks, discount offers, and more

For support files and downloads related to your book, please visit www.PacktPub.com.

Did you know that Packt offers eBook versions of every book published, with PDF and ePub files available? You can upgrade to the eBook version at www.PacktPub.com and as a print book customer, you are entitled to a discount on the eBook copy. Get in touch with us at service@packtpub.com for more details.

At www.PacktPub.com, you can also read a collection of free technical articles, sign up for a range of free newsletters and receive exclusive discounts and offers on Packt books and eBooks.

https://www2.packtpub.com/books/subscription/packtlib

Do you need instant solutions to your IT questions? PacktLib is Packt's online digital book library. Here, you can search, access, and read Packt's entire library of books.

Why subscribe?

- Fully searchable across every book published by Packt
- Copy and paste, print, and bookmark content
- On demand and accessible via a web browser

Free access for Packt account holders

If you have an account with Packt at www.PacktPub.com, you can use this to access PacktLib today and view 9 entirely free books. Simply use your login credentials for immediate access.

Table of Contents

Preface   **vii**

Chapter 1: Task Automation   **1**

  Before we begin   3
  About Logology   3
  Why use Gulp for task automation?   4
  Setting up your app's directory structure   5
  Installing Gulp   10
  Creating your first Gulp configuration file   12
  Creating a modular Gulp configuration   14
  Copying assets   17
  Performing substitutions   18
  How to execute Cordova tasks   24
  Managing version numbers   31
  Supporting ES2015   32
  Linting your code   35
  Uglifying your code   37
  Putting it all together   38
  Summary   39

Chapter 2: ECMAScript 2015 and Browserify   **41**

  Getting started   42
  Benefits of ES2015   42
    Block scope   43
    Arrow functions   44
    Simpler object definitions   47
    Default arguments   48
    Variable arguments   49
    Destructuring and named parameters   51
    String interpolation   54

Promises and a taste of ES2016	56
Classes	60
Modules	63
More information	64
Using Browserify	**65**
Including Node.js packages	68
Summary	**70**
Chapter 3: Sassy CSS	**71**
Getting started	**71**
Learning Sass	**72**
Comments	73
Calculation	73
Variables	76
Nesting	82
Mixins and functions	84
Object-oriented CSS	86
Modules and partials	87
Integrating Sass with Gulp	**88**
Including the Stylesheets installed via npm	90
Summary	**91**
Chapter 4: More Responsive Design	**93**
Getting started	**94**
Pixel densities	**94**
The CSS3 units	**97**
Media queries	**101**
Image sizing	**104**
Using flex-box layout	**111**
Summary	**118**
Chapter 5: Hybrid Application Accessibility	**119**
Getting started	**120**
Types of accessibility features	**120**
Color vision deficient	120
Low vision	121
Blindness	122
Auditory disabilities	123
Motor disabilities	123
Dyslexia	123
Seizures	124
Accessibility for free	**124**

What is WAI-ARIA?   **126**
The WAI-ARIA roles   128
Accessibility examples   **131**
Separation of presentation and content   131
Accessible icon buttons   132
Accessible navigation   133
Accessible lists   135
Accessible alerts and dialogs   136
Fitting in with native accessibility features   **138**
Installing the Mobile Accessibility Plugin   139
Detecting the user's preferred text size   140
Detecting a screen reader   140
Speaking custom text   141
Useful tools   **142**
Summary   **142**

Chapter 6: Testing and UI Automation   **143**
Getting started   **144**
An introduction to assertions   **144**
Writing tests using Chai   **146**
Language chains   151
Logical words   151
Testing existence and types   152
Testing equality   152
Testing collections   153
Running test suites using Mocha   **154**
Writing UI automation tests   **160**
Installing Appium   161
Exploring your app with Appium   163
Creating test cases   177
Running UI Automation tests using Appium and Mocha   **182**
Integrating our tests with Gulp   **184**
Summary   **186**

Chapter 7: IndexedDB   **187**
Getting started   **188**
IndexedDB support and polyfills   **188**
Differences between relational and key-object storage   **189**
Creating a database   **193**
Creating an object store within the database   **197**
Handling database upgrades   **200**
Transactions   **203**

Storing objects	**204**
Getting objects	**206**
Deleting objects	**207**
Using cursors and indexes	**208**
Closing the database	**211**
Additional resources	**211**
Summary	**212**
Chapter 8: Web SQL Database	**213**
Getting started	**214**
Web SQL Database support	**214**
The Cordova SQLite plugin	**215**
Creating and opening databases	**215**
Transactions	**219**
Creating tables	**221**
Inserting data and binding values	**227**
Querying data (single table, joins, and so on)	**231**
Deleting data	**236**
The SQLite utilities	**236**
Summary	**237**
Chapter 9: Transferring Files	**239**
Getting started	**239**
Configuring the whitelist	**240**
Downloading files from a server	**242**
Receiving files using PHP on a server	**247**
Uploading files to a server	**252**
Monitoring progress	**254**
Aborting transfers	**256**
Security concerns	**257**
Summary	**257**
Chapter 10: Performance	**259**
Getting started	**259**
Defining performance	**260**
The performance difference between desktop browsers, emulators, and physical devices	**261**
Desktop browser performance differences	261
Power availability and consumption	262
Battery life	262
Browser impacts	263
Memory	263
Storage	263
Lag	264

Emulator performance differences   266
Profiling your app   **269**
Profiling on Android   270
Profiling on iOS   271
Caveats   276
Correcting input lag   **276**
Correcting visual stutters   **279**
Reaching 60 fps   280
Correcting memory problems   **282**
Splitting up and delegating long computations   **285**
Summary   **287**

Chapter 11: Graphical Assets   **289**
Getting started   **289**
App icon requirements   **290**
Creating an app icon   **292**
Launch screen requirements   **298**
Creating a Launch Screen   **302**
Configuring your app   **304**
Useful resources   **308**
Summary   **310**

Chapter 12: Deployment   **311**
Build modes   **311**
Distribution methods   313
Signing up for developer accounts   **314**
Becoming an Apple iOS developer   315
Becoming a Google Play Store developer   327
Generating signed release builds   **333**
Managing the iOS signing identities   333
Managing iOS App IDs   335
Managing iOS devices   339
Managing the iOS provisioning profiles   340
Creating an Android keystore   343
Signing the release build   346
Deploying ad hoc releases   **348**
Deploying via e-mail   348
Deploying via URL   350
Deploying via Diawi   350
Deploying app store releases   **350**
Deploying to the Apple App Store   350
Deploying to the Google Play Store   356

Resources   **359**
Summary   **360**
Index   **361**

Preface

PhoneGap/Cordova, as a technology to create hybrid mobile apps, relies heavily upon JavaScript, HTML, and CSS in order to present your apps to your users. This is ideal in many ways, especially since you can rely upon your knowledge of web-based technologies in order to create cross-platform mobile apps. Being able to build on your existing knowledge set is a major plus when it comes to recommending Cordova, and generally, one can build their first simple app using Cordova pretty easily. But when it comes to building larger, more complex apps, it is useful to explore various technologies and tools that allow us to more efficiently develop mobile apps. The first few chapters of this book focus exactly on this need. We'll cover task runners such as Gulp, packagers such as Browserify, and a method of writing CSS that's easier to maintain using Sassy CSS.

In this book we generally refer to PhoneGap and Cordova simply as Cordova—PhoneGap itself is a distribution of Cordova and supplies additional features and utilities. If there is a specific difference we need to mention, we will do so in at the appropriate time.

One particular hallmark of large, complex apps is a requirement for a way to store complex data efficiently. There comes a point when using the Local Storage and File API become unwieldy, and so it is important to learn about other methods to store data, such as IndexedDB and Web SQL Database.

Quite often, it's also necessary for apps to transfer large amounts of data between the device and external servers. You can imagine a social photography app might need to upload images, and an e-book app would need to download files that represent books. We'll devote an entire chapter to this topic as well.

Of course, most developers want to get their apps out into the devices of as many users as possible. This is why creating accessible applications is important. Not every user has perfect vision. Some users may have trouble reading small text or text with low contrast. Other users may have problems discerning various color shades. And other users may not be able to hear your app's sounds very well. With assistive technologies on many mobile platforms, it is a very good idea to build our apps so that as many users as possible can use them effectively.

Deployment, ultimately, is our goal, and so the latter portion of the book will deal exactly with that: how to create launch screens and icons for our app, how to create a release build, and ultimately, how to deploy the app to the various app stores.

Along the way, we'll also deal with other concepts, such as tips you can use to make your app's user interface respond appropriately to the various form factors it finds itself running on. You'll also find tools that can verify that your app is working as you expect, as well as tips on how to find and fix performance issues.

When you're finished with this book, you should hopefully have the knowledge necessary to tackle large scale and more complex apps that are accessible, performant, and responsive.

In this book, we'll focus on the iOS and Android platforms. Cordova, however, supports many other platforms. In general, most of what is covered in this book applies to these other platforms as well. However, there are some third-party plugins that are used. If you do want to support another platform, you'll want to verify that the same or a similar plugin is available.

What this book covers

Chapter 1, *Task Automation*, introduces you to the process of automating your common development tasks, including copying and transforming files in various ways as part of your build steps. Sections deal specifically with creating an extensible build system that can transpile JavaScript, minify code automatically, perform Cordova CLI tasks, and lint your code to catch syntax errors.

Chapter 2, *ECMAScript 2015 and Browserify*, is a short introduction to many of the new features in ECMAScript 2015 and beyond, including string interpolation, object destructuring, named and default parameters, lexically bound functions, and more. The chapter also introduces Browserify as a way to package your own code and reuse great code modules from other JavaScript developers.

Chapter 3, *Sassy CSS*, introduces you to the world of CSS transpilers, notably the Sassy CSS language. Specifically, the chapter covers variables, nesting, and mixins, all of which make it easier to write readable and maintainable CSS code.

Chapter 4, More Responsive Design, focuses on the steps and features you can use to create hybrid apps that respond appropriately to the form factors of various devices. This chapter explores logical and physical pixels, important CSS units, media queries, image sizing, and using the flex box model to design complex yet responsive user interfaces.

Chapter 5, Hybrid Application Accessibility, explores the various methods you can use as a developer to make your app accessible to users who may need assistance seeing, hearing, or utilizing the content within your application.

Chapter 6, Testing and UI Automation, addresses the very real need to ensure that the apps we build actually function correctly. The chapter introduces you to testing concepts as well as various tools to automate tests. Finally, the chapter addresses how to automate the user interface as another method to test on real devices.

Chapter 7, IndexedDB, introduces you to a method of persistent storage other than Local Storage or the File API. The chapter covers how to create new object stores, save, retrieve and search for data, and more.

Chapter 8, Web SQL Database, introduces you to relational databases and how they can be used within Cordova using a third-party plugin. The chapter focuses on how to store and retrieve data using SQL.

Chapter 9, Transferring Files, covers how to download content from an external server into your app as well as how to upload content from your app and transfer it to an external server.

Chapter 10, Performance, discusses methods you can use to check how well your application performs on real devices, and also provides tips you can use to improve the performance if necessary.

Chapter 11, Graphical Assets, discusses how to create launch screens and icons for your application. The chapter provides tips on how to create a memorable icon and a good launch screen.

Chapter 12, Deployment, shows you how to create developer accounts for the Google Play Market and Apple App Store step by step so that you can deploy your apps to the world. Once your accounts are created, the chapter guides you through the process of uploading your app's graphical assets, defining metadata, and finally, uploading your app itself.

What you need for this book

To build/run the code supplied for the book, the following software is required (divided by platform where appropriate):

	Windows	Linux	OS X
For iOS Apps			
IDE			XCode 7+
OS			OS X 10.10.5+
SDK			iOS 7+
For Android Apps			
IDE	Not required; you can use Android Studio if you want an IDE		
OS	Vista or newer	Any modern distro supporting: GNU C library 2.15+, if 64-bit, must be able to run 32-bit apps. Ubuntu must be 15.04+	OS X 10.8.5+
Java*	JDK 7 or higher	JDK 7 or higher	JDK 7 or higher
SDK Level	Version 19+	Version 19+	Version 19+
For All Platforms			
Apache Cordova / Phonegap	5.x** or better	5.x** or better	5.x** or better
ANT	1.9.4+	1.9.4+	1.9.4+

* A JRE is not sufficient.

** The code accompanying this book has been tested with Cordova 6.0.0. It should work with any 5.x or 6.x version. The code also relies on core and third-party plugins, as well as various other software and node packages; check the README file in the code package for this book for specific plugin, software, and package versions, if applicable.

While not required, it is considered good practice to work using source control. Git is an easy-to-use source control management solution, and the one the author uses.

Websites and download locations:

- Xcode: https://developer.apple.com/xcode/
- iOS SDK: https://developer.apple.com/devcenter/ios/index.action
- Android SDK: http://developer.android.com/sdk/index.html
- Apache Cordova: http://cordova.apache.org
- PhoneGap: http://phonegap.com
- Git: http://git-scm.com/downloads

Who this book is for

If you are a developer using Cordova to create hybrid mobile applications and wish to take your app to the next level by including any of the following features, this book is for you:

- Automate code transformation, syntax checking, and build steps
- Package your code more efficiently, and use npm packages to speed development
- Use responsive design techniques so that your app can respond appropriately to different form factors and orientations
- Increase your app's audience by making it more accessible
- Verify correctness using automated tests and UI automation tools
- Store structured data using databases
- Transfer files between the app and external servers
- Locate and fix performance issues
- Create signed release versions of your app, ready for deployment

This book assumes that the reader has the following knowledge and abilities:

- Understand how to use the operating system's command-line interface, whether Mac OS X, Linux, or Windows
- Can install and configure Android and iOS SDKs
- Has a basic understanding of the Cordova CLI, and the typical workflow
- Understands typical HTML5, CSS, and JavaScript code
- Has some knowledge of the browser's Document Object Model or DOM

Conventions

In this book, you will find a number of text styles that distinguish between different kinds of information. Here are some examples of these styles and an explanation of their meaning.

Code words in text, database table names, folder names, filenames, file extensions, pathnames, dummy URLs, user input, and Twitter handles are shown as follows: "We can include other files through the use of the import keyword."

A block of code is set as follows:

```
function mul(a, b, log) {
  var ans = a * b;
```

```
    if (log === true) {
      console.log ([a, b, ans]);
    }
  }
```

When we wish reference a portion of code in the following text, the code is marked with a commented number, like so:

```
  function mul(a, b, log) {
    var ans = a * b;
    if (log === true) { // [1]
      console.log ([a, b, ans]);
    }
  }
```

We use the strict equality operator in [1] to avoid type coercion.

Any command-line input or output is written as follows:

```
$ gulp copy && gulp init
```

New terms and **important words** are shown in bold. Words that you see on the screen, for example, in menus or dialog boxes, appear in the text like this: "Right-click on **An Element** and then on **Inspect Element**."

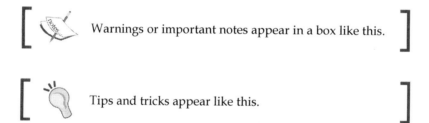

Warnings or important notes appear in a box like this.

Tips and tricks appear like this.

Reader feedback

Feedback from our readers is always welcome. Let us know what you think about this book—what you liked or disliked. Reader feedback is important for us as it helps us develop titles that you will really get the most out of.

To send us general feedback, simply e-mail feedback@packtpub.com, and mention the book's title in the subject of your message.

If there is a topic that you have expertise in and you are interested in either writing or contributing to a book, see our author guide at www.packtpub.com/authors.

Customer support

Now that you are the proud owner of a Packt book, we have a number of things to help you to get the most from your purchase.

Downloading the example code

You can download the example code files from your account at `http://www.packtpub.com` for all the Packt Publishing books you have purchased. If you purchased this book elsewhere, you can visit `http://www.packtpub.com/support` and register to have the files e-mailed directly to you.

The code package for this book is also available on GitHub: `https://github.com/kerrishotts/Mastering-PhoneGap-Code-Package`.

Downloading the color images of this book

We also provide you with a PDF file that has color images of the screenshots/diagrams used in this book. The color images will help you better understand the changes in the output. You can download this file from `http://www.packtpub.com/sites/default/files/downloads/1234OT_ColorImages.pdf`.

Errata

Although we have taken every care to ensure the accuracy of our content, mistakes do happen. If you find a mistake in one of our books—maybe a mistake in the text or the code—we would be grateful if you could report this to us. By doing so, you can save other readers from frustration and help us improve subsequent versions of this book. If you find any errata, please report them by visiting `http://www.packtpub.com/submit-errata`, selecting your book, clicking on the **Errata Submission Form** link, and entering the details of your errata. Once your errata are verified, your submission will be accepted and the errata will be uploaded to our website or added to any list of existing errata under the Errata section of that title.

To view the previously submitted errata, go to `https://www.packtpub.com/books/content/support` and enter the name of the book in the search field. The required information will appear under the **Errata** section.

Piracy

Piracy of copyrighted material on the Internet is an ongoing problem across all media. At Packt, we take the protection of our copyright and licenses very seriously. If you come across any illegal copies of our works in any form on the Internet, please provide us with the location address or website name immediately so that we can pursue a remedy.

Please contact us at `copyright@packtpub.com` with a link to the suspected pirated material.

We appreciate your help in protecting our authors and our ability to bring you valuable content.

Questions

If you have a problem with any aspect of this book, you can contact us at `questions@packtpub.com`, and we will do our best to address the problem.

1
Task Automation

While developing your app, there are often many tasks that need to be executed on a recurring basis. Although these tasks are rarely difficult or terribly time-consuming, over time, the effort adds up and it quickly becomes tiresome and error-prone.

Task automation simplifies these tiresome rituals. Automation lets you define the steps for tasks that you frequently execute (and even those that you execute *infrequently*, which may be even more useful). In a way, you could consider task automation similar to macros in other productivity applications you might use (such as Microsoft Word).

Individual tasks can also depend on other tasks, so you can simplify your manual processes to one or two easy-to-remember and easy-to-type commands. Furthermore, most task automation utilities provide a mechanism to watch for changes made to your project, automatically executing various tasks when any changes have been detected.

Technically, task automation isn't required while developing a PhoneGap / Cordova app; but as your apps grow larger and more complex, it becomes increasingly beneficial. There is some initial overhead, of course, which is often why small projects never implement task automation. But when an app has several views, lots of modules, and a good number of dependencies, the initial overhead quickly pays off.

Although this book is titled *Mastering PhoneGap Mobile Application Development*, we will be using *Cordova* to refer to PhoneGap and Cordova. PhoneGap is derived from Cordova and everything we do using Cordova will also work with PhoneGap. Where this doesn't hold true, we'll mention it explicitly.

Also, when we're referring to Cordova and PhoneGap, we are referring to the command-line utilities. There is a PhoneGap Build service available that performs compilation and packaging in the cloud; but if you want to use it, you'll need to adapt the content in this book appropriately. If you want to learn more, see the README.md file in the code package for this book.

There are several different task automation utilities available. Because one generally writes the majority of their Cordova app in HTML, CSS, and JavaScript, it makes sense to select a task automation system based on JavaScript. At the time of this writing, Gulp (http://gulpjs.com) and Grunt (http://gruntjs.com) are the most popular of the various available utilities.

In this chapter, you will learn about:

- Logology, the demonstration app
- Why use Gulp for Task Automation
- Setting up your app's directory structure
- Installing Gulp
- Creating your first Gulp configuration file
- Creating a modular Gulp configuration
- Copying assets
- Performing substitutions
- Executing various Cordova tasks
- Managing version numbers
- Supporting ES2015
- Linting your code
- Minifying/uglifying your code

Before we begin

This book comes with a code bundle that is available at `https://github.com/kerrishotts/Mastering-PhoneGap-Code-Package`. If you haven't downloaded it yet, I strongly advise you to do so. It contains all the code for each chapter as well as lots of snippets that demonstrate some of the examples in most chapters. Furthermore, the chapters in the book focus mostly on snippets—to see the topics in use in an actual application, you'll definitely want to look at the demonstration app's code.

Before continuing with this chapter, ensure that you have met the pre-requisites as listed in this book's preface. Software and hardware requirements are also listed in the code package for this book in the `README.md` file.

If you want to build and deploy the demonstration application from the code bundle, you'll need to install the earlier mentioned tools. Because the Cordova projects and platform-specific files are considered build artifacts, you'll need to execute the following in each chapter's directory in order to build each version of the app:

```
# On Linux / Mac OS X (using Bash shell)
$ npm install && gulp init

% On Windows
> npm install
> gulp init
```

About Logology

Before we go any further, let's describe the demonstration app we'll be building through the course of this book.

I've called it **Logology**. If you're familiar with any Greek words, you might have already guessed what the app will be: a dictionary. Now, I understand that this is not necessarily the most amazing app, but it is sufficient for our purposes. It will help you learn how advanced mobile development is done.

By the end of the book, the app will have the following features:

- **Search**: The user will be able to search for a term
- **Responsive design**: The app will size itself appropriately to any display size
- **Accessibility**: The app will be usable even if the user has visual difficulties
- **Persistent storage**: The app will persist settings and other user-generated information

Although the app sounds relatively simple, it's complex enough to benefit from task automation. Since it is useful to have task automation in place from the very beginning, in this chapter we'll install Gulp and verify that it is working with some simple files first. As such, the app in the code package for this first chapter is very simple; it exists solely to verify that our tasks are working correctly.

You may think that working through configuring task automation is very time-consuming, but it will pay off in the long run. Once you have a workflow that you like, you can take the workflow and apply it to any other apps you may build in the future. This means that future apps can be started almost immediately (just copy the configuration from the previous app). Even if you don't write other apps, the time you save from having a task runner will outweigh the initial setup time.

Why use Gulp for task automation?

Gulp (`http://gulpjs.com`) is a task automation utility using the Node.js platform. Unlike some other task runners, one configures Gulp by writing a JavaScript code. The configuration for Gulp is just like any other JavaScript file, which means that if you know JavaScript, you can start defining the automation tasks quickly.

Gulp also uses the concept of *streams* (again, from Node.js). Although you can think of a stream as a file, streams are actually more powerful. Plugins can be inserted within steam processing to perform many different transformations, including beautification or uglification, transpilation (for example, ECMAScript 6 to ECMAScript 2015), concatenation, packaging, and much more.

 If you've performed any sort of piping on the command line, Gulp should feel familiar to you, because it operates on a similar concept. The output from one process is piped to the next process, which performs any number of transformations, and so on, until the final output is written to another location.

Gulp also tries to run as many dependent tasks in parallel as possible. Ideally, this makes it possible to run Gulp tasks faster, although this really depends on how your tasks are structured. Other task runners such as Grunt perform their task steps in a sequence that may result in a slower output, although it may be easier to follow the steps from input to output when they're performed sequentially.

That's not to say that Gulp is the best task runner—there are many that are quite good, and you may find that you prefer one of them over Gulp. The skills you will learn in this book can easily be transferred to other task automation utilities.

Here are some other task runners that are useful:

- **Grunt** (`http://www.gruntjs.com`): The configuration is specified through settings, not code. The tasks are performed sequentially.

- **Cake** (`http://coffeescript.org/documentation/docs/cake.html`): It usesCoffeeScript and the configuration is specified via code, as it is seen in Gulp. If you like using CoffeeScript, you might prefer this over Gulp.

- **Broccoli** (`https://github.com/broccolijs/broccoli`): It also uses configuration through code.

Setting up your app's directory structure

Before we install Gulp, we should create the directory structure for our app. Keep in mind that there's no single correct way to structure your application, and your opinion on how apps should be structured is likely to change as you gain more experience. That said, this section will show you how I like to structure my projects.

My typical structure starts with the project's root directory. If you look at the code bundle for this book, you'll notice that the project's root directory is called `logology-v01/`.

 I wouldn't normally append the version number on a project — that's what a version control system is for. However, since it is important that you be able to see changes from version to version, the code package splits these changes out by chapter — hence the version number

Within the project's root directory are some additional directories:

- `config/`: Configuration files needed during the tasks are stored in this directory.

- `src/`: All the app's source code and image assets are stored in this directory. This is the *source* that we supply to Gulp. Gulp then transforms the source and stores it in a directory of our choosing (typically the `build` directory).

- `build/`: This directory contains the transformed HTML, CSS, and JavaScript code, as well as the native portions of a Cordova project.

 The `build/` directory will not be present in the code bundle for this book. It is considered a build artifact, and as such, you can always regenerate it.

Within the `src/` directory lives our app's source code. I like to structure the code and assets as follows:

```
project-root/
  src/
    config.xml              # Template file for our Cordova app's
                            # configuration
    res/                    # Icons & splash screens (covered in
                            # Chapter 11)
    www/                    # HTML, JavaScript, and CSS, and other
                            # web assets
      index.html            # Initial HTML file (as specified in
                            # config.xml)
      html/                 # Additional HTML files, if any
      img/                  # Image files, if we need them
      scss/                 # Sassy CSS files (see Chapter 3)
        lib/                # Utility functions
        themes/             # Themes (appearance of the app)
        views/              # Styles specific to views in our app
      js/                   # JavaScript
        lib/                # Third-party library code and support
                            # code
        app/                # Our application code
          index.js          # The entry point for our app
          controllers/      # View controllers live here
          lib/              # App-specific utility files
          localization/     # Language translations
          models/           # Data models go here
          views/            # Views and templates live here
```

If you look at the directory structure of this chapter in the code bundle, you will notice that a lot of it is missing. This is because it's not necessary at this point; we'll fill it out in the future chapters.

If you're wondering where the Cordova files are, you're paying attention. There aren't any. *Yet.* This is because they are considered to be **build artifacts**. Build artifacts are files that are created when you compile your app. If this feels both a little strange and a little familiar at the same time, there's a good reason behind it: the Cordova projects already have portions that are considered to be build artifacts. The strange part is that you're probably used to editing the www/ folder within the Cordova project, and executing cordova build to create the remaining build artifacts (namely, the native wrappers around your code, typically in platforms/).

In this book, however, we're going to take a higher level approach and consider the *entire Cordova project* as a build artifact. Why? Because Cordova has been extended by several other projects (such as Steroids: http://www.appgyver.com/steroids) and they usually have their own project formats and build steps. If you ever want to target these platforms, you can readily do so since your code doesn't live within a Cordova project. Furthermore, you might find that you want to target other technologies entirely, such as Electron (http://electron.atom.io) which encapsulates your code with a Chromium webview suitable for desktop execution. The build steps and project structure for Electron are different than what you might expect for a Cordova project. In short, it's a way to avoid tying yourself down.

All said, when we're done with the chapter, you'll have a Cordova app filled with your source code. That project will be present in the build/ directory.

> If you ever need to execute Cordova commands outside Gulp, you'll need to change to the build/ directory first or the command will fail. This is because the Cordova CLI expects be to run within a Cordova project, and our app's root directory isn't a Cordova project. Only build/ contains a valid Cordova project.

A crucial part of our workflow is going to be our project's package.json file. This file will contain the app's version information, Cordova configuration, and more. If you're starting from scratch, you will need to create this file yourself by changing to the project's root directory and executing npm init:

> If you are using the code bundle for this chapter, the package.json file is already built for you.

```
# (in your project's root directory)
$ npm init [ENTER]
This utility will walk you through creating a package.json file.
It only covers the most common items, and tries to guess sane
defaults.
```

...

```
name: (logology-v01) Logology [ENTER]
version: (1.0.0) [ENTER]
description: Logology and PhoneGap demonstration app [ENTER]
entry point: (index.js) [ENTER]
test command: [ENTER]
git repository: [ENTER]
keywords: dictionary word study phonegapcordova html5 javascript
css [ENTER]
author: Kerri Shotts<kerrishotts@gmail.com> [ENTER]
license: (ISC) MIT [ENTER]
About to write to .../logology-v01/package.json:


Is this ok? (yes) [ENTER]
```

At this point, you have the `package.json` file is created, but it will need a few more edits. Open the `package.json` file in your favorite editor and remove the `scripts` section. Then, add the following (for the full contents of this file you can refer to the code package):

```
{ ...,
"cordova": {
  "name": "Logology",
  "id": "com.packtpub.logologyv1",
  "description": "Dictionary application",
  "author": {
    "name": "Kerri Shotts",
    "email": "kerrishotts@gmail.com",
    "site": "http://www.photokandy.com"
  },
  "template": "../blank",
  "platforms": [ "ios", "android" ],
  "preferences": {
    "permissions": "none",
    "fullscreen": "false",
    "orientation": "default",
    "stay-in-webview": "false",
    "ShowSplashScreenSpinner": "false",
    "AutoHideSplashScreen": "false",
    "disable-cursor": "false",
```

```
      "KeyboardDisplayRequiresUserAction": "false",
      "target-device": "universal",
      "prerendered-icon": "true",
      "webviewbounce": "false",
      "DisallowOverscroll": "true",
      "exit-on-suspend": "false",
      "deployment-target": "7.0",
      "detect-data-types": "false",
      "SupressesIncrementalRendering": "true",
      "android-minSdkVersion": "14",
      "android-installLocation": "auto",
      "android-windowSoftInputMode": "adjustResize",
    },
    "plugins": [
      "cordova-plugin-device@1.1.0",
      "cordova-plugin-network-information@1.1.0",
      "cordova-plugin-globalization@1.0.2",
      "cordova-plugin-whitelist@1.1.0",
      "ionic-plugin-keyboard@1.0.8",
      "cordova-plugin-inappbrowser@1.0.1"
      ]
    }
  }
```

The preceding code should be fairly self-explanatory. With it, we are essentially duplicating the contents of Cordova's `config.xml` file. Because the Cordova project itself is considered to be a build artifact, it makes sense to manage plugins, platforms, and preferences somewhere else and, because `package.json` handles the other configuration aspects of our project, it makes sense to include these configuration settings here.

 This doesn't remove the need for a `config.xml` file. We'll cover this later on in this chapter.

At this point, we're ready to install Gulp and any other dependencies our project might need.

Installing Gulp

Installing Gulp is easy, but is actually a two-step process. The first step is to install Gulp globally. This installs the command-line utility; but Gulp won't work without also being installed *locally* within our project. If you aren't familiar with Node.js, the packages can be installed locally and/or globally. A locally installed package is local to the project's root directory, while a globally installed package is specific to the developer's machine. Project dependencies are tracked in `package.json`, which makes it easy to replicate your development environment on another machine.

Assuming you have Node.js installed and `package.json` created in your project directory, the installation of Gulp will be very easy. Be sure you are positioned in your project's root directory and then execute the following:

```
$ npm install -g gulp@3.9.0
$ npm install --save-dev gulp@3.9.0
```

If you receive an error while running these commands on OS X, you may need to run them with `sudo`. For example: `sudo install -g gulp`.

You can usually ignore any `WARN` messages.

Notice that we're specifying version numbers here – these are the versions that I used while writing the code for this book. You can try later versions if you want, as long as they are minor revisions. Major revisions may work, but you may also have to make modifications to the code in this book in order to support them.

It's a good idea to be positioned in your project's root directory any time you execute an `npm` or `gulp` command. On Linux and OS X, these commands generally locate the project's root directory automatically; but this isn't guaranteed on all platforms, so it's better to be safe than sorry.

That's it! Gulp itself is very easy to install, but most workflows require additional plugins that work with Gulp. In addition, we'll also install the Cordova dependencies for this project.

If you're working with the code bundle for this chapter, you can install all the following dependencies by executing `npm install`.

First, let's install the Cordova dependencies:

```
$ npm install --save-dev cordova-lib@5.4.1 cordova-ios@3.9.2 cordova-android@4.1.1
```

`cordova-lib` allows us to programmatically interact with Cordova. We can create projects, build them, and emulate them—everything we do with the Cordova command line can be done with `cordova-lib`. `cordova-ios` and `cordova-android` refer to the iOS and Android platforms that `cordova platform add ios android` would add. We've made them dependencies for our project, so we can easily control which version we will build it with.

> While starting a new project, it's wise to start with the most recent version of Cordova and the requisite platforms. Once you begin, it's usually a good practice to stick with a specific platform version, unless there are serious bugs or security issues that require updating to a newer platform version..

Next, let's install the Gulp plugins we'll need:

```
$ npm install --save-dev babel-eslint@4.1.1 cordova-tasks@0.2.0 gulp-babel@5.2.1 gulp-bump@0.3.1 gulp-concat@2.6.0 gulp-eslint@1.0.0 gulp-jscs@3.0.2 gulp-notify@2.2.0 gulp-rename@1.2.0 gulp-replace-task@0.10.1 gulp-sourcemaps@1.3.0 gulp-uglify@1.4.0 gulp-util@3.0.6 merge-stream@1.0.0 require-all@1.1.0 rimraf@2.4.3
```

These will take a few moments to install; but when you're done, take a look at `package.json`. Notice that all the dependencies we added are also added to the `devDependencies` section in the file. This makes it easy to install all the project's dependencies at a later date (say, on a new machine) simply by executing `npm install`.

Before we go on, let's quickly go over what each of the earlier mentioned utilities do. We'll go over them in more detail as we progress through the remainder of this chapter:

- `gulp-babel`: Converts ES2015 JavaScript into ES5. If you aren't familiar with ES2015, it has several new features and an improved syntax that make writing mobile apps easier. Unfortunately, because most browsers don't yet natively support the ES2015 features and syntax, it must be transpiled to the ES5 syntax. Of course, if you prefer other languages that can be compiled to ES5 JavaScript, you could use those as well (these would include CoffeeScript and so on).

- `gulp-bump`: This small utility manages the version numbers in `package.json`.

- `gulp-concat`: This concatenates streams together. We can use this to bundle files together.

- `gulp-jscs`: This performs the JavaScript code style checks against your code. It supports ES2015.

- `gulp-eslint`: This lints your JavaScript code. It supports ES2015.

- `babel-eslint`: This provides ES2015 support to `gulp-eslint`.

- `gulp-notify`: This is an optional plugin, but it comes in handy, especially when some of your tasks take a few seconds to run. This plugin will send a notification to your computer's notification panel when something of import occurs—perhaps an error or a completion message. If the plugin can't send it to your notification panel, it will be logged to the console.

- `gulp-rename`: This renames the streams.

- `gulp-replace-task`: This performs text searches and replaces within the streams.

- `gulp-sourcemaps`: While transpiling ES2015 to ES5, it can be helpful to have a mapping between the original source and the transpiled source. This plugin creates them automatically for you.

- `gulp-uglify`: This uglifies/minifies your code. While useful for code obfuscation, it also reduces the size of the code.

- `gulp-util`: This provides additional utilities for Gulp, such as logging.

- `merge-stream`: This merges multiple tasks.

- `require-all`: This lets us import an entire directory of code into an object at once.

- `rimraf`: Easy file deletion. Akin to `rm` on the command line.

Creating your first Gulp configuration file

Gulp tasks are defined by the contents of the project's `gulpfile.js` file. This is a JavaScript program, so the same skills you have with JavaScript will apply here. Furthermore, it's executed by Node.js, so if you have any Node.js knowledge, you can use it to your advantage.

> This file should be placed in the root directory of your project and must be named `gulpfile.js`.

The first few lines of your Gulp configuration file will *require* the Gulp plugins you'll need to complete the tasks. The following lines will then specify how the various tasks need to be performed. For example, a very simple configuration might look as follows:

```
var gulp = require("gulp");
gulp.task("copy-files", function () {
  gulp.src(["./src/**/*"])
      .pipe(gulp.dest("./build"));
});
```

This configuration only performs one task: it moves all the files contained within `src/` to `build/`. In many ways, this is the simplest form of a build workflow, but it's a bit too simple for our purposes.

 Note the pattern we used to match all the files. If you need to see the documentation on what patterns are supported, see `https://www.npmjs.com/package/glob`.

To execute the task, you can execute `gulp copy-files`. Gulp would then execute the task and copy all the files from `src/` to `build/`.

What makes Gulp so powerful is the concept of task composition. Tasks can depend on any number of other tasks and those tasks can depend on yet more tasks. This makes it easy to create complex workflows out of simpler pieces. Furthermore, each task is asynchronous, so it is possible for many tasks with no shared dependencies to operate in parallel.

Each task, as you can see in the prior code, is comprised of a selection of a series of source files (`src()`), optionally performing some additional processing on each file (via `pipe()`) and then writing those files to a destination path (`dest()`). If no additional processing is specified (as in the prior example), Gulp will simply copy the files that match the wildcard pattern. The beauty of streams, however, is that one can execute any number of transformations before the final data is saved. So, the workflows can become very complex.

Now that you've seen a simple task, let's get into some more complicated tasks in the next section.

Creating a modular Gulp configuration

Although you can add all the tasks that you want to run to a single configuration file, this quickly becomes unwieldy as you add more tasks to your environment. In order to keep your configuration maintenance easy, it's best to split everything up into separate files.

This means that aside from our project's directory structure, our Gulp configuration has its own structure. The following shows how I like to structure my configuration:

```
project-root/
  gulpfile.js              # Stub (loads in everything else)
  gulp/
    config.js              # Configuration - files to copy,
                           # output paths, etc.
    settings.js            # values of command-line flags
    tasks.js               # Stub (loads in all the tasks)
    tasks/                 # Contains each task, in its own
      some-task.js         # JavaScript file
      another-task.js
    utils/                 # Utility functions all tasks share
      paths.js             # path manipulation methods
```

Let's go over the code that is in some of the above files. First, let's look at a simplified `gulp/config.js` file, which stores the base paths, as well as source and destination paths for our project:

```
var config = {
    paths: {
        base: process.cwd(), // [1]
        dest: "build",       // [2]
        src: "src",          // [3]
        config: "config"     // [4]
    },
    assets: { // [5]
        copy: [ // [6]
                {src:  "www/*.*",         dest: "www"},
                {src:  "www/html/**/*",   dest: "www/html"},
                {src:  "www/img/**/*",    dest: "www/img"},
                {src:  "www/js/lib/**/*", dest: "www/js/lib"},
                {src:  "res/**/*",        dest: "res"}
            ]
    }
}
module.exports = config; // [7]
```

This is a fairly simple configuration file—we'll end up adding much more to it as the book progresses.

The first section defines the various paths that Gulp will need to know in order to copy our project files as well as those necessary for transforming our code. The `base` path (`[1]`) is used as the foundation for every other path, and as such, every other path you see will be relative, not absolute.

The output directory is specified in `[2]`, and the source directory is specified in `[3]`. Configuration files that we might need for code transformation and style checking are specified in `[4]`. Each one is relative to the `base` path.

Every project has a set of assets, and ours is no exception – these are specified in section `[5]`. In this case, we don't have very many, but even so, they need to be specified so that our tasks know what files they need to work with. We may have many different assets, some of which may require different processing, so we can add to this section as we need. For now, we just need to copy some files, and so we add them to the copy section (`[6]`). Notice that we specify them in terms of a source wildcard string and a destination path. These will automatically be made relative to the `src` (`[3]`) and `dest` (`[2]`) paths.

The final line (`[7]`) is used to export the information out of this file. We can then `require` the file later in another file (and most of our tasks and the like will do so). This means that our asset and path configuration only needs to be maintained in one place.

Gulp can accept custom command-line arguments, and these can be used to control how various tasks operate. A typical argument might specify the amount of logging that is generated. This is all handled by the `gulp/settings.js` file. Let's take a look:

```
var gutil = require("gulp-util");
var settings = {
    VERBOSE: gutil.env.verbose ? (gutil.env.verbose === "yes")
                               : false
}
module.exports = settings;
```

Right now, there's not a lot going on in this file, and that's because we really don't have tasks that need to be configured using command line arguments. But we'll be adding to this file as the book goes on.

By itself, this file doesn't do much. All it is doing is using `gutil.env` to read the arguments passed on the command line. In this case, it's checking to see if we passed `verbose` on the command line. If we did, and the value was `yes`, `settings.VERBOSE` would be set to `true`. If we didn't (or if we did and the value was `no`), `settings.VERBOSE` would be set to `false`. If we want to take advantage of this setting later on in a task, we can do so.

There's one other file in the `gulp/` directory, so let's take a look at `gulp/tasks.js`:

```
var path = require("path");
var tasks = require("require-all")(path.join(__dirname, "tasks"));
module.exports = tasks;
```

As you can see, it's a very short file. All it does is find all the tasks within `gulp/tasks/` and load them into the `tasks` object. Right now that would return an empty object, but by the end of the chapter, the `tasks` object will contain several methods that Gulp can use. We use the `require-all` package to make life easier on us—that way we don't have to individually `require` each and every task. Later on, when we add additional tasks to our Gulp configuration, it means we don't have to later come back and edit this file.

Next, let's look at `gulp/utils/paths.js`:

```
var path = require("path"),
    config = require("../config"); // [1]
function makeFullPath(filepath, relativeTo) {
    var pathComponents = [config.paths.base];
    if (relativeTo) {
        pathComponents.push(config.paths[relativeTo]);
    }
    pathComponents = pathComponents.concat(filepath.split("/"));
    return path.join.apply(path, pathComponents);
}
module.exports = {
    SRC: "src",
    DEST: "dest",
    CONFIG: "config",
    makeFullPath: makeFullPath
};
```

This utility file provides a mechanism our tasks can use to craft paths that are relative to the source, destination, configuration, and base paths in our project. It makes heavy use of Node.js' `path` library so that our Gulp tasks can work across different platforms.

Finally, we need to create the actual `gulpfile.js` file that kicks everything off. It doesn't do much on its own; instead it loads everything else in and configures any available tasks with Gulp:

```
require ("babel/register"); // [1]
var gulp = require("gulp"),
    tasks = require("./gulp/tasks"); // [2]
Object.keys(tasks).forEach(function(taskName) { // [3]
    var taskOpts = tasks[taskName];
    if (typeof taskOpts === "function") {
        gulp.task(taskName, taskOpts); // [4]
    } else {
        gulp.task(taskName, taskOpts.deps, taskOpts.task); // [5]
    }
});
```

The first line ([1]) imports Babel so that we can use ES2015 code in our tasks should we choose to. The third line ([2]) imports all the tasks that are available. Right now this will be an empty object, but as we add tasks, it will contain more and more functions that Gulp can use to copy and transform files.

The code starting at [3] just takes all the available tasks and creates a corresponding Gulp task. Each task can either be a function, or it can be an object that specifies dependencies (and more), hence the two different method invocations at [4] and [5].

Copying assets

Now that we've created the basic Gulp configuration structure, let's create our first task to copy our app's assets from the source path to the destination path.

We can call this file `gulp/tasks/copy-assets.js`, and it should look like this:

```
var merge = require("merge-stream"),
    gulp = require("gulp"),
    config = require("../config"),
    paths = require("../utils/paths");

function copyAssets() {
  return merge.apply(merge, config.assets.copy.map(function(asset)
  {
    var fqSourcePath = paths.makeFullPath(asset.src, paths.SRC);
    var fqTargetPath = paths.makeFullPath(asset.dest, paths.DEST);
    return gulp.src([fqSourcePath])
      .pipe(gulp.dest(fqTargetPath));
  });
```

```
  }

  module.exports = {
    task: copyAssets
  }
```

The method, `copyAssets` simply copies a lot of files based upon the project's file structure as specified in `gulp/config.js`. The code here could be simpler, but you may find that you need to change which files need and don't need substitutions later. So, we've made it configurable. All you need to do is to change the files and destinations within `config.assets.copy` in `gulp/config.js` and this task will react accordingly.

Let's go over what this task is really doing:

- We're using our utility method `paths.makeFullPath` (which uses `path.join`) to ensure that our configuration works across multiple platforms. On Unix-like systems, the path separator is `/`; but on Windows systems, the path separator is actually `\`. In order to simplify the configuration, however, we're using `/` in `config.assets.copy`. `makeFullPath` splits (`/`)each one of the strings into arrays, and uses `path.join` (which knows the correct path separator) to create the final path.

- `map` iterates over an array and returns a new array using a given transformation. For example, `[1, 2, 3].map(function(x) {return x*2;})` will return a new array of `[2, 4, 6]`. In our case, we're returning an array of `gulp.src(...).pipe(gulp.dest(...))` chains. We can then `apply` the array to `merge` in order to combine all the tasks together.

- `apply` is a way to call a function that accepts multiple arguments using an array instead. For example, `console.log.apply(console,[1,2,3])` will log `1  2  3`. This is different from `console.log([1,2,3])` which instead will log `[1, 2, 3]`.

At this point, you can type the following on the command line and copy the project assets from their source location to their destination:

```
$ gulp copy-assets
```

Performing substitutions

Many times, we need to convert certain keywords in a Gulp stream into some other values. A simple example is to transform `{{{VERSION}}}` your app's version number—for example, into `1.23.4456`. Doing this is pretty simple, but it opens up a large number of possibilities.

To do this, we'll use the `gulp-replace-task` plugin. This plugin will replace all the instances of a particular regular expression with a replacement value. These expressions can become very complex; but in our case, we'll keep them simple.

We'll only need to support substitutions in our code files, so let's create a new task that is designed to copy our code files and apply any necessary substitutions along the way. We'll call it `gulp/tasks/copy-code.js`. The file should start as follows:

```
var gulp = require("gulp"),
    replace = require("gulp-replace-task"),
    concat = require("gulp-concat"),
    pkg = require("../../package.json"),
    config = require("../config"),
    paths = require("../utils/paths");
```

Next, we need to define a method that will perform substitutions on the input streams. Remember, these will be the files matched by the pattern provided to `gulp.src()`:

```
function performSubstitutions() {
  return replace({
    patterns: [
      {
        match: /{{{VERSION}}}/g,
        replacement: pkg.version
      }
    ]
  });
}
```

Next, let's define another configuration setting that specifies the code files that *do* need substitutions and where they should be stored. In `gulp/config.js`, add a code section to the `config.assets` object, like this:

```
assets: {
  copy: [ ... ],
  code: {src: "www/js/app/**/*.js", dest: "www/js/app"}
}, ...
```

Next, we need to define the code that will copy the files specified by `config.assets.code` to the appropriate destination. This will be added to `gulp/tasks/copy-code.js`, and it should look like this:

```
function copyCode() {
  return gulp.src([paths.makeFullPath(config.assets.code.src,
                   paths.SRC)])
```

```
        .pipe(performSubstitutions())
        .pipe(concat("app.js"))
        .pipe(gulp.dest(paths.makeFullPath(
            config.assets.code.dest, paths.DEST)));
}
module.exports = {
    task: copyCode
}
```

The `copyCode` method is pretty simple to follow. First, all the JavaScript files are located using the configuration we've specified. These are all passed through `performSubstitutions()`. The results of the substitutions are then packaged together in a neat little bundle with `concat`. So, even if we have multiple JavaScript files, they will all be packaged into a single file (`app.js`).

 You don't *have* to concatenate your files if you don't want to. When you have multiple JavaScript files, however, it means that you have to include each one in your `index.html` file. Whereas if you bundle them into a single file, you reduce the number of `script` tags you have in your `index.html` file.

To test these tasks, we can create two simple files. The first should be placed in `src/www/` and named `index.html`:

```html
<!DOCTYPE html>
<html>
  <head>
    <script src="cordova.js" type="text/javascript"></script>
    <script src="js/app/app.js" type="text/javascript"></script>
  </head>
  <body>
    <p>Hello!</p>
    <div id="demo"></div>
  </body>
</html>
```

The second file should be in `src/www/js/app/` and named `index.js`:

```javascript
document.getElementById("demo").textContent = "{{{VERSION}}}";
```

The JavaScript file itself is very simple, obviously. The idea is simply to prove that our Gulp tasks work. If you execute `gulp copy-assets`, you'll find that `index. html` has been copied from `src/www/` to `build/www/`. Likewise, if you execute `gulp copy-code`, you'll find that `index.js` has been copied from `src/www/js/app/` to `build/www/js/app/` and renamed to `app.js`. If you open the latter file in an editor, you'll also see that `{{{VERSION}}}` has been replaced with `1.0.0` (which came from `package.json`).

As you may recall, we indicated earlier in this chapter that we still need a `config. xml` file. This is true, but we've specified everything we need in `package.json`. Wouldn't it be great to generate a valid `config.xml` file from a template? This means that we need more substitutions and a proper template.

Let's define our template first. This should be in `src/config.xml` (see the code package for the entire file):

```xml
<?xml version='1.0' encoding='utf-8'?>
<widget id="{{{ID}}}" version="{{{VERSION}}}"
        xmlns="http://www.w3.org/ns/widgets"
        xmlns:cdv="http://cordova.apache.org/ns/1.0"
        xmlns:gap="http://phonegap.com/ns/1.0">
    <name>{{{NAME}}}</name>
    <description>
      {{{DESCRIPTION}}}
    </description>
    <author email="{{{AUTHOR.EMAIL}}}"href="{{{AUTHOR.SITE}}}">
      {{{AUTHOR.NAME}}}
    </author>
    <content src="index.html" />
      {{{PREFS}}}
    <access origin="*" />
...
</widget>
```

Notice that there are a lot of substitution variables in the preceding code. Most of them are pretty simple: `{{{ID}}}`, `{{{NAME}}}`, and so on. One of them is a little more complex: `{{{PREFS}}}`. This will need to render our simpler list of preferences in `package.json` into the XML format required by Cordova.

Let's create a new utility file named `gulp/utils/performSubstitutions.js` with a new version of the `performSubstitutions` method. We'll need this new version in two tasks, hence the need to split it out into its own file. The new file should look like this:

```js
var pkg = require("../../package.json"),
    replace = require("gulp-replace-task");
```

```
function performSubstitutions() {
  function transformCordovaPrefs() {
    var template = '<preference name="{{{NAME}}}" ' +
                   'value="{{{VALUE}}}" />';
    if (pkg.cordova &&
      pkg.cordova.preferences instanceof Object) {
      return Object.keys(pkg.cordova.preferences).map(
        function(prefName) {
          var str = template.replace(/{{{NAME}}}/g,
            prefName)
            .replace(/{{{VALUE}}}/g,
              pkg.cordova.preferences[prefName]);
          return str;
        }).join("\n  ");
    }
  }

  return replace({
    patterns: [
      {
        match: /{{{VERSION}}}/g,
        replacement: pkg.version
      },
      {
        match: /{{{ID}}}/g,
        replacement: pkg.cordova.id
      },
      {
        match: /{{{NAME}}}/g,
        replacement: pkg.cordova.name
      },
      {
        match: /{{{DESCRIPTION}}}/g,
        replacement: pkg.cordova.description
      },
      {
        match: /{{{AUTHOR.NAME}}}/g,
        replacement: pkg.cordova.author.name
      },
      {
        match: /{{{AUTHOR.EMAIL}}}/g,
        replacement: pkg.cordova.author.email
      },
      {
```

```
                match: /{{{AUTHOR.SITE}}}/g,
                replacement: pkg.cordova.author.site
            },
            {
                match: /{{{PREFS}}}/g,
                replacement: transformCordovaPrefs
            }
        ]
    });
}
module.exports = performSubstitutions;
```

Next, we'll need to edit `gulp/copy-code.js` to include this new version. Remove the `performSubstitutions` method from this file first, and then add the following `require` to the top of the file:

```
var …,
    performSubstitutions = require("../utils/performSubstitutions");
```

Finally, let's add another task that can copy the configuration file. We'll call it `gulp/tasks/copy-config.js`, and it should look like this:

```
var gulp = require("gulp"),
    performSubstitutions =
        require("../utils/performSubstitutions"),
    config = require("../config"),
    paths = require("../utils/paths");

function copyConfig() {
    return gulp.src([paths.makeFullPath("config.xml", paths.SRC)])
            .pipe(performSubstitutions())
            .pipe(gulp.dest(paths.makeFullPath(".",
              paths.DEST)));
}
module.exports = {
    task: copyConfig
}
```

Of course, we don't want to have to run lots of individual tasks just to copy files. So let's create a simple task that depends upon these three tasks. By doing so, Gulp will run all of these tasks with a single command.

Let's create the new task with the name `gulp/tasks/copy.js`. The file should contain the following:

```
module.exports = {
    deps: ["copy-assets", "copy-config", "copy-code"],
}
```

This is the shortest task so far. All it does is list the other three tasks as dependencies. This means that they will be executed prior to `copy`. Since `copy` doesn't contain any additional code, it's just a simple way to execute several tasks at once. If you execute `gulp copy`, you'll find that you have a new `config.xml` file under `build`. It should look a lot like the following:

```
<?xml version='1.0' encoding='utf-8'?>
<widget id="com.packtpub.logologyv1" version="1.0.0"
        xmlns="http://www.w3.org/ns/widgets"
        xmlns:cdv="http://cordova.apache.org/ns/1.0"
        xmlns:gap="http://phonegap.com/ns/1.0">
  <name>Logology</name>
  <description>
    Dictionary application for Mastering PhoneGap book
  </description>
  <author email="kerrishotts@gmail.com"
   href="http://www.photokandy.com">
    Kerri Shotts
  </author>
  <content src="index.html" />

  <preference name="permissions" value="none" />
  <preference name="fullscreen" value="false" />
  <preference name="orientation" value="default" />
  ...
  <access origin="*" />
</widget>
```

Now that you've mastered the method of performing substitutions, you will learn how to interact with Cordova programmatically in the next section.

How to execute Cordova tasks

It's tempting to use the Cordova command-line interface directly, but there's a problem with this: there's no great way to ensure what you write works across multiple platforms. If you are certain you'll only work with a specific platform, you can go ahead and execute shell commands instead; but what we're going to do is a bit more flexible.

The code in this section is inspired by `https://github.com/kamrik/CordovaGulpTemplate`.

The Cordova CLI is really just a thin wrapper around the `cordova-lib` project. Everything the Cordova CLI can do, `cordova-lib` does as well.

Because the Cordova project will be a build artifact, we need to be able to create a Cordova project in addition to building the project. We'll also need to emulate and run the app. To accomplish this, we'll need to create a new utility file named `gulp/utils/cordova-tasks.js`. At the top we require `cordova-lib` and other packages we'll need:

```
var cordovaLib = require("cordova-lib"),
    pkg = require("../../package.json"),
    config = require("../config"),
    path = require("path"),
    settings = require("../settings"),
    paths = require("../utils/paths");
var cordova = cordovaLib.cordova.raw;
```

Next, let's create the code to create a new Cordova project in the `build` directory:

```
var cordovaTasks = {
  // CLI: cordova create ./build com.example.app app_name
  //                --copy-from template_path
  create: function create() {
    return cordova.create(paths.makeFullPath(".", paths.DEST),
      pkg.cordova.id, pkg.cordova.name,
      {
        lib: {
          www: {
            url: path.join(process.cwd(), pkg.cordova.template),
            link: false
          }
        }
      });
  }
}
module.exports = cordovaTasks;
```

Although it's a bit more complicated than `cordova create` is on the command line, you should be able to see the parallels. The `lib` object is passed simply to provide a template for the project (equivalent to `--copy-from` on the command line). In our case, `package.json` specifies that this should come from the `blank/` directory in the code bundle of this book. If we don't do this, all our apps would be created with the sample Hello World app that Cordova installs by default.

> Our blank project template resides in `../blank` relative to the project root. Yours may reside elsewhere (since you're apt to reuse the same template), so `package.json` can use whatever path you need. Or, you might want the template to be within your project's root; in which case, `package.json` should use a path inside your project's root directory.

We won't create a task to use this just yet. We need to define several other methods to build and emulate the Cordova app. First, we need to add some additional settings to `gulp/settings.js`:

```
var settings = { ...,
  PLATFORM = gutil.env.platform ? gutil.env.platform :"ios",
  BUILD_MODE = gutil.env.mode ? gutil.env.mode :"debug",
  BUILD_PLATFORMS = (gutil.env.for ? gutil.env.for
                                   : "ios,android").split(","),
  TARGET_DEVICE = gutil.env.target ? "--target=" +
                  gutil.env.target : ""
}
```

Next, let's continue to add the additional methods we need to the `cordovaTasks` object:

```
var cordovaTasks = {
  create: function create() {
    /* as above */
  },
  cdProject: function cdProject() {
    process.chdir(paths.makeFullPath("www", paths.DEST));
  },
  cdUp: function cdUp() {
    process.chdir("..");
  },
  // cordova plugin add ...
  addPlugins: function addPlugins() {
    cordovaTasks.cdProject();
    return cordova.plugins("add", pkg.cordova.plugins)
      .then(cordovaTasks.cdUp);
  },
```

```
// cordova platform add ...
addPlatforms: function addPlatforms() {
  cordovaTasks.cdProject();
  function transformPlatform(platform) {
    return path.join(process.cwd(), "node_modules",
      "cordova-" + platform);
  }
  return cordova.platforms("add",
    pkg.cordova.platforms.map(transformPlatform))
    .then(cordovaTasks.cdUp);
},
// cordova build <platforms> --release|debug
//                          --target=...|--device
build: function build() {
  var target = settings.TARGET_DEVICE;
  cordovaTasks.cdProject();
  if (!target || target === "" ||
    target === "--target=device") {
    target = "--device";
  }
  return cordova.build({
    platforms: settings.BUILD_PLATFORMS,
    options: ["--" + settings.BUILD_MODE, target]
  }).then(cordovaTasks.cdUp);
},
// cordova emulate ios|android --release|debug
emulate: function emulate() {
  cordovaTasks.cdProject();
  return cordova.emulate({
    platforms: [settings.PLATFORM],
    options: ["--" + settings.BUILD_MODE,
      settings.TARGET_DEVICE]
  }).then(cordovaTasks.cdUp);
},
// cordova run ios|android --release|debug
run: function run() {
  cordovaTasks.cdProject();
  return cordova.run({
    platforms: [settings.PLATFORM],
    options: ["--" + settings.BUILD_MODE, "--device",
      settings.TARGET_DEVICE]
  }).then(cordovaTasks.cdUp);
},
init: function() {
```

```
        return cordovaTasks.create()
          .then(cordovaTasks.copyConfig)
          .then(cordovaTasks.addPlugins)
          .then(cordovaTasks.addPlatforms);
    }
};
```

 If you aren't familiar with promises, you might want to learn more about them. `http://www.html5rocks.com/en/tutorials/es6/promises/` is a fantastic resource.

Most of the previous tasks should be fairly self-explanatory; they correspond directly to their Cordova CLI counterparts. A few, however, need a little more explanation:

- `cdProject` / `cdUp`: These change the current working directory. All the `cordova-lib` commands after `create` need to be executed from within the Cordova project directory, not our project's root directory. You should notice them in several of the tasks.

- `addPlatforms`: The platforms are added directly from our project's dependencies, rather than from the Cordova CLI. This allows us to control the platform versions we are using. As such, `addPlatforms` needs to do a little more work to specify the actual directory name of each platform.

- `build`: This executes the `cordova build` command. By default, CLI builds every platform. Since we will want to control the platforms that are built, hence we can use `BUILD_PLATFORMS` to control this behavior. On iOS, the build for an emulator is different than the build for a physical device. So, we also need a way to specify this, which is what `TARGET_DEVICE` does. This will look for emulators with the name specified for `TARGET_DEVICE`. But we might want to build for a physical device; in which case, we will look for `device` (or no target specified at all) and switch over to the `--device` flag which forces Cordova to build for a physical device.

- `init`: This does the hard work of creating the Cordova project, copying the configuration file (and performing substitutions), adding plugins to the Cordova project, and then adding platforms.

Now is also a good time to mention that we can specify various settings with switches on the Gulp command line. In the earlier snippet, we're supporting the use of `--platform` to specify the platform to emulate or run, `--mode` to specify the build mode (`debug` or `release`), `--for` to determine what platforms Cordova will build for, and `--target` to specify the target device. The code will specify reasonable defaults if these switches aren't specified; but they also allow the developer extra control over the workflow, which is very useful. For example, we'll be able to use commands like the following:

```
$ gulp build --for ios,android --target device
$ gulp emulate --platform ios --target iPhone-6s
$ gulp run --platform ios --mode release
```

Next, let's write the code to actually perform various Cordova tasks. It isn't difficult, but we need to create a lot of files. Each file name in the code below is in comments:

```js
// gulp/tasks/clean.js
var paths = require("../utils/paths"),
    config = require("../config"),
    rimraf = require("rimraf");
function clean(cb) {
    var BUILD_PATH = paths.makeFullPath(".", paths.DEST);
    rimraf(BUILD_PATH, cb);
}
module.exports = {
    task: clean
}

// gulp/tasks/init.js
var cordovaTasks = require("../utils/cordova-tasks");
module.exports = {
  deps: ["clean"],
  task: cordovaTasks.init
};

// gulp/tasks/build.js
var cordovaTasks = require("../utils/cordova-tasks");
module.exports = {
  deps: ["copy"],
  task: cordovaTasks.build
};

// gulp/tasks/emulate.js
var cordovaTasks = require("../utils/cordova-tasks");
```

```
module.exports = {
  deps: ["copy"],
  task: cordovaTasks.emulate
};

// gulp/tasks/run.js
var cordovaTasks = require("../utils/cordova-tasks");
module.exports = {
  deps: ["copy"],
  task: cordovaTasks.run
};
```

There's a catch with the `init` task: it will fail if anything is already in the `build/` directory. As you can guess, this could easily happen; so we also created a `clean` task. This uses `rimraf` to delete a specified directory, which is equivalent to using `rm -rf build`. We then ensured that `init` depends on clean. So, whenever we execute `gulp init`, the old Cordova project is removed and a new one is created for us.

Finally, note that all the `build` (and other) tasks depend on `copy`. This means that all our files in `src/` will be copied (and transformed, if necessary) to `build/` prior to executing the desired Cordova command. As you can see, our tasks are already becoming very complex, while remaining comprehensible when they are taken singularly.

This means that we can now use the following tasks in Gulp:

```
$ gulp init                        # create the cordova project;
                                   # cleaning first if needed
$ gulp clean                       # remove the cordova project
$ gulp build                       # copy src to build; apply
                                   # transformations; cordova build
$ gulp build --mode release        # do the above, but build in
                                   # release mode
$ gulp build --for ios             # only build for iOS
$ gulp build --target=device       # build device versions instead of
                                   # emulator versions
$ gulp emulate --platform ios      # copy src to build; apply
                                   # transformations;
                                   # cordova emulate ios
$ gulp emulate --platform ios --target iPhone-6
                                   # same as above, but open the
                                   # iPhone 6 emulator
```

```
$ gulp run --platform ios          # copy src to build;
                                    # apply transformations;
                                    # cordova run ios --device
```

Now, you're welcome to use the previous code as it is or you can use an NPM package that takes care of the `cordovaTasks` portion for you. This has the benefit of drastically simplifying your Gulp configuration. We've already included this package in our `package.json` file as well as our Gulp configuration. It's named `cordova-tasks` and was created by the author. It shares a lot of similarities to the earlier code. To see how it works (and how much simpler the tasks become), see `logology-v01/gulp` in the code package for this book.

This was one of the complex sections; so if you've come this far, take a coffee break. Next, we'll worry about managing app version numbers.

Managing version numbers

Although we've set up our `copy-config` and `copy-code` tasks to substitute the version number whenever `{{{VERSION}}}` is encountered, we don't have any tasks that actually change the version. We could just edit `package.json`, of course. But this is tedious and it can't be included automatically in any other Gulp task. Instead, let's use the `gulp-bump` plugin to take care of this for us.

`gulp-bump` is a very simple plugin: it is designed to take a `package.json` (or similar) file and edit the `version` property based on specific commands. Most versions are of the `major.minor.patch` form and we can ask it to increment any portion by one. If you wanted, you could increment the `patch` portion of the version to automatically track build numbers, for example.

Doing this is pretty simple. Let's first create another utility file, this time called `gulp/utils/bump.js`:

```
var gulp = require("gulp");
var bump = require("gulp-bump");

module.exports = function bump(importance) {
  return gulp.src([path.join(process.cwd(), "package.json")])
             .pipe(bump({type: importance}))
             .pipe(gulp.dest(process.cwd()));
}
```

The `importance` variable can be one of the following strings: `major`, `minor`, or `patch`. Next, let's create three tasks that will allow us to call this method directly (again, these are in three separate files, indicated in the comment):

```
// gulp/tasks/version-bump-patch.js
var bump = require("../utils/bump");
module.exports = {
    task: bump.bind(null, "patch")
}


// gulp/tasks/version-bump-minor.js
var bump = require("../utils/bump");
module.exports = {
    task: bump.bind(null, "minor")
}


// gulp/tasks/version-bump-major.js
var bump = require("../utils/bump");
module.exports = {
    task: bump.bind(null, "major")
}
```

Now you can directly bump the version number by executing `gulp version-bump-patch`. This, however, only edits `package.json`. If you want the files in `build/` to reflect this, you will need to also execute `gulp copy` (or `build` and so on).

Supporting ES2015

We've already mentioned ES2015 (or EcmaScript 2015) in this chapter. Now is the moment to start using it. First, though, we need to modify our `copy-code` task to transpile from ES2015 to ES5, or our code will not run on any browser that doesn't support the new syntax (which is still quite a few mobile platforms).

There are several transpilers available. I prefer Babel (`https://babeljs.io`).

 We used Babel 5.x. Although Babel 6 has recently been released, as of this writing, the demonstration app and corresponding Gulp configurations have not been updated to Babel 6.x.

There is a Gulp plugin that we can use, which makes this transpilation transform extremely simple. To do this, we need to add the following to the top of gulp/tasks/copy-code.js:

```
var ...,
    babel = require("gulp-babel"),
    sourcemaps = require("gulp-sourcemaps"),
    gutil = require("gulp-utils");
```

 Source maps are an important piece of the debugging puzzle. As our code will be transformed by the time it runs on our device, debugging could become a little more difficult, since the line numbers and the like don't match. Sourcemaps provide the browser with a map between your ES2015 code and the final result so that debugging is a lot easier.

Next, let's modify our projectTasks.copyCode method:

```
function copyCode() {
    var isRelease = (settings.BUILD_MODE === "release");
    return gulp.src([paths.makeFullPath(config.assets.code.src,
      paths.SRC)])
                .pipe(cordovaTasks.performSubstitutions())
                .pipe(settings.BUILD_MODE === "debug" ?
                  sourcemaps.init() : gutil.noop())
                .pipe(babel())
                .pipe(concat("app.js"))
                .pipe(settings.BUILD_MODE === "debug" ?
                  sourcemaps.write() : gutil.noop())
                .pipe(gulp.dest(paths.makeFullPath(
                  config.assets.code.dest, paths.DEST)));
}
```

Our task is now a little more complex; but this is only because we want to control when source maps are generated. When babel() is called, it will convert the ES2015 code to ES5 and also generate a sourcemap of the changes. This makes debugging easier, but it also increases the file size (sometimes by quite a bit). As such, when we're building in release mode, we don't want to include the sourcemaps. So, we will call gutil.noop instead, which will just do nothing.

The sourcemap functionality requires us to call sourcemaps.init prior to any Gulp plugin that might generate sourcemaps. After the plugin that creates the sourcemaps is executed, we also have to call sourcemaps.write to save the sourcemap back in the stream. We could also write the sourcemap to a separate .map file by calling sourcemaps.write("."). But you would need to be careful about cleaning up that file while creating a release build.

`babel` does the actual hard work of converting ES2015 code into ES5. But it does need a little help in the form of a small support library. We'll add this library to `src/www/js/lib/` by copying it from the `gulp-babel` module:

```
$ cp node_modules/babel-core/browser-polyfill.js src/www/js/lib
```

 If you don't have the `src/www/js/lib/`directory yet, you'll need to create it before you execute the previous command.

Next, we need to edit `src/www/index.html` to include this script. While we're at it, let's make a few other changes:

```html
<!DOCTYPE html>
<html>
  <head>
    <script src="cordova.js" type="text/javascript"></script>
    <script src="./js/lib/browser-polyfill.js"
            type="text/javascript"></script>
    <script src="./js/app/app.js"
            type="text/javascript"></script>
  </head>
  <body>
    <p>This is static content...,
        but below is dynamic content.</p>
    <div id="demo"></div>
  </body>
</html>
```

Finally, let's write some ES2015 code in `src/www/js/app/index.js`:

```javascript
function h(elType, ...children) {
  let el = document.createElement(elType);
  for (let child of children) {
    if (typeof child !== "object") {
      el.textContent = child;
    } else if (child instanceof Array) {
      child.forEach(el.appendChild.bind(el));
    } else {
      el.appendChild(child);
    }
  }
  return el;
}

function startApp() {
```

```
document.querySelector("#demo").appendChild(
  h("div",
    h("ul", h("li", "Some information about this app..."),
      h("li", "App name: {{{NAME}}}"),
      h("li", "App version: {{{VERSION}}}")
    )
  )
);
}

document.addEventListener("deviceready", startApp, false);
```

This chapter isn't about *how* to write the ES2015 code, so I won't bore you with all the details. We'll cover that in the next chapter. Suffice it to say, the earlier code generates a few list items when the app is run using a very simple form of DOM templating. But it does so using the ... (spread) syntax for variable parameters: the `for ... of` loop and `let` instead of `var`. Although it looks a lot like JavaScript, ES2015 is different enough that it will take some time to learn how best to use the new features.

Linting your code

You could execute `gulp emulate --platform ios` (or `android`) right now; the app should work. But how do we know whether our code will work when it is built? Better yet—how can we *prevent* a build if the code isn't valid?

We do this by adding **lint** tasks to our Gulp configuration. Linting is a lot like compiling; the linter checks your code for obvious errors and aborts if it finds any. There are various linters available (some better than others), but not all of them support ES2015 syntax yet. The best one that does is ESLint (http://www.eslint.org). Thankfully, there's a very simple Gulp plugin that uses it.

We could stop at linting and be done, but code style is also important, and can catch out potentially serious issues as well. As such, we're also going to be using the JavaScript Code Style checker or JSCS (https://github.com/jscs-dev/node-jscs).

Let's create tasks to lint and check our coding style. First, we need to add some additional configuration to `gulp/config.js`:

```
var config = { ...,
    lint: "src/www/js/app/**/*.js",
    "code-style": "src/www/js/app/**/*.js"
}
```

Now, let's create the associated tasks. Let's start with linting—this will live in the `gulp/tasks/link.js` file:

```
var gulp = require("gulp"),
    eslint = require("gulp-eslint"),
    config = require ("../config"),
    settings = require("../settings"),
    paths = require("../utils/paths");
function lintCode() {
    return gulp.src(paths.makeFullPath(config.lint))
        .pipe(eslint(paths.makeFullPath("eslint.json",
          paths.CONFIG)))
        .pipe(eslint.format());
}
module.exports = {
    task: lintCode
}
```

The task for checking our code style will be named `gulp/tasks/code-style.js`. It should have the following code:

```
var gulp = require("gulp"),
    jscs = require("gulp-jscs"),
    config = require ("../config"),
    settings = require("../settings"),
    paths = require("../utils/paths");
function checkCodeStyle() {
    return gulp.src(paths.makeFullPath(config["code-style"]))
        .pipe(jscs({
            configPath: paths.makeFullPath("jscs.json",
                         paths.CONFIG),
            esnext: true
        }))
        .pipe(jscs.reporter())
        .pipe(jscs.reporter('fail'));
}
module.exports = {
    task: checkCodeStyle
}
```

Now, before you run either task, you'll need two configuration files to tell each task what should be an error and what shouldn't be. We suggest using the files from the code bundle for this chapter for now (you can find them in the `logology-v01/config` directory). If you want to change the settings, you can do so; the sites for ESLint and JSCS both have information on how to modify the configuration files.

`config/eslint.json` must contain `"parser"`: `"babel-eslint"` in order to force it to use the ES2015 syntax. This is set for JSCS in the Gulp configuration, however.

`config/jscs.json` must exist and must not be empty. If you don't need to specify any rules, use an empty JSON object ({ }).

Now, if you were to execute `gulp lint` and our source code had a syntax error, you would receive an error message. The same goes for code styles; `gulp code-style` would generate an error if it didn't like the look of the code.

Next, you should add these two tasks to our build, emulate, and run tasks. Here's what the `module.exports` of `gulp/tasks/build.js` looks like after doing this:

```
module.exports = {
    deps: ["copy", "lint", "code-style"],
    task: …
}
```

Now, if you execute `gulp build` and there is a linting or code style error, the build will fail with an error. This gives a little more assurance that our code is at least syntactically valid prior to distributing or running the code.

 Linting and style checks do not guarantee that your code works *logically*. It just ensures that there are no syntax or style errors. If your program responds incorrectly to a gesture or processes some data incorrectly, a linter won't necessarily catch these issues.

Uglifying your code

Code uglification or minification sounds a bit painful, but it's a really simple step we can add to our workflow. It will reduce the size of our applications when we build in release mode. Uglification also tends to obfuscate our code a little bit, but don't rely on this for any security—obfuscation can be easily undone.

To add code uglification, add the following line of code to the top of our `gulp/tasks/copy-code.js` file:

```
var …,
    uglify = require("gulp-uglify");
```

We can then uglify our code by adding the following code immediately after `.pipe(concat("app.js"))` in our `projectTasks.copyCode` method:

```
.pipe(isRelease ? uglify({preserveComments: "some"}) :
gutil.noop())
```

Notice that we added the `uglify` method only when the build mode was `release`. This means that we'll only trigger it if we execute `gulp build --mode release`.

You can, of course, specify additional options. If you want to see all the documentation, visit `https://github.com/mishoo/UglifyJS2/`. Our options include certain comments (which most likely are license-related) while stripping out all the other comments.

Putting it all together

You've accomplished quite a bit, but there's one last thing we want to mention: the `default` task. If `gulp` is run with no parameters, it will look for a default task to perform. This can be anything you want.

To specify this, just add the following task at `gulp/tasks/default.js`:

```
module.exports = {
    deps: ["build"]
}
```

Now, if you execute `gulp` with no specific task, you'll actually start the `build` task instead. What you want to use for your default task is largely dependent upon your preferences.

Your Gulp configuration is now quite large and complex. We've added a few additional features to it in the code package, so it wouldn't be a bad idea to take a look at our final version in the code bundle of this book. We've also added several other features to the configuration, which you might want to investigate further. They are as follows:

- BrowserSync for rapid iteration and testing
- The ability to control whether or not any errors prevent further tasks from being executed
- Help text

Summary

In this chapter, you've learned why a task runner is useful and how to install Gulp and create several tasks of varying complexity to automate the building process of your project and other useful tools. We're not yet done with Gulp, though. In the next ~~~~~~~~~~~ ularization using Browserify and how to integrate

2
ECMAScript 2015 and Browserify

JavaScript has quickly become the *lingua franca* of the Web and the language's syntax and semantics have long been in need of improvements. ECMAScript 2015 introduces a lot of syntactic sugar that makes writing JavaScript easier. It also provides many new useful concepts that simplify application development. We briefly introduced you to ES2015 in the previous chapter. We'll be delving deeper into ES2015, as it's important that you become familiar with what the new syntax looks like.

Furthermore, it can be extremely useful to reuse your own work and that of others as well. But doing so would require you to manage your dependencies and ensure that the appropriate libraries are included. Doing this manually can be painful; but you can leverage a tool such as Browserify to assist. Browserify is a utility that not only packages your JavaScript files along with their dependencies, but also provides a Node.js-like environment for the browser. This means that you can reuse the majority of the huge JavaScript repository that Node.js uses. After all, why reinvent the wheel if someone has already done the hard work?

In this chapter, we'll cover:

- New ES2015 syntax
- Using Browserify

Getting started

Several of the snippets in this chapter are also available using the interactive snippet playground that accompanies the code package of this book. Instructions to launch the playground are in the README.md file in the code package. Once it starts, select **2: ES2015 and Browerify** and then browse and experiment with the examples in the adjacent dropdown. Where applicable, each section and snippet will indicate which example you should select.

Benefits of ES2015

Although we briefly touched upon ES2015 (ECMAScript 2015) in the previous chapter, it's possible that you may not be very familiar with it. Most browsers (especially mobile) do have full support for ES2015, if any at all. This is unfortunate, because there are tremendous improvements in syntax and semantics that make it easier to create complex mobile applications.

Thankfully, as you saw in the previous chapter, there are tools that port this functionality back to ES5, which is *very* well supported in modern browsers. These tools convert the ES2015 syntax and semantics into their ES5 equivalent (where possible). Where a perfect equivalence is not possible, the conversion will get as close as possible, which will still bring us great benefit.

We can't go over *every* new change in ES2015 in this book; but we do need to go over some common examples, especially if you aren't familiar with the syntax.

If you are developing for older devices, you will want to pay special attention to the performance characteristics of your application if you intend on using ES2015 code. ES2015 code is not necessarily faster than ES5, especially when it is transpiled. Unfortunately, even the native implementations of ES2015 aren't always faster, so you must balance the benefits of developer productivity and program readability with that of the actual performance of your app.

Block scope

Correctly understanding variable scope is one very common developer pitfall developers encountered in ES5. Instead of being block-scoped (which is typical of most languages that have the block concept), the variables were function-scoped. Variable definitions were hoisted to the top of the function definition, which meant that it was easy to use variables before they were actually assigned a value and it was also easy to redefine variables (often typical in `for` loops). Because this hoisting wasn't obvious from the source code, it was very easy to end up with nasty surprises.

Block-scoped variables, on the other hand, allow us to indicate that a variable is valid for a very specific portion of a function. We can reuse the name of the variable when we like (benefiting `for` loops) without worrying about unwanted side effects or surprises. Let's look at the difference in how these are defined and assigned:

ES5	ES2015	Explanation
`var x;`	`let x;`	x is defined, but has no value
`var y = 5;`	`let y = 5;`	y is defined and has the value 5
N/A	`const z = 5;`	z can never be reassigned
`for(var i=0,l=5;i<l;i++)`	`for(let i=0,l=5;i<l;i++)`	Iterate 5 times

 The snippets in this section are located at `snippets/02/ex1-block-scope/a` and `snippets/02/ex1-block-scope/b` in the code package of this book. Using the interactive snippet playground, select **2: ES2015 and Browserify** in the first dropdown and examples **1a** and **1b** in the second.

What's not terribly obvious in the previous examples is the difference in block scope. Consider this example in ES5:

```
// Snippet Example 1a
// Snippet Example 1a
var i = 10, // [1]
    x = 0;
console.log(i); // 10
for (var i = 0, l = 5; i < l; i++) { // [2]
  x += i;
}
console.log(x); // 10 (0+1+2+3+4)
console.log(i); // 5 [3]
console.log(l); // 5
```

Notice that the value of i defined in [1] is overwritten by the for loop in [2] (as you can see in [3]). Based upon the way the code is written, this is a surprise, especially to anyone who doesn't understand that the variable is function-scoped. Now, let's see the code in ES2015:

```
// Snippet Example 1b
let i = 10,
    x = 0;
console.log(i); // 10
for (let i = 0, l = 5; i < l; i++) {
  x += i;
}
console.log(x); // 10 (0+1+2+3+4)
console.log(i); // 10
console.log(l); // Error: Can't find variable: l
```

Note that i is no longer overwritten—a new variable was created for the duration of the loop. Furthermore, note that l is not available *at all*; it fell out of scope when the loop terminated.

Preventing multiple definitions of variables is another important feature of let and const. ES5 didn't complain when a variable was defined more than once, which is what lead to the nasty surprise in the preceding example. ES2015, on the other hand, *will* complain if you attempt to redefine a variable within the same scope. For example:

```
let i = 10;
let i = 20; // Error: Duplicate definition "i"
```

 It's vital that you recognize that var has not gone away; it's perfectly valid to define a variable using var. If you do, however, you need to be aware that such variables operate using function-scope and do not inherit any ES2015 behavior.

Arrow functions

JavaScript has always relied upon the function keyword heavily and this has often resulted in some hard-to-read code with a lot of boilerplate. Consider this ES5 snippet:

```
// Snippet Example 2a
[1, 2, 3].map(function(val) {
  return val * 2;
}).forEach(function(val) {
```

```
    console.log(val);
});
// console displays:
// 2
// 4
// 6
```

 The snippets in this section are located at `snippets/02/ex2-fat-arrow-functions/a` and `snippets/02/ex2-fat-arrow-functions/e` in the code package of this book. Using the interactive snippet playground, select **2: ES2015 and Browserify** in the first dropdown and examples **2a-2e** in the second dropdown.

Although this snippet is pretty simple to follow, it's a little annoying to type `function` and `return` all the time. With ES2015, we can use the following arrow syntax instead:

```
// Snippet Example 2b
[1, 2, 3].map(val => val * 2)
  .forEach(val => console.log(val));
// console displays the same output as before
```

The form of these arrow functions differ based on the required number of parameters. Here are some examples:

```
// no parameters; note the empty parentheses
[1, 2, 3].map(() => 2); // [2, 2, 2]

// one parameter; no parentheses required
[1, 2, 3].map(val => val * 2); // [2, 4, 6]

// multiple parameters; parentheses required
[1, 2, 3].map((val, idx) => val * idx); // [0, 2, 6]
```

Notice the lack of any `return` keyword; the result of the expression after the arrow is assumed to be returned. Assuming the implicit `return` is valid only for a single expression; if you need multiple statements, you must use braces and supply `return`, as follows:

```
[1, 2, 3].map((val, idx) => {
  console.log(val);
  return val * idx;
});
```

Arrow functions also have the concept of a *lexical* `this` value. What exactly `this` refers to at any point in time in JavaScript has always been a bit difficult to wrap one's mind around, especially while learning the language. It still often trips up even experienced developers. The problem arises when you do something like the following:

```
// Snippet Example 2c
var o = {
  a: [1, 2, 3],
  b: 5,
  doMul: function() {
    return this.a.map(function(val) {
      return val * this.b;
    });
  }
}
console.log(o.doMul());
```

Although this seems like a perfectly innocuous segment of code (we would expect [5, 10, 15] on the console), it will actually throw an error: `undefined is not an object (evaluating this.b)`. The `this` reference inside `doMul` refers to the object `o`, but when `this` is used inside the mapping function, it doesn't refer to `o`. We can get around this by changing the code slightly, as follows:

```
// Snippet Example 2d
var o = {
  ...,
  doMul: function() {
    return this.a.map(function(val) {
      return val * this.b;
    }, this); // map accepts a this parameter to apply to the callback
  }
}
```

For any methods that don't accept a `this` parameter, we could also use `bind` and its cousins. But what if we didn't have to worry about it at all? In ES2015, we can write it as follows:

```
// Snippet Example 2e
let o = {
  a: [1, 2, 3],
  b: 5,
  doMul() {
    return this.a.map(val => val * this.b);
  }
}
```

ES2015 doesn't eliminate the various vagaries with this, so you still need to be on the lookout for any misuse of this in your own code. But the lexical this value definitely helps in easing this particular pain point.

Because arrow functions have their own lexical context, however, you can't use them everywhere you might use regular functions. If the function needs to be supplied with many different contexts using bind (or similar), you'll want to use a regular function instead.

Simpler object definitions

Object definitions in JavaScript are fairly verbose. For example, consider the following code snippet:

```
// Snippet Example 3a
function makePoint(x, y) {
  return {
    x: x,
    y: y
  };
}
console.log(makePoint(5, 10)); // {x: 5, y: 10}
```

The snippets in this section are located at snippets/02/ex3-object-definitions/a and snippets/02/ex3-object-definitions/b in the code package of this book. Using the interactive snippet playground, select **2: ES2015 and Browserify** in the first dropdown and examples **3a** and **3b** in the second dropdown.

In the previous example, it seems a bit redundant to specify x and y twice, doesn't it? Although, in this example, it's not particularly onerous, in ES2015, we can write the following, which is much more concise:

```
// Snippet Example 3b
function makePoint (x, y) {
  return {x, y};
}
console.log(makePoint(5,10)); // {x: 5, y: 10}
```

In ES2015, the key name is optional. If it isn't provided, ES2015 assumes the key name should match that of the variable. In the preceding example, the resulting object will have two keys, namely x and y, and they will have the values passed to the routine.

Functions can also be specified using this shorthand, as you saw in the previous section. Instead of typing `myFunction: function() {...}`, ES2015 allows you to specify `myFunction() {...}`.

Default arguments

It is very common to write functions that have optional parameters. When these parameters aren't supplied, a default value is supplied instead. Unfortunately, the way this is often implemented is fraught with issues and potential surprises, and has led to many bugs. In ES5, default parameters are often handled as follows:

```
// Snippet Example 4a
function mul(a, b, log) {
  var ans = a * b;
  if (log === true) {
    console.log(a, b, ans);
  }
}
mul(2, 4); // doesn't log anything
mul(4, 8, true); // logs 4 8 32
```

The snippets in this section are located at `snippets/02/ex4-default-arguments/a` and `snippets/02/ex4-default-arguments/b` in the code package of this book. Using the interactive snippet playground, select **2: ES2015 and Browserify** in the first dropdown and examples **4a** and **4b** in the second dropdown.

While this *technically* works, it is far from ideal in because it isn't obvious from a quick read over the code that `log` really is optional from a quick read over the code. Furthermore, if the variable isn't checked correctly, it's easy to end up in surprising situations (for example, `if (log)` is *not* the same thing as `if (log===true)`).

It's also quite common to see the following pattern:

```
function repeat (a, times) {
  for (var I = 0; i < (times || 1) /*[1]*/; i++) {
    console.log(a);
  }
}
```

Unfortunately this will lead to incorrect behavior if we were to call this method with `times` set to zero. Because zero is falsy, the expression in [1] will actually evaluate to one, not zero.

It would be nice if we could avoid this mess entirely. ES2015 lets us write the earlier code in the following way:

```
// Snippet Example 4b
function mul(a, b, log = false) {
  var ans = a * b;
  if (log === true) { // [1]
    console.log(a, b, ans);
  }
}
```

This does nothing regarding JavaScript's concept of truthiness (so, we should still include the check in [1]). However, it does make it obvious to the reader that log is optional, and if it isn't supplied, what value it will receive.

Variable arguments

Another common pattern in JavaScript is to write methods that accept a variable number of arguments. A common example is the console.log method — it accepts several values and logs each to the console. We can follow its example to write a simple sum method. Let's see this first in ES5:

```
// Snippet Example 5a
function sum() {
  var args = [].slice.call(arguments);
  return args.reduce(
    function(prev, cur) {
      return prev + cur;
    }, 0);
}
console.log(sum(1, 2, 3, 4, 5)); // 15
```

 The snippets in this section are located at snippets/02/ex5-variable-arguments/a...d in the code package of this book. Using the interactive snippet playground, select **2: ES2015 and Browserify** in the first dropdown and examples **5a...5d** in the second dropdown

Of course, this isn't ideal—it's not immediately obvious that this method can accept any number of parameters. ES2015 lets us indicate this explicitly by writing the code as follows:

```
// Snippet Example 5b
function sum(...items) {
  return items.reduce((prev, cur) => (prev + cur), 0);
}
```

There's not a significant difference so let's take a look at a slightly more complex example, again in ES5 first:

```
// Snippet Example 5c
function interpolate(str) {
  var args = [].slice.call(arguments, 1 /*[1]*/);
  return args.reduce(function(prev, cur, idx) {
    return prev.replace(new RegExp(":" + (idx + 1), "g"), cur);
  }, str);
}
console.log(interpolate("My name is :1 and I say :2",
  "Bob", "Hello"));
  // My name is Bob and I say Hello
```

As before, this function signature doesn't indicate that `interpolate` accepts multiple parameters. Furthermore, we had to modify the code that parses all the additional parameters slightly—notice we added 1 while calling `slice` at `[1]`. This is because we needed to avoid including the first named parameter when performing the interpolation.

In ES2015, we can write the following instead:

```
// Snippet Example 5d
function interpolate(str, ...items) {
  return items.reduce((prev, cur, idx) => prev.replace(
    new RegExp(":" + (idx + 1), "g"), cur), str);
}
```

The ... operator can be used in another form in ES2015 by calling `interpolate` this way:

```
console.log(interpolate("My name is :1 and I say :2", ...["Bob",
  "Hello"]));
```

Granted, it looks a little silly when we hard-code the array. But if we need to write this in ES5, we'd have to use `interpolate.apply (null,["...","Bob","Hello"])` to achieve the same functionality. This proves incredibly useful when an array is passed to you; you can easily call a function that accepts a variable number of parameters

Destructuring and named parameters

A fairly typical pattern in JavaScript is extracting values from objects. For example, it's very common to see functions that accept an `options` object that modifies the way the function works. In ES5, this takes quite a bit of work. Consider the following snippet—it searches the **DOM (document object model)** for any elements matching a given query:

```
// Snippet Example 6b
function findElements(options) {
  var first = false,
      query,
      els;
  if (options !== undefined && typeof options === "object") {
    if (options.first !== undefined) {
      first = options.first;
    }
    if (options.query !== undefined) {
      query = options.query;
    }
  }
  els = [].slice.call(document.querySelectorAll(query));
  if (first === true) {
    els = [els[0]];
  }
  return els;
}
console.log(findElements({
  query: "a",
  first: true
}).map(function(o) {
    return o.textContent;
  }));
```

The snippets in this section are located at `snippets/02/ex6-destructuring/a...d` in the code package of this book. Using the interactive snippet playground, select **2: ES2015 and Browserify** in the first dropdown and examples **6a ... 6d** in the second dropdown.

The first several lines are devoted to supplying appropriate defaults and extracting values out of the `options` object. This is largely boilerplate; but if it is incorrect, bugs can arise. It would be so much better if we could avoid this entirely.

In ES2015, we can extract these values easily using a new feature called **destructuring**. It lets us write code like the following:

```
// Snippet Example 6a
let {a, b} = {
  a: 5,
  b: 10
};
console.log(a, b); // 5 10
```

We can do this safely, even if the object doesn't contain one of the keys we're asking for — the value will simply be `undefined`. Or, we can specify defaults:

```
let {a, b = 10} = {
  a: 5
}; // a = 5, b = 10
```

We can also drill into the object, as follows:

```
let {a: {b, c=10}} = {
  a: {
    b: 5
  }
};
console.log(b, c); // 5, 10, a is undefined
```

The same applies to arrays, as seen in the following snippet:

```
let [state, capitol] = ["Illinois", "Springfield"];
```

If there are more items than you care about, you can skip them:

```
let [a, , c] = [1, 2, 3];
console.log (a, c); // 1 3
```

You can use the . . . operator as well, should you wish to collect all the remaining values:

```
let [a, ...b] = [1, 2, 3];
console.log(a, b); // 1, [2, 3]

let {c, ...d} = {
  c: 5,
  d: 10,
  e: 15
}
console.log(c, d); // 5, {d: 10, e: 15}
```

Once we put all this together, we can rewrite our original code snippet as follows (in ES2015):

```
// Snippet Example 6c
function findElements({query, first = false}) {
  let els = [].slice.call(document.querySelectorAll(query));
  if (first === true) {
    els = [els[0]];
  }
  return els;
}
console.log(findElements({
  query: "a",
  first: true
}).map(o => o.textContent));
```

Although it may not be immediately obvious, this also gives us another feature: named parameters. It's not quite as nice as it is in other languages that support named parameters, but it's good enough. It also means that our code is even more self-documenting.

We can use this to approximate multiple return values as well:

```
// Snippet Example 6d
function doSomethingThatErrors() {
  let error = 5,
    message = "Element could not be found";
  return {
    error,
    message
  };
}
let {error, message} = doSomethingThatErrors();
console.log(error, message); // 5 Element could not be found
```

String interpolation

Many template and interpolation libraries have been developed for JavaScript, but ES2015 now provides built-in string interpolation.

 The snippets in this section are located at `snippets/02/ex7-string-interpolation/a` in the code package of this book. Using the interactive snippet playground, select **2: ES2015 and Browserify** in the first dropdown and example **7** in the second dropdown.

If you recall, we have already written an interpolation method named interpolate in the *Variable Arguments* section. For example, `interpolate("My name is :1", "Bob")` would return `My name is Bob`. In ES2015, we can achieve the same thing with the following:

```
let name = "Bob",
    str = `My name is ${name}`;
```

For most interpolation libraries, this is where it stops. But ES2015 allows us to evaluate arbitrary expressions:

```
let x = 2,
    y = 4,
    str = `X=${x},Y=${y},X+Y=${x + y}`; // X=2,Y=4,X+Y=6
```

 Anything that is an expression will work, including accessing object properties and methods.

As an added bonus, this new syntax also permits multiline strings:

```
let str = `SELECT * FROM
            FROM aTable`;
```

Of course, all whitespace is included, which means the string actually becomes `"SELECT *\n                FROM aTable"`. If spacing is important, you would need to take the necessary steps to strip the whitespace.

You can also define your own *interpolations*, which can be very useful. Let's consider a common security problem—SQL injection. For example, some developers are a bit lax when it comes to how they construct their SQL statements, as in the following example:

```
var sql = "SELECT * FROM customers WHERE customer_name = \"" +
    name + "\"";
```

Unfortunately, it's possible to inject arbitrary SQL code into this statement by supplying a specially crafted customer name. Now, before you think that ES2015 interpolation has saved you from security issue, be careful. The following construct is just as insecure:

```
let sql = `SELECT * FROM customers WHERE customer_name = ${name}`;
```

 Do not ever write code like the prior code! Ever!

Instead, most libraries that work with SQL commands allow you to craft *prepared statements*. These statements are comprised of two parts: a SQL template and an array of variables that are slotted into their appropriate positions in the template. This sounds an awful lot like interpolation, and it is. The difference is that these libraries use the database's own code to properly handle values such that SQL injection becomes impossible.

It looks something like the following in practice:

```
var preparedStatement = {
  sql = "SELECT * FROM customers WHERE customer_name = ?",
  binds: ["Bob"]
};
```

It's not terribly difficult to write SQL statements this way; but with ES2015, we *can* write our own interpolation handler that will make writing prepared statements even easier:

```
function sql(s, ...binds) {
  let len = binds.length;
  return {
    sql: s.map((val, idx) => (`${val}${idx < len ? "?" : ""}`))
      .join(""),
    binds
  };
}

let name = "Bob";
let preparedStatement = /*[1]*/ sql`SELECT * FROM customers WHERE
customer_name = ${name}`;
console.log(JSON.stringify(preparedStatement, null, 2));
// Console outputs
// {
//   sql: SELECT * FROM customers WHERE customer_name= ?
//   binds: ["Bob"]
// }
```

Take a look at `[1]` in the prior code. This is ES2015's way of indicating that the `sql` method is to be called in order to interpolate the string. Internally, this converts to `sql(["SELECT * FROM CUSTOMERS WHERE customer_name = ", ""], ["Bob"]);`.

Promises and a taste of ES2016

One often needs to write asynchronous code in JavaScript, *especially* when using Cordova plugins and also if one needs to make an `XMLHttpRequest`. This means that you will typically end up writing code as follows:

```
// Snippet Example 8a
function slowDiv(a, b, callback) {
  setTimeout(function() {
    if (b === 0) {
      callback("Can't divide by zero");
    } else {
      callback(undefined, a / b);
    }
  }, 2500 + Math.random() * 10000);
}
slowDiv(10, 5, function(err, result) {
  if (err !== undefined) {
    console.log(err);
    return;
  }
  console.log(result);
});
```

 The snippets in this section are located at `snippets/02/ex8-promises/a` and `snippets/02/ex8-promises/d` in the code package of this book. Using the interactive snippet playground, select **2: ES2015 and Browserify** in the first dropdown and examples **8a-8d** in the second dropdown

The previous example implements a very simple asynchronous method called `slowDiv` which it returns the results of a division operation after a short random period of time. If the divisor is zero, an error is returned instead.

The callback function accepts both the `err` and `result` parameters. If `err` has some value other than `undefined`, then we know that an error has occurred and we can handle it appropriately. Otherwise, we can log the result of the operation.

The `(err, result)` pattern is typical in Node.js applications.

Another similar callback pattern looks like the following – this is what you'll commonly see when using Cordova plugins:

```
// Snippet Example 8b
function slowDiv(a, b, success, failure) {
  setTimeout(function() {
    if (b === 0) {
      failure("Can't divide by zero");
    } else {
      success(a / b);
    }
  }, 2500 + Math.random() * 10000);
}
slowDiv(10, 5, function success(result) {
  console.log(result);
}, function failure(err) {
  if (err !== undefined) {
    console.log(err);
    return;
  }
});
```

The previous two code snippets do exactly the same thing—they return their result of division *very* slowly. This doesn't look too bad as long as you only need to do it once. But if you need to chain divisions together, the resulting code will quickly become very ugly.

To help combat the "pyramid of doom" and the resulting difficulty in understanding the code, **promises** were developed. These allow you to write a function which promises that it will return a result at some point in the future. Promises can also be chained by calling the `then` method on the resulting promise. Errors can be caught by supplying a `catch` handler as well.

There have been many libraries that provide promises to JavaScript. ES2015, however, makes promises a part of the language. This doesn't necessarily obviate the need for other libraries (they may provide other interesting features), but it does mean that you can use promises without a library.

A full primer on promises is beyond the scope of this chapter. If you want to learn more on promises, see `https://developer.` `mozilla.org/en-US/docs/Web/JavaScript/Reference/` `Global_Objects/Promise` and `https://www.promisejs.org`.

With promises and other ES2015 syntax, we can rewrite the previous code as follows:

```
// Snippet Example 8c
function slowDiv(a, b) {
  let p = new Promise((resolve, reject) => {
    setTimeout(() => {
      if (b === 0) {
        reject("Can't divide by zero");
      } else {
        resolve(a / b);
      }
    }, 2500 + (Math.random() * 10000));
  });
  return p;
}
slowDiv(10, 5)
  .then(result => console.log(result))
  .catch(err => console.log("error", err));
```

This is better than the example with callbacks; how much things improve will become obvious when we chain two slow divisions together, as follows:

```
slowDiv(10, 5)
  .then(result => slowDiv(20, result))
  .then(result => console.log(result)) // 20 / ( 10 / 5 ) = 10
  .catch(err => console.log("error", err));
```

As great as this is (and it's been heavily adopted by many JavaScript developers), it still doesn't feel like natural code. Instead it would be nice if we could write our asynchronous code as if it were synchronous.

With ES2015, we can't. We can come close with a combination of generators and a generator runner, but this still isn't quite natural. The next version of ECMAScript (ES2016), however, gives us a way to do almost exactly what we want: the `await` and `async` keywords.

If you want to see how to simulate `await` in ES2015, see `http://davidwalsh.name/async-generators`.

With these two keywords, we can now write our chained division as follows:

```
async function doCalculation_a() {
  try {
    let result1 = await slowDiv(10, 5);        // 2, eventually
    let result2 = await slowDiv(20, result1); // 10, eventually
    console.log(result2);
  } catch (err) {
    console.log("error", error);
  }
}
```

There are a few things to be noted in the previous example. First, there's a new `async` keyword (see [1])—this marks any function that returns an asynchronous result. Second, `await` is used to mark where our asynchronous function is waiting for a value from a promise (see [2]). Finally, it looks almost identical to the equivalent synchronous code! This means that we can reason how our code works even more easily.

There's only one problem: `await` must exist within an `async` function, and this means that any calling functions must also properly handle the asynchronicity. As such, you can't just use it wherever you want without planning for it. Even with this caveat, it's extremely useful.

 The syntax for `await` and `async` has not yet been finalized. Unlike ES2015, which has been accepted by the standards body, it is possible that the syntax (and perhaps even the semantics) for this feature will change in the future. As such, be wary of using `await` and `async` in production code.

You can also use `await` in expressions. So, we can write our `doCalculation` method as follows:

```
async function doCalculation() {
  try {
    // 10, eventually
    console.log( await slowDiv(20, await slowDiv(10, 5)));
  } catch (err) {
    console.log("error", error);
  }
}
```

How you use `await` is largely up to you; the second example is a little harder to read, but it does the same thing.

 Using ES2016 features is considered experimental. As such, Babel won't recognize it by default. We'll address this in the *Modifying our Gulp configuration* section later in this chapter.

Classes

Classes are probably one of the more controversial features added to ES2015. But in reality, they are simply syntactic sugar for JavaScript's existing prototypical nature. You don't have to use ES2015 classes if you don't want to – you can still create objects the same way you did before. From a readability perspective, however, there are some definite benefits.

 The snippets in this section are located at `snippets/02/ex9-classes/a` in the code package of this book. Using the interactive snippet playground, select **2: ES2015 and Browserify** in the first dropdown and example **9** in the second dropdown.

Let's start off with a quick look at the new syntax. In the following snippet, we define a simple `Point` class that represents an x and y coordinate on a two-dimensional plane:

```
class Point {
  constructor(x = 0, y = 0) { // [1]
    [this._x, this._y] = [x, y];
  }

  get x() { // [2]
    return this._x;
```

```
    }
    set x(x) { // [3]
      this._x = x;
    }
    get y() {
      return this._y;
    }
    set y(y) {
      this._y = y;
    }

    toString() {
      return `(${this.x}, ${this.y})`;
    }
    copy() {
      return new Point(this.x, this.y);
    }
    equal(p) {
      return (p.x === this.x) && (p.y === this.y);
    }
  }
```

Notice that we defined a constructor using the constructor keyword ([1]).
Property getters and setters are defined using get ([2]) and set ([3]), respectively.
Now, let's imagine that we want to create a rectangle. We could simply specify
the top left and the bottom right points; let's allow the developer to specify the *size*
instead. Although we could make the size a point, it would be more convenient to
use w and h instead of x and y. That's easy to accomplish, as seen in this snippet:

```
class Size extends Point { // [1]
  constructor(w = 0, h = 0) {
    super(w, h);
  }
  get w() {
    return this.x;
  }
  set w(w) {
    this.x = w;
  }
  get h() {
    return this.y;
  }
  set h(h) {
    this.h = h;
  }
```

```
    copy() {
      return new Size(this.w, this.h);
    }
  }
}
```

Notice the new `extends` keyword ([1])—this allows you to indicate that one class is based on another. The new class gains all the previous properties and methods automatically. Better yet, the subclass can call its parent's methods using `super`.

Now we can create a `Rectangle` class:

```
class Rectangle {
  constructor(origin = (new Point(0, 0)),
                  size = (new Size(0, 0))) {
    [this._origin, this.size] = [origin.copy(), size.copy()];
  }
  get origin() {
    return this._origin;
  }
  set origin(origin) {
    this._origin = origin.copy();
  }
  get size() {
    return this._size;
  }
  set size(size) {
    this._size = size.copy();
  }
  copy() {
    return new Rectangle(this.origin, this.size);
  }
  toString() {
    return `${this.origin}:${this.size}`;
  }
  equal(r) {
    return this.origin.equal(r.origin) && this.size.equal(r.size);
  }
  equalSize(r) {
    return this.size.equal(r.size);
  }
}
```

We can use all of these objects just as we expect:

```
let pointA = new Point(10, 50);
let sizeA = new Size(25, 50);
let rectA = new Rectangle(pointA, sizeA);
console.log(`${rectA}`); // (10,50):(25,50)
```

> When objects are used with string interpolation, `toString` is called automatically.

Modules

The final new ES2015 feature that we'll cover in this section is modules. There have been many ways to approach modularization in JavaScript, but ES2015 brings modularization into the language itself. The syntax is pretty simple; but if you aren't familiar with modules, it might take a while for you to absorb it fully.

In ES2015, a module is a separate JavaScript file that has one or more methods or variables marked with `export`. This is a new keyword that allows you to indicate that a value or method should be available to the other parts of your program. You can choose to provide a default export using `export default`.

Conversely, your code consumes a module with `import`. You can choose to import everything that the module exports with `import *` or you can pick and choose.

Let's consider an example. First, let's define a simple module:

```
// math.js
export function add(a, b) {
  return a + b;
}
export function sub(a, b) {
  return a - b;
}
```

We can use this module in another JavaScript file, as follows:

```
// another.js
import * from "math.js";
// the above line is equivalent to the following
// import {add, sub} from "math.js"
console.log(add(2, 5));
```

Now, imagine that we want to make an advanced math library, but we want to pass on the simpler methods to the consumer. We can export methods and values directly from another file, as follows:

```
// advancedMath.js
export * from "math.js"
export function mul(a, b) {
  return a * b;
}
```

None of this is terribly earth shattering—most developers use something similar, but it is nice to have it baked in. Furthermore, it does provide a little more flexibility, since you can pick and choose what you want to import and export.

Unfortunately, you need a packaging utility that provides support for this feature—it won't work by default with Babel. We'll cover that in the *Using Browserify* section later in this chapter.

More information

You've read a lot of information, but it's going to be critical to understand while reading the code in the rest of this book. Take some time to familiarize yourself with the information provided in this chapter. Then, I suggest that you read up some of the other features we didn't go over. The following websites provide a good starting point:

- http://www.2ality.com
- https://babeljs.io/docs/learn-ES2015/
- https://babeljs.io/docs/learn-es2015/

 Not every ES2015 feature is supported by the transpiler that we are using, namely Babel. For specifics on what Babel supports, see http://kangax.github.io/compat-table/es6/.

In order to test your comprehension of all the ES2015 features, or if you just want to play around, Babel has an excellent sandbox, where you can write ES2015 code, see the results of the transpilation, and then verify that whether the code works. You can access it online at https://babeljs.io/repl/.

Using Browserify

Very few applications require completely custom code. Most applications can benefit from modularization and code reuse, and it's important to use modularization to your benefit so that you can build apps more efficiently.

There's a syndrome common to many developers (and even some companies): the not-invented-here syndrome. The afflicted developer (or company) is extremely hesitant to use code, algorithms, or any other assets that they themselves didn't create. It's easy to see where this syndrome comes from—it ensures that one can't be held liable for third-party code, one can't be sued for improperly licensing assets, and so on; but it also means that one must continually reinvent the wheel. This invariably results in buggier, less secure algorithms, as everyone is always attempting to build their apps completely from scratch.

If you've worked through other books on mobile application development, chances are you've already been introduced to modularizing your own code. Rather than having one large monolithic JavaScript file that contains *everything*, you can separate your code so that it is easier to understand (and so that each concern is clearly separated).

It's extremely useful, however, to extend this to the JavaScript world at large; there are a large number of open source modules with permissive licenses that you can base your application upon. This means that one has to worry about properly abiding with licensing requirements, but it also enables you to assemble well-tested building blocks upon which your application is built.

Browserify (http://browserify.org) is a tool that lets you use the huge repository of Node.js packages. Many of these packages work fine in the browser as-is, but Node.js does have a different global environment. Browserify shims this Node.js environment into the browser, which means that just about any Node.js package can work within the browser environment. Most packages will indicate if the browser isn't supported in the documentation.

 Browserify is also used to package all your app's dependencies into one or more large files. This is useful in production, when you might want to supply one minified file containing all your code.

Furthermore, since we can use Node.js packages, we may as well use the Node.js package manager, npm. We've been using this already to install development dependencies, such as Cordova, Gulp, and more. But we can use npm to manage our application's dependencies as well.

You should take a moment and browse https://www.npmjs.com. It should be apparent that there's a *lot* there. The ability to leverage npm as a resource can greatly speed your own development.

Modifying our Gulp configuration

Unfortunately, in order to use Browserify and ES2015 together, we need to modify our Gulp configuration. Whereas, before we call babel directly to convert our code, we have to get a little fancy; browserify has to be called and browserify will call babel on its own. It's a subtle distinction, perhaps, but it is an important one.

First, let's install our new development dependencies:

```
$ npm --save-dev install vinyl-source-stream@1.1.0 vinyl-buffer@1.1.0
browserify@11.2.0 babelify@6.3.0

$ npm --save install babel@5.8.23

$ npm --save-dev uninstall gulp-babel
```

 The first two modules that we are installing will allow us to convert the output from browserify into something that Gulp can handle.

Then, we need to add some configuration at the top of our configuration file (gulp/config.js):

```
assets: { ...,
    code: {src: "www/js/app/index.js", dest: "www/js/app"}
}
```

Next, we need to modify the gulp/tasks/copy-code.js file. First, we need to add additional require statements to the top:

```
var ...,
    babelify = require("babelify"),
    browserify = require("browserify"),
    buffer = require("vinyl-buffer"),
    source = require("vinyl-source-stream");
```

Then, we modify copyCode to look like this:

```
function copyCode() {
  var isRelease = (settings.BUILD_MODE === "release");
  return browserify(paths.makeFullPath(config.assets.code.src,
                    paths.SRC), { // [1]
    debug: !isRelease, // [2]
```

```
      standalone: "app"
    }).transform(babelify.configure({ // [3]
      stage: 0, // allow experimental features // [4]
    }))
    .bundle()
    .on("error", function(error) {
      this.emit("end"); // [5]
    }).on("error", notify.onError(function(error) {
      return "BABEL: " + error.message; // [6]
    }))
    .pipe(source("app.js")) // [7]
    .pipe(buffer()) // [8]
    .pipe(cordovaTasks.performSubstitutions())
    .pipe(isRelease ? gutil.noop() : sourcemaps.init({
      loadMaps: true
    })) // loads map from browserify file
    .pipe(isRelease ? uglify({
      preserveComments: "some"
    }) : gutil.noop())
    .pipe(isRelease ? gutil.noop() : sourcemaps.write())
    .pipe(gulp.dest(paths.makeFullPath(config.assets.code.dest,
        paths.DEST)))
    .pipe(browserSync.stream());
}
```

The second half of the earlier code should look pretty familiar—it's what we had in the previous chapter, but the top half is completely new. Let's go over it a little more in detail.

First, instead of using `gulp.src`, we called `browserify` directly ([1]). In the previous chapter, we asked Gulp to concatenate all our JavaScript files into one file. Browserify, on the other hand, will discover all the files it needs to package together by following the dependency tree from our main file. Files that aren't dependencies will be automatically left out of the final output. This alone is a pretty nice feature.

While calling `browserify`, we ask it to create sourcemaps by setting the `debug` property ([2]). We would only want to do this if we are developing, so we make this based upon the `--mode` setting we pass on to Gulp.

We also want to be able to access our application's state globally while testing. By default, Browserify would package everything up into a neat bundle, but we wouldn't have direct access to the objects our application might create. Passing `standalone:"app"` to Browserify in allows us to specify a single global variable (app)that will give us access to our entire app. This isn't required for production code; but during development, it definitely helps when it comes to debugging.

Next, we transform the code using `babelify` ([3]). Browserify will then call `babel` for us automatically. We also pass `stage: 0` ([4])so that we can use ES2016 features such as `await` and `async`.

A couple of error handlers are also added so that we can be notified if Browserify encounters issues while transforming our code. The first one ([5]) ends the stream (which is important if you ever want to have Gulp watch your code), and the second ([6]) generates an error message.

Finally, we enter the Gulp territory—the first two `pipe` methods are where we bring Gulp into the picture ([7], [8]). Because we aren't actually asking Gulp to look for specific files, we used the two `vinyl` modules we installed earlier to pass the output from Browserify into a form that Gulp can work with. From this point onward, our code is identical to the code in *Chapter 1, Task Automation*.

Including Node.js packages

Including a Node.js package is very simple. First, you need to find a package you like from npm. In our example, we'll add a module called `yasmf-h`. It's not a complex package and it's essentially a fancier version of our little templating method in `index.js` from *Chapter 1, Task Automation*.

To install the package, enter the following:

```
$ npm --save install yasmf-h
```

Next, we need to modify `src/www/js/app/index.js` so that we can use the package:

```
import 'babel/polyfill'; // [1]
import h from 'yasmf-h'; // [2]

export var app = {
  start() {
    var n = h.el("div",
      h.el("ul",
        h.el("li", "Some information about this app..."),
        h.el("li", "App name: {{{NAME}}}"),
```

```
            h.el("li", "App version: {{{VERSION}}}")
        )
    );
    h.renderTo(n, document.querySelector("#demo"));
  }
};

document.addEventListener("deviceready", app.start, false);
```

This isn't entirely different from what we had in *Chapter 1, Task Automation*. Notice the two `import` statements. The first line of code (`[1]`) imports the `polyfill` that is necessary to support Babel, the ES2015 transpiler we have been using. The second (`[2]`) imports the code from the `npm` module we installed and assigns it to the `h` variable.

We need to modify our `src/www/index.html` file slightly as well, namely, to remove a line. Take a look at the following:

```html
<!DOCTYPE html>
<html>
  <head>
    <script src="cordova.js" type="text/javascript"></script>
    <script src="./js/app/app.js" type="text/javascript"></script>
  </head>
  <body>
    <p>This is static content..., but below is dynamic content.</p>
    <div id="demo"></div>
  </body>
</html>
```

Everything is the same, except that we've removed the following line:

```html
<script src="./js/lib/browser-polyfill.js" type="text/javascript"></script>
```

We don't need to include the ES2015 polyfill in our `index.html` file anymore simply because we've imported it in our `index.js` file. The fewer scripts we need to include in `index.html`, the better.

At this point, you can use `gulp build` to rebuild the project with the new changes. It will run exactly as before, but you're now using a module from a third party that *you didn't write*!

Of course, it's incredibly important to remember a few things while using modules you didn't write:

- Check the license, always. npm packages are usually pretty permissive, but it is wise to double-check. The package we included is MIT-licensed, and the requirements only ask for the original copyright to be included somewhere in the output. Because the license is included in the package's code, it is transferred into our output code. But it is up to you to ensure that you properly license any code you include in your project. You should also include a list of packages that you use in a visible portion of your app as well, perhaps in your app's **About** or **Settings** section.

- Review the package prior to installing it. Look at the code or any documentation, and see whether there are any big issues you can't work around. If a package has tests, even better — you can verify that the package actually works.

Summary

We've covered quite a bit in this chapter — most of it is related to the new syntax and features that ES2015 is bringing. Furthermore, we covered how to import npm modules and utilize them in our own code.

In the next chapter, we'll work on building modular CSS files with Sass. We'll also see how to integrate this into our build process.

3
Sassy CSS

Although JavaScript is critical for our application's functionality, CSS is critical for our application's appearance. Although CSS is extremely powerful, the version supported by most mobile browsers (CSS3) lacks many features that would make development easier. CSS also tends to be verbose; it's quite easy to end up with long, tangled stylesheets that are difficult to understand and maintain.

Sass (Syntactically Awesome Style Sheets) is an attempt to improve upon CSS3 and make it easy to write and maintain. It adds features like variables, interpolation, computations, mixins, modularity, and much more. We can use Sass to our benefit to make our CSS easier to read and write.

 You can learn more about Sass by visiting `http://sass-lang.com`.

In this chapter, we'll focus on the following:

- Learning Sass
- Integrating Sass with Gulp

Getting started

Several of the snippets in this chapter are also available using the interactive snippet playground that accompanies the code package of this book. Instructions to launch the playground are in the `README.md` file in the code package. Once it starts, select **3: Sassy CSS** and then browse and experiment with the examples. Where applicable, each section and snippet will indicate which chapter and example you should select.

Learning Sass

We've already briefly mentioned the benefits of Sass, but it will require a little effort to learn how to use it. That said, it's important to recognize a very important fact about Sass, which makes it easier to learn: every CSS file is a valid SCSS file. Sass itself understands two formats; but the format we'll be using is similar to the CSS syntax and uses the `.scss` extension. This means that you can write pure CSS and Sass will recognize it without a problem. This allows you to learn features at your own rate without losing productivity. In cases where you don't know a Sass feature, you can write regular CSS. Later, when you've learned more, you can rewrite the CSS using Sass.

 The other format that Sass understands uses indentation rather than brackets in order to define the structure of the file. These files use the `.sass` extension.

Before we delve deeper into the benefits of Sass, it is important to remember that browsers don't support the SCSS syntax. This means that we have to use a tool to transform the SCSS file into a CSS file that the browser understands. You're already familiar with converting ES2015 code into ES5, and this process is very similar.

Sass is highly based on the DRY concept—that is, don't repeat yourself. CSS, on the other hand, is often full of repetition, so the Sass code can be much more modular and compact than the equivalent CSS. While writing Sass code, one should look for opportunities to reduce repetition and encourage code reuse.

Sass contains imperative control structures such as control flow and loops as well as constructs that look and act like functions. This means that Sass code can sometimes read a bit more like a program than a style sheet. Thus, it is easy to abstract lots of complicated functions in reusable modules; but it also means that one has to be familiar with how Sass works. That said, if there's ever any confusion, consulting the resulting CSS file usually helps clear things up.

We can't cover every feature that Sass provides. Instead, we'll cover the features that we'll tend to use in our code for this book. If you want, you can always learn more by browsing the Sass documentation (`http://sass-lang.com/documentation/file.SASS_REFERENCE.html`).

Comments

CSS allows comments in the form of /* ... */. These types of comments are useful for licenses and other text that should be downloaded by a client. But typically, developers will strip out any other comment in production-ready CSS files in order to reduce the size of the file. Sass addresses this issue by providing a single-line comment feature. This single-line comment will never be rendered in the output CSS file, so you can use it as much as you want without worrying about the size of the output file. Single-line comments start with a double forward slash (//). Sass will continue rendering /* ... */ comments, so this is also a useful way of controlling which comments remain in the final output.

Sass can also be configured to eliminate all the comments. If you use this feature, you can still force certain comments to be included in the final output by using /! ... */. This might be useful if you need to include a license in the final output.

Calculation

CSS has long been riddled with *magic* numbers—values that are rather opaque as to their meaning or how the developer arrived at their value. Consider the following example:

```
.some-element {
    width: 560px;
}
```

Other than knowing that something is 560px wide, this snippet doesn't tell you how the width was determined. This means that it's difficult to come back and later modify the value appropriately. It could be the width of an image or it could be the result of a series of mathematical operations.

With CSS3, we can perform runtime calculations, which are extremely useful. So, we could write the following:

```
.some-element {
    width: calc((960px / 12) * 7);
}
```

This begins to provide some context—we have a 960px grid with 12 columns and the element should be 7 columns wide. So, when we come back later to modify it, we will know what we were initially thinking.

Although most modern mobile browsers support this, it's unwise to use `calc` in this way, because it incurs a performance hit since it must be continually evaluated. Because this number never changes, it would be faster if the result of the calculation could be determined only once and inserted into the output CSS.

Sass allows this by allowing us to specify calculations inline with our styles. Consider the following example:

```
.some-element {
  width: (960px / 12) * 7;
}
```

When Sass generates the CSS file, it will write `560px`, which means that the browser doesn't have to worry about recalculating this value. But when we look at our own code, it's much easier to read and understand why `560px` is the final result.

 The snippets in this section are located at `snippets/03/ex1-calculation/` in the code package of this book. When using the interactive snippet playground, select **3: Sassy CSS** and **Example 1: Calculation**.

The expected mathematical operators are available, including addition (+), subtraction (-), multiplication (*), and division (/). Modulo (%) is also supported. If any operand is missing its unit, the unit is inferred based on the previous operands. This means that `5px + 3` becomes `8px` and `10px * 3` is calculated as `30px`.

It should be noted that Sass does not perform mixed unit calculations. One cannot add `em` units to `px` units, for example. This would cause an error. If you need to do these kind of calculations, CSS3's `calc` is your only option.

You can, however, convert a ratio into a percentage. For example:

```
.some-element {
    width: ((960px / 12) * 7) / 960px * 100%;
}
```

In the preceding example, we're trying to move from a `960px` grid to a percentage-based layout while maintaining the same ratio. The result of the previous calculation will be `58.3333%`. The multiplication by `100%` converts our calculation into a percentage.

The division operator is somewhat special—the symbol is also used frequently in CSS. What should the result of the following be?

```
.some-element {
    width: 500px / 20;
}
```

In the prior example, Sass would output `500px / 20`, not `25px`. This is because CSS shorthand also uses the forward slash to separate some values. For example, `font` accepts the size and the line height (for example, `20px/50px` specifies a `20px` font size and `50px` line-height). Because every the CSS file is also a valid Sass file and the expectation is that the resulting output would match the original CSS files, Sass can't perform any division in this case. To force division in this case, we can wrap the expression in parentheses, as follows:

```
.some-element {
    width: (500px / 20);
}
```

We can also use various functions to operate on numbers. `round(1000px / 3)` would be translated to `333px`, not `333.3333px`. For a list of all the available functions, see `http://sass-lang.com/documentation/Sass/Script/Functions.html`.

Calculations can also be performed on colors; but it is easier to use color functions (these are listed in the previous link) than it is to use calculations to achieve the desired result.

If you need to perform string concatenation, you can use the addition operator.

For more information regarding Sass calculations, please see `http://sass-lang.com/documentation/file.SASS_REFERENCE.html#operations`.

Variables

One of the most obvious problems with vanilla CSS is the lack of variables. CSS instead often specifies the same colors, sizes, and images over and over. While this can be mitigated using the cascading nature of CSS, not everyone does so. Let's take a look at a couple of examples. Each example will duplicate the following simple layout:

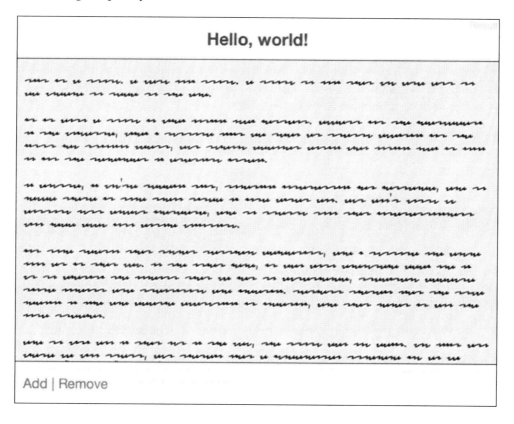

The HTML we're using for each example is as follows (it won't change for any of our following snippets):

```
<div class="ui-view-container">
  <div class="ui-navigation-bar">
    Hello, world!
  </div>
  <div class="ui-scroll-container">
    <p>...</p> ...
  </div>
  <div class="ui-tool-bar">
```

```
        <a href="#">Add</a> | <a href="#">Remove</a>
    </div>
</div>
```

 The snippets in this section are located at `snippets/03/ex2-variables/a...c` in the code package of this book. When using the interactive snippet playground, select **3: Sassy CSS** and examples from **2a** to **2c**.

Although this layout looks pretty simple, it is easy to see how the resulting CSS can quickly grow out of control. See the following example:

```
// Snippet Example 2a
.ui-view-container {
    position: absolute;
    padding: 10px; margin: 10px;
    border: 1px solid black;
    background-color: #EEE;
    top: 0; left: 0;
    bottom: 0; right: 0;
    box-sizing: border-box;
    font: 16px "Helvetica Neue", Helvetica, Arial, sans-serif;
}
.ui-navigation-bar {
    position: absolute;
    height: 50px; line-height: 50px;
    top: 0;
    left: 0; right: 0;
    border-bottom: 1px solid black;
    background-color: rgba(255,255,255,.95);
    color: #333;
    box-sizing: border-box;
    text-align: center;
    font-size: 20px;
    font-weight: bold;
    z-index:1;
}
.ui-scroll-container {
    position: absolute;
    top: 0; left: 0;
    right: 0; bottom: 0;
    padding: 50px 10px;
    overflow: auto;
}
```

```
.ui-tool-bar {
    position: absolute;
    bottom: 0;
    left: 0; right: 0;
    padding: 0 10px;
    line-height: 50px; height: 50px;
    box-sizing: border-box;
    background-color: rgba(255,255,255,.95);
    color: #333;
    border-top: 1px solid black;
    z-index:1;
}


.ui-tool-bar a {
    color: #369;
    text-decoration: none;
    display: inline-block;
    line-height: 50px;
}
```

Now, this isn't good CSS—it's very repetitive and it isn't taking advantage of CSS's cascading nature. So, let's rewrite it to be a bit less repetitive and easier to maintain:

```
//Snippet Example 2b
.ui-view-container, .ui-navigation-bar, .ui-tool-bar,
.ui-scroll-container {
    box-sizing: border-box;
    position: absolute;
}
.ui-view-container, .ui-scroll-container {
    top: 0; left: 0;
    bottom: 0; right: 0;
}
.ui-navigation-bar, .ui-tool-bar {
    background-color: rgba(255,255,255,.95);
    color: #333;
    height: 50px;
    left: 0; right: 0;
    padding: 0 10px;
    z-index: 1;
}
.ui-navigation-bar, .ui-tool-bar, .ui-tool-bar a {
    line-height: 50px;
}
.ui-view-container {
```

```
        border: 1px solid black;
        background-color: #EEE;
        font: 16px "Helvetica Neue", Helvetica, Arial, sans-serif;
        margin: 10px;
        padding: 10px;
    }
    .ui-navigation-bar {
        border-bottom: 1px solid black;
        font-size: 20px;
        font-weight: bold;
        text-align: center;
        top: 0;
    }
    .ui-scroll-container {
        overflow: auto;
        padding: 50px 10px;
    }
    .ui-tool-bar {
        border-top: 1px solid black;
        bottom: 0;
    }
    .ui-tool-bar a {
        color: #369;
        display: inline-block;
        text-decoration: none;
    }
```

The prior code has improved, but it still isn't clear and it has a lot of magic numbers whose meanings aren't immediately clear (this becomes worse in larger style sheets). With variables, we can start eliminating these magic numbers and improve our code's readability. We can also make it easy to adjust our app's appearance in the future by changing variables in a single location rather than having to search all over our style sheet looking for specific occurrences and making replacements.

Sass defines variables in the following manner:

```
$variable: value;
```

With this knowledge, we can now write a theme-able version of our CSS using just a few variables:

```
//Snippet Example 2c
$text-color: #333;
$font: "Helvetica Neue", Helvetica, Arial, sans-serif;
$text-font: 16px $font;
```

```scss
$text-title-size: 20px;
$text-title-weight: bold;
$tint-color: #369;
$bar-background-color: rgba(255,255,255,.95);
$view-background-color: #EEE;
$separation-border: 1px solid black;
$separation-size: 10px;
$bar-height: 50px;

.ui-view-container, .ui-navigation-bar, .ui-tool-bar,
.ui-scroll-container {
    box-sizing: border-box;
    position: absolute;
}
.ui-view-container, .ui-scroll-container {
    top: 0; left: 0;
    bottom: 0; right: 0;
}
.ui-navigation-bar, .ui-tool-bar {
    background-color: $bar-background-color;
    color: $text-color;
    height: $bar-height;
    left: 0; right: 0;
    padding: 0 $separation-size;
    z-index: 1;
}
.ui-navigation-bar, .ui-tool-bar, .ui-tool-bar a {
    line-height: $bar-height;
}
.ui-view-container {
    border: $separation-border;
    background-color: $view-background-color;
    font: $text-font;
    margin: $separation-size;
    padding: $separation-size;
}
.ui-navigation-bar {
    border-bottom: $separation-border;
    font-size: $text-title-size;
    font-weight: $text-title-weight;
    text-align: center;
    top: 0;
}
.ui-scroll-container {
```

```
    overflow: auto;
    padding: $bar-height $separation-size;
}
.ui-tool-bar {
    border-top: $separation-border;
    bottom: 0;
}
.ui-tool-bar a {
    color: $tint-color;
    display: inline-block;
    text-decoration: none;
}
```

If you're counting lines, you may notice that this example is actually longer than our previous example. So, at first, this may not appear to offer much benefit. Once you study the code, however, you'll notice several improvements, including the following points:

- The code is more readable and understandable. We don't have to guess what 50px might mean—the code specifically indicates that it is the height of a bar widget.

- The code has fewer magic numbers. Nearly every value (other than zero oro one) is represented by a variable instead of an opaque number. This isn't to say that every value in your Sass should be a variable; but when you find yourself typing the same value over and over in similar contexts, it might be a good time for you to use a variable.

- It's easy to change the resulting appearance. All we have to do is modify the first few lines of the preceding code and change our values. If we want the bars to be 44px high instead of 50px, it would be an easy change. In the second snippet, it's still easy, but we'd have to make the change in several places. If we did a search and replace, we'd have to make the untenable assertion that each instance of 50px should be changed. In our particular case, this would be safe, but in large files, it's less likely to be correct.

Sass variables are scoped to the selector in which they are declared. So, if a variable was declared in .ui-tool-bar, it would not be accessible to any other selectors. You can force such a variable to be global by appending !global. But if you find yourself doing this, you may as well take the variable itself out of the selector.

While using variables, you may also find that it is useful to use interpolation. Consider the following snippet:

```
.ui-navigation-bar {
    font: $text-title-weight #{$text-title-size}/#{$bar-height}
        $font;
  //font: bold 20px/50px"Helvetica Neue", Helvetica, Arial,
        sans-serif;
}
```

The preceding interpolation (identified with #{$variable-name}) is useful to avoid parsing issues. In the previous example, the forward slash could be interpreted in many different ways (including division). To avoid ambiguity (and possibly the wrong result), we can use interpolation.

We could also use interpolation in other places. Consider the following example:

```
$button-class: button;
a.#{$button-class} {
  ...
}
```

This translates to the following CSS:

```
a.button {
  ...
}
```

In the earlier example, we must use interpolation; using a.$button-class would result in an error.

Nesting

When you read HTML, it's pretty obvious that a hierarchical and nested structure is present. This is quickly lost in most CSS code. This can make it hard to understand how the CSS is accomplishing the final look. We can use Sass's nesting feature to make our code easier to write and understand.

 The snippets in this section are located at snippets/03/ex3-nesting/ in the code package of this book. When using the interactive snippet playground, select 3: **Sassy CSS** and Example 3.

Let's continue using the layout we discussed in the previous section. There are two anchors in the toolbar. Although the anchors are clearly nested within the `div` toolbar, it isn't quite as obvious that this is the case while reading the CSS. We can, however, write our Sass as follows:

```
.ui-tool-bar {
    border-top: $separation-border;
    bottom: 0;
    a {
      color: $tint-color;
      display: inline-block;
      text-decoration: none;
    }
}
```

Now, it's quite clear that we are styling anchors that live inside toolbars. The generated CSS creates two rules: `.ui-tool-bar` and `.ui-tool-bar a` out of this nesting.

While nesting, there is a special placeholder we can use: the ampersand (`&`). This is useful when we need to use pseudo-elements such as `:hover` or the like. This lets us write a rule like the following:

```
.ui-tool-bar {
    ...
    a {
        ...
        &:hover {
            text-decoration: underline;
        }
    }
}
```

Sass also provides another form of nesting. CSS often groups properties together. For example, `font-family`, `font-size` and `font-weight` are all related to the element's. In CSS, we'd have to specify each property separately (or use CSS shorthand). But in Sass, we can do as follows:

```
.some-element {
    font: {
        family: sans-serif;
        size: 16px;
        weight: bold;
    }
}
```

Mixins and functions

As we mentioned before, Sass is all about reducing repetition and increasing abstraction. Sass provides mixin and function directives that let us create reusable components, which we can later insert into our styles.

 The snippets in this section are located at `snippets/03/ex4-mixins/a...d` in the code package of this book. When using the interactive snippet playground, select **3: Sassy CSS** and Example **4a** to **4d**.

Supporting vendor prefixes makes for a good example. It's not uncommon to see something like the following in many style sheets:

```
.some-element {
  -webkit-box-sizing: border-box;
  -moz-box-sizing: border-box;
  -ms-box-sizing: border-box;
  -o-box-sizing: border-box;
  box-sizing: border-box;
}
```

Not only is this a bit painful to look at, it's also incredibly repetitive. With Sass, however, we can write a mixin that does this work for us. First, we will define the mixin:

```
// Snippet Example 4a
@mixin box-sizing($value) {
  -webkit-box-sizing: $value;
  -moz-box-sizing: $value;
  -ms-box-sizing: $value;
  -o-box-sizing: $value;
  box-sizing: $value;
}
```

This looks quite a bit like the previous snippet. Remember, a mixin is essentially a macro or a template that you can include elsewhere. To use it, we can create the following rule:

```
.some-element {
  @include box-sizing(border-box);
}
```

Of course, with variable interpolation, we could go a step further and make this even more abstract, as in the following snippet:

```
// Snippet Example 4b
@mixin prefix($property, $value...) {
  -webkit-#{$property}: $value;
  -moz-#{$property}: $value;
  -ms-#{$property}: $value;
  -o-#{$property}: $value;
  #{$property}: $value;
}

@mixin box-sizing($value) {
  @include prefix (box-sizing, $value);
}
```

 The ... token in the previous example is used to indicate that the parameter may take multiple parameters. This is similar to the ... operator in ES6.

Finally, we can abstract this one step further:

```
// Snippet Example 4c
$prefixes: "-webkit-","-moz-","-ms-","-o-","";
@mixin prefix($property, $value...) {
  @each $prefix in $prefixes {
    #{$prefix}#{$property}: $value;
  }
}
```

This is an example of the control flow and looping that Sass provides. It is important to remember, however, that there is no runtime performance impact—Sass will unroll the loop when the preceding is converted into CSS.

 This `prefix` mixin won't handle every case where vendor prefixes are used; but for our example, it is sufficient. One case our mixin doesn't handle is that of vendor prefixes in property values.

If you find yourself reusing the same calculation over and over, the `function` directive may come in handy. For example, let's assume that we want to work with a `960px` grid, but we don't want to have a lot of calculations throughout our code. We could write a function as follows:

```
// Snippet Example 4d
$grid-width: 960px;
$grid-columns: 12;
@function grid-size($columns) {
  @return ($grid-width / $grid-columns) * $columns;
}
```

We can use this as follows:

```
.some-element {
  width: grid-size(5);
}
```

 You can pass parameters by name to mixins and functions as well. For example, `grid-size($columns: 5)`.

Object-oriented CSS

While mixins provide a great way to reuse code, there's yet another way we can reduce repetition and encourage abstraction. Sass provides us with a mechanism called the `@extend` directive.

Let's consider a simple CSS example:

```
.button {
  ...
}
.shiny-button {
  ...
}
```

If we want to create a shiny button, we will need two classes attached to the element (`button shiny-button`). This can be error-prone, since we need to remember to include both classes; it can also create lengthy class lists. Sass's `@extend` keyword can simplify this. Consider the following version:

```
.button {
  ...
}
.shiny-button {
```

```
    @extend .button
    ...
}
```

When we create an HTML element with a class of `shiny-button`, it will automatically receive all the rules given to `button` without us having to explicitly list it in the class list.

Sometimes, however, we may want to reuse styles without cluttering our CSS. If the base class is never going to be used on its own, there's little reason to generate a class name for it. In this case, Sass has the concept of placeholders. Consider the following example:

```
%button {
    ...
}
.shiny-button {
    @extend %button
    ...
}
```

Now, we can create an HTML element with a class of `shiny-button` like we did earlier, but we can't create an element with just a class of `button`, because this class doesn't exist.

> There is a form of object-oriented CSS called OOCSS. If you want to learn more, see `http://appendto.com/2014/04/oocss/`. I've used object-oriented in the title of this section simply because it is the best way to describe what Sass does while using `@extend`.

Modules and partials

CSS lets us import styles from other style sheets and Sass extends this a little further by allowing your Sass files to import other Sass files. The syntax is largely the same as CSS, except that the file extension is omitted. Consider the following example:

```
@import "utils", "grid";
```

The previous command will look for an `util.scss` and a `grid.scss` file in the same directory and import their rules. If you ever need to import a CSS file, you can:

```
@import "vanilla.css";
```

An imported Sass file may not be something that you would wish to have translated to CSS on its own. If this is the case, you can prepend an underscore to the filename in the filesystem. For instance, using our preceding example, we could have a _util.scss file instead of util.scss. @import would look and work the same, but Sass will never attempt to create a _util.css file (without the underscore, it would attempt to create an util.css file). Which one you use depends largely on whether or not you desire a corresponding CSS file to be generated.

Integrating Sass with Gulp

Before we use Sass, we need to install it in our project and then add some additional code to gulpfile.js. Thankfully, all the steps are fairly simple. The steps are as follows:

1. Install a version of Sass that Gulp can use by executing the following command:

    ```
    $ npm install --save-dev gulp-sass@2.0.4
    ```

2. Next, modify gulp/config.js to define where our SCSS files live, and where the output should be placed:

    ```
    assets: {
        copy: [...],
        code: {...},
        styles: {src:  "www/scss/app.scss",
                dest:  "www/css"}
    }
    ```

3. Now, create gulp/tasks/copy-scss.js:

    ```
    var gulp = require("gulp"),
        sass = require("gulp-sass"),
        notify = require("gulp-notify"),
        sourcemaps = require("gulp-sourcemaps"),
        gutil = require("gulp-util"),
        config = require("../config"),
        settings = require("../settings"),
        paths = require("../utils/paths");

    function copySCSS() {
      var isRelease = (settings.BUILD_MODE === "release");
      var includePaths = []; // [1]
      var includeModules = config.sass &&
            config.sass.includeModules;
      if (includeModules instanceof Array) {
    ```

```
        includePaths = includePaths.concat(
          includeModules.map(function(moduleName) {
            var module = require(moduleName);
            return module.includePath;
          }));
      }
    var moreIncludePaths = config.sass &&
        config.sass.includePaths;
    if (moreIncludePaths instanceof Array) {
      includePaths = includePaths.concat(moreIncludePaths);
    }
    return gulp.src(paths.makeFullPath(
                    config.assets.styles.src,
                    paths.SRC)) //[2]
      .pipe(isRelease?gutil.noop():sourcemaps.init()) //[3]
      .pipe(sass({
        includePaths: includePaths, //[4]
        outputStyle: (isRelease?"compressed":"nested") //[5]
      }))
      .on("error", function(error) {
        this.emit("end");
      })
      .on("error", notify.onError(function(error) {
        return "SASS: " + error.message;
      }))
      .pipe(isRelease?gutil.noop():sourcemaps.write()) //[3]
      .pipe(gulp.dest(paths.makeFullPath(
          config.assets.styles.dest, paths.DEST)));
  }
module.exports = {
  task: copySCSS
}
```

This should look somewhat familiar—there are several lines in here that are pretty close to the `copy-code.js` task we worked on in the previous chapter. That said, let's go over a few of the details:

- Near the beginning of the file ([1]), we check our configuration file to see whether there are any directories we want Sass to search through while executing `@import`. We can either specify these paths in `sass.includePaths` as an array, or we can specify various npm modules that have exposed `includePath` by listing them in the `sass.includeModules` array. We'll go over an example of this shortly. These paths are actually utilized in [3].

- Notice that we only passed one file to `gulp.src()` (`[4]`). Just like `babelify` in the previous chapter, we only need to pass the top-level Sass file. Sass will discover the other files it needs to process based on the imports contained within the top-level file. Then, we'll only need to include one style sheet in our `index.html` file. That said, if you want to process multiple Sass files, nothing will stop you from including multiple files.

- Like in the prior chapter, we will only render source maps if we're not building for production (`[3]`). Having source maps is extremely useful for debugging, but they take up space, which we don't need to pass on to the user.

- `outputStyle` is compressed when we are building in the release mode (`[5]`). The resulting output is not intended to be human-readable, but the browser still understands it just fine. This helps in saving some space on the end user's device.

Before we can actually use this method, we need to modify the `gulp/tasks/copy` task to look as follows :

```
module.exports = {
  deps: ["copy-assets", "copy-scss", "copy-code"]
}
```

At this point, we can execute `gulp copy` and it will process `app.scss` in the `src/www/scss/` folder. When it is finished, there will be an `app.css` file in `build/www/css/`. At this point, you can modify `src/www/index.html` to include the style sheet by adding the following line to the `head` section:

```
<link rel="stylesheet" type="text/css "href="./css/app.css">
```

Including the Stylesheets installed via npm

npm isn't solely for JavaScript—there are several modules that include the Sass stylesheets that we can utilize. Let's use a stylesheet "reset" (which clears out the various styles that browsers apply to the various elements) as a simple example. This "reset" is useful for obtaining visual consistency across different browsers and rendering engines, since different browsers may have different default styling for elements.

 Note: You may prefer normalizing element styles rather than clearing them. If that's the case, take a look at https://www.npmjs.com/package/normalize-scss.

First, execute the following command:

```
$ npm install --save node-reset-scss@1.0.1
```

Next, let's add the following object to `gulp/config.js`:

```
"sass": {
  "includeModules": [
    "node-reset-scss"
  ]
}
```

At this point, we can use `@import "reset";` at the top of our Sass file. If we didn't use `includePaths` in our Gulp configuration, we would need to use `@import "../../../node_modules/node-reset-scss/scss/reset";`. Personally, I'll take the former—it's a lot easier to type!

There's no guarantee that a module will expose the location of its style sheets via `includePath`, though. If it doesn't, we can specify the path directly, as follows:

```
"sass": {
  "includePaths": [
    "./node_modules/node-reset-scss/scss"
  ]
}
```

Summary

In this chapter, you were introduced to Sass—a language that allows us to write modular and less repetitive CSS. You also integrated Sass into your build process. At this point, you finished setting up your build process.

In the next chapter, we'll cover some advanced responsive design, which will help us create the look and feel of our application.

4
More Responsive Design

One very common question asked about Cordova and PhoneGap is *how does one properly handle different screen sizes?* Unfortunately, this question is often asked when it's already very late in the development process, at which point it is difficult to introduce the appropriate fixes into the code. The developer has built the app with hard-coded sizes, usually ignoring aspect ratio differences, and any fix is now expensive to implement. As such, it is critical to implement your app such that it responds to the size of your user's device from the very start of your app's development.

HTML is naturally responsive, but it's easy to break this natural responsiveness if you use pixel-based origins and sizes. As long as you avoid these pitfalls where possible and use percentages and absolute and relative positioning, your app will naturally scale to whatever screen it finds itself on. The results may not be what you desire (too much whitespace or too cramped), but these can be easily solved using CSS.

Images aren't so easy: it's one thing while dealing with an icon—it's apt to be the same size and shape on any device, but it is a very different thing when we're dealing with background images or images that fill the width or height of the screen. Images are very sensitive to aspect ratio, and it's usually immediately obvious to the viewer when an image's aspect ratio isn't quite right. CSS3 provides mechanisms that help us here as well.

In this chapter, we'll be covering the following:

- Pixel densities
- CSS3 units, including the rem and viewport units
- Media queries
- Image sizing
- Flex-box

Getting started

Several of the snippets in this chapter are also available using the interactive snippet playground that accompanies the code package of this book. Instructions to launch the playground are in the README.md file in the code package. Once it starts, select **4: Responsive design** and then browse and experiment with the examples. Where applicable, each section and snippet will indicate which chapter and example you should select.

Although we've concentrated solely upon the build process for the demonstration app in this book, the full code using the techniques in this chapter is present in /logology-v04/ in the code package for this book. You should probably read the logology-readme.md file to get a better feel for the underlying code and structures. You can follow the instructions in the readme.md file in the code package in order to build and execute the app on your devices.

Pixel densities

Devices of many different screen dimensions dominate today's mobile landscape. Some are small with 4.5-inch screens and others are quite large with 6-inch screens. Tablets, of course, are even larger at 7 inches, 8.9 inches, 10 inches, and so on (the recently released iPad Pro is 12.9 inches).

To further complicate matters, the resolutions of these screens are also very different. The physical dimension of a screen tells you very little about how many pixels it contains—a 4.5-inch screen might have a resolution of 320 x 480 pixels or it might be 640 x 960, or 1280 x 800. Slightly larger screens may have significantly more pixels – a 6-inch phone may have a resolution of 2560 x 1600.

Most developers are used to thinking about pixels as discrete units over which they have direct control. In other words, the developer has the idea that they can determine the color and brightness of each and every pixel on the screen individually. While it is indeed possible to control each pixel individually, one quickly encounters problems with regard to the size of text and other elements when it comes to rendering web content. There weren't any problems as long as devices used large pixels (corresponding to a low pixel density). But the moment high density displays became popular, web browsers had a real problem. If browsers enforced a 1:1 pixel mapping, then any content that would be easy to read on a desktop display of 1440 x 900 pixels would be exceedingly small on a smaller mobile device with a much higher pixel density. This might not seem like much for very young eyes, but it is usually difficult to read lots of text at extremely small point sizes for extended periods, regardless of how clear or sharp the rendering may be.

Mobile browsers faced a conundrum. They could require users to scale their web pages up to whatever they found comfortable or the mobile browser could scale the site automatically. Mobile browser vendors chose the latter. In order to ensure that websites still rendered with the same layout, mobile browsers also lied to the site by indicating that the screen contained fewer pixels than in reality. The ratio of reported pixels to the actual pixels is called a "**scaling factor**". Most devices would report an integer scaling factor, often 2:1. Newer devices have such high-density displays that they report 3:1.

This scaling factor or scaling ratio indicates the number of physical pixels contained within each logical pixel. A **logical pixel** is simply a group of physical pixels combined together into one addressable unit. The developer doesn't necessarily have control over every pixel in the group—this is the device's responsibility. This makes it easy for new devices with different scaling factors to render content reasonably close to how the designer wants it. Text and vector graphics can automatically benefit from the higher density screens, maintaining sharpness. Images, in the worst case, appear a little blurrier (since the device must up-sample the image to fit it on more pixels). Once a pixel density becomes popular enough, the designer can generate a higher resolution image for these particular devices.

Okay, enough words. Some of us are visual learners, so here's a diagram on how this works out:

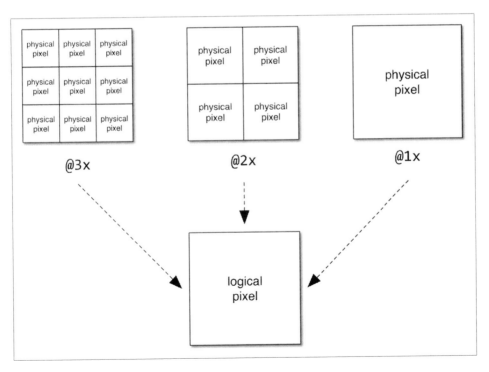

Note that, at the top, there are three different pixel densities represented by the scaling factor. **@3x** (alternatively 3:1) indicates the ratio of nine physical pixels to one logical pixel (3 x 3). **@2x** (2:1) maps four physical pixels to a single logical pixel (2 x 2). Finally, **@1x** (1:1) indicates that there is a direct one-to-one mapping between the physical and logical pixels.

While working with CSS and HTML, in nearly every case, we'll be working with logical pixels, not physical pixels. The only times when this doesn't completely apply are when we're working with images or when we're working with the HTML5 canvas. We aren't going to be discussing the HTML5 canvas in this book, but we will have to render sharp images on screens with many different pixel densities.

Unfortunately, not all the scaling factors are integers. This means that one logical pixel may not always completely align with the discrete physical pixels. Consider the following image:

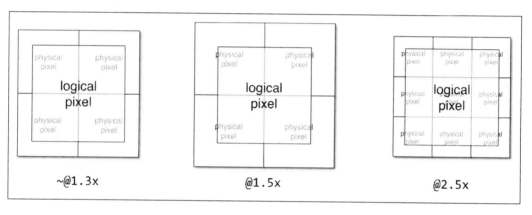

Notice how the physical pixels don't fit entirely within the logical pixel? This means that there is no way to ensure pixel perfection; you'll always have some degree of blending, where one physical pixel blends the colors from two logical pixels. On high-density displays (such as the iPhone 6s+), this isn't very obvious, because the physical pixels themselves are very small. But on other displays (such as the 2012 Nexus 7), this becomes very obvious due to the larger physical pixel size. It is at this point that you should recognize that any hope of achieving true pixel perfection is gone, and that you should lay that dream aside. HTML was never about pixel perfection anyway.

This isn't to say that there are no ways of addressing each and every physical pixel—there are. This usually requires a good deal of hard work. It's important to note that even Apple's iPhone 6s+ doesn't render pixel perfect while using native user interface widgets. You have to fall back on OpenGL in this specific example.

The previous image isn't a perfect representation of how the device blends logical pixels into physical pixels. It depends on the device and what logical pixel one is addressing. So, sometimes, it will appear as if a particular line or border isn't being blended, while another line or border will. It just depends on where the logical pixels happen to fall on the physical pixel grid Take a look at the following image – although each line is drawn with a single pixel stroke, depending upon where the line is drawn, different physical pixels are used to render the final result. If the pixels are large, this is pretty obvious.

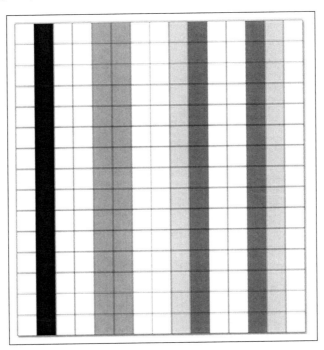

The CSS3 units

You're probably familiar with the typical CSS units such as px (pixel), pt (point), and em (font-size). There are others that are used more often in print situations, such as in (inch) and cm (centimeter). You should also be familiar with specifying percentages so that your content can resize appropriately.

Unfortunately, these units, though very well supported, aren't as flexible as modern application development may require. Thankfully, CSS3 has added several new units that we can use to our advantage, and they are becoming reasonably well supported on mobile platforms.

The em unit indicates font-size for a specific element. If an element's font-size is 20px, then 1em is also 20px. This has been useful in the past, because it is easy to adjust the size of elements based upon the font-size. The rem unit is an extension of this unit. rem is short for root em and it allows us to specify a root em size that is consistent throughout the document. That is, if we specify font-size: 16px on the html element, we can then use 1rem anywhere within the document, and it will evaluate to 16px regardless of any font-size, the element might have otherwise inherited.

```
<html> { font-size: 10px; }

  <body>

    <div> { font-size: 200%;  /*  20px */
            width:     20em;  /* 400px */
            height:    20em;  /*   "   */
          }

      =   { font-size: 200%;  /*  20px */
            width:    40rem;  /* 400px */
            height:   40rem;  /*   "   */
          }

                        <div> { width: 10em;  /*200px*/      <div> { width: 20em;  /*200px*/
                                height:10em;  /*  "  */              height:20em;  /*  "  */
                              }                                    }
                          =   { width: 20rem; /*200px*/       =   { width: 20rem; /*200px*/
                                height:20rem; /*  "  */              height:20rem; /*  "  */
                              }                                    }
```

The prior image should help make the relationship clear. Notice that the number of pixels that the em unit represents varies based on the font-size of the element (or that of its parent). But, the rem unit is always consistent: it always equals the font-size of the html element.

Other useful units are the viewport units. There are four:

- vw: This equates to 1% of the viewport's width
- vh: This equates to 1% of the viewport's height
- vmin: This equates to 1% of the viewport's shortest side
- vmax: This equates to 1% of the viewport's longest side

Technically, the first two elements would be equivalent to using percentages, assuming that the nearest positioned element filled the entire browser viewport. Of course, if the element didn't fill the browser viewport, using percentages won't achieve the same effect, which is why these new units are so useful.

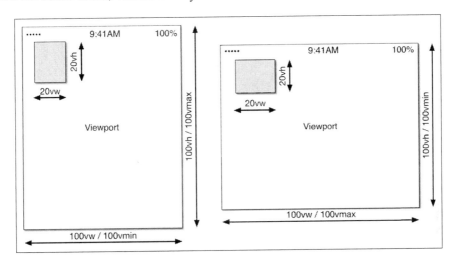

The prior image should make clear how these units work: the vw and vh units always represent 1/100th of the viewport's width and height, respectively. The vmin and vmax units, however, are based solely on the shortest and longest axes.

There's another unit we'd like to mention briefly, though you may not immediately think of it as such: calc. If you recall, in *Chapter 3, Sassy CSS* we discussed how we could use Sass to perform calculations for us. We mentioned that operands were required to be of the same units. The CSS3 calc expression, however, can work with mixed units, allowing us to write calc(25% + 25rem) or calc(25rem + 2vw), or just about any expression we'd like. The following image shows this visually:

```
<html> { font-size: 10px; }

<body>

<div> { width: 100rem; /* 1000px */ }

<div>                      <div>
{                          {
    width: 25%;                width: calc(25% + 25rem);
        /* 250px */                /* 500px */
}                          }
```

All this is great until we talk about browser compatibility. Desktop browsers support these units very well and, surprisingly, so do many modern mobile browsers. There are some caveats, however:

- Viewport units are supported on iOS 6.1 and higher, and Android 4.4 and higher (see `http://caniuse.com/#feat=viewport-units`). Unfortunately, iOS 6 and 7 do some funny things with viewport units. There's a buggyfill that takes care of the problem online at `https://github.com/rodneyrehm/viewport-units-buggyfill`. Unfortunately, Android 4.3 or lower are out of luck, so a fallback is a must if these versions of Android are targeted.

- Root EM units are well supported on iOS 4.1 and higher, and Android 2.1 and higher (see `http://caniuse.com/#feat=rem`). Feel free to use as much as you like. But there may be some Android devices out there that have issues with it, as indicated on the linked page.

- Dynamic calculations are supported in iOS 6 and higher, though iOS 6 requires a `-webkit-` prefix. Android support is lacking, however. Partial support for addition and subtraction is present as of 4.4, but full support didn't arrive until version 37 of the Android browser. This means you probably should only use addition and subtraction, and you'll definitely need a fallback for any Android device running 4.3 or lower. If possible, consider using Sass's `calc` function instead, since it will work on every browser.

If you're targeting very recent, modern platforms, you may find that you don't need to worry about fallbacks. For example, as of this writing, you could reach 92% of the iOS market solely by targeting iOS 8, which doesn't need the viewport buggyfill. On the other hand, only Android 4.4 and higher support CSS3 `calc` function in any capacity, and unfortunately, only 67% of the install base is on 4.4 or higher, as of this writing.

 You can determine the install base of any Android version by visiting `https://developer.android.com/about/dashboards/index.html`. For iOS, visit `https://developer.apple.com/support/appstore/`. For an alternate view based on the stats from one app, see `http://david-smith.org/iosversionstats/`.

We have a short example that demonstrates these units in the code package of this book. You can run it in your browser or on your device if you wish. It is located at `snippets/04/ex1-css3-units/`. If you are using the interactive snippet playground, select **4: Responsive Design, Example 1**.

Media queries

Media queries are exceptionally powerful constructs that allow us to build responsive layouts based on the properties of the device on which our code is running. For example, we can change the styling of various elements based upon the width or height of the screen or the pixel density. Alternatively, we could detect various device capabilities, such as color depth, or we could determine whether we're working with a screen or a printer. In this section, however, we're going to focus on how to detect screen size and pixel density.

Media queries can be defined using CSS `@import` rules, style sheet links, and `@media` rules. We'll focus on the latter, since it is of the typical form.

A media query often looks as follows:

```
@media only screen and (max-width: 768px) and
(max-resolution: 2dppx) {
  /* some CSS rules that apply when this query is true */
}
```

The syntax is fairly flexible and you can probably already guess what the preceding rule does. But let's go over how you can craft media queries:

- `only`: This is used to prevent older browsers that understand media types but not media queries from applying styles.
- `screen`: This specifies that this query applies only to screens, not paper or other devices. Since we're targeting mobile devices in this book, `screen` makes the most sense (as we aren't usually printing content). Note that media types (such as `screen`) aren't specified using parentheses.
- `and`: This joins filters together. All the filters must be matched for the query to match. It is equivalent to JavaScript's `&&` operator.
- Comma (`,`): This joins filters together, but only one of the filters must be matched for the query to match. It is equivalent to JavaScript's `||` operator.
- `not`: This negates the query. This applies to the entire query if `and` is used to join the filters, or only to a single filter if a comma is used to join the filters.
- Filters are enclosed with parentheses and are of the `media-feature:value` form.
- Styles within the media query are applied if and only if the entire query is matched.

Sass adds one additional feature to media queries: we can specify them inside a selector. This allows us to keep any media queries that might affect our layout or styling close to the item that is being modified, as in the following example:

```
.someElement {
    width: 100%;
    min-width: 320px;
    @media only screen and (max-width: 320px) {
        display: none; // hide this element on screens that
                       // aren't wide enough to show it.
    }
}
```

There are many features that we can filter upon. Let's go over some common ones:

- The `width` filters are based on the width of the viewport. `min-width` puts a lower bound on the width, while `max-width` places a higher limit on the width. For example, a filter of `max-width: 320px` would match any viewport with a width of 0 to 320 logical pixels, but wouldn't match a viewport with a width of 400 pixels. `min-width: 320px`, on the other hand, would match all the viewports with a width of 320 logical pixels or more. If `width` is used (without a `min-` or `max-` prefix), it is only matched if the width of the viewport matches the specified width exactly.

- The `height` filters are based on the height of the viewport. For instance, `width`, `min-height`, and `max-height` can all be used, and they work the same as in the prior point (except they use height instead of width).

- The `aspect-ratio` filters are based on the aspect ratio of the viewport. Aspect ratio is the ratio of the width of the viewport to the height. `aspect-ratio`, `min-aspect-ratio`, and `max-aspect-ratio` are supported.

- The `orientation` filters are based on whether or not the viewport is in a landscape orientation or a portrait orientation. Note that this does not necessarily indicate the device's orientation. For the purposes of this feature, `landscape` orientation is matched when the viewport is wider than it is tall, and `portrait` is the opposite. As such, it's possible on a mobile device to trigger a change in this value by displaying the soft keyboard while the device is physically in a portrait orientation, causing the viewport to become wider than it is tall, which would be treated as `landscape` for this filter.

- The `device-pixel-ratio` filters are based on the physical to logical pixel ratio. For example, a 1:1 display will have a ratio of 1. A 2:1 display will have a ratio of 2. This feature is no longer the preferred way to detect the pixel density of a device, but it's still commonly used by iOS and Android versions lower than 4.4. Each of these platforms use a `-webkit-` prefix as well. They support `min-device-pixel-ratio` and `max-device-pixel-ratio` can also be used.

- The `resolution` filters are based on the resolution of the device. Two units are most often used: `dpi` and `dppx`. The former matches based on the number of pixels there are in an inch, while the latter is essentially equivalent to `device-pixel-ratio`. Because of browser support, you need to handle both of the units in your queries. `min-resolution` and `max-resolution` are also supported.

> If you're familiar with media queries at all, you may be thinking that we're missing some very obvious features here. You'd be right—we haven't listed the `-device-` features. These features aren't based upon the actual viewport, but on the device itself. A lot of developers use these to detect which device they are rendering on; but as screen sizes and resolutions continuously change as new devices are released, this becomes a never-ending battle. Furthermore, if you modify your layout based upon these features, you may not actually get the result you expect, since it is possible for the browser viewport to not fill the entire screen, especially if multiple apps are on the screen at once. From my perspective, it's best to avoid using these features and rely only on the viewport-specific features for layout.

There are many more features you can use for detection. A full discussion on media queries is out of the scope of this book. If you want to learn about media queries in depth, see `https://developer.mozilla.org/en-US/docs/Web/Guide/CSS/Media_queries`.

The benefit of this kind of feature detection is that we can create layouts that do more than simply scale up and down to the size of the viewport. We can actually modify the entire layout of our app based on the size of the viewport. For example, on iOS, this might mean displaying two views side by side if the app is running on an iPad or an iPhone 6s+, but on smaller devices the app would render only a single view. This gives us a tremendous amount of control over the appearance of our user interface without having to write a lot of JavaScript code.

Being able to detect pixel density is also critical. This isn't so much for layout, since layout works with logical pixels, but for images and icons, which use a mix of logical and physical pixels.

Image sizing

Most HTML elements are responsive by default, assuming we don't use pixel-based units with regard to their origin or size. Bitmap (or raster) images are a different story; they aren't resizable without losing information, so we have to deal with them separately.

There are three scenarios with respect to images:

- Rendering an image with a specific size, such as an icon or a thumbnail
- Rendering an image that needs to resize itself to the width of the viewport, as in a header image
- Rendering a background image that needs to fill the viewport

In all these cases, we want the image to be as sharp as possible and require as little up sampling as possible, since this will result in blurry images. If we're rendering icons, we should also attempt to avoid down sampling as much as possible, since this can also result in poorly rendered icons.

When it comes to describing the differences between rendering on a display with a 1:1 pixel mapping (otherwise known as low density, loDPI, or nonretina) and the same image being rendered on a 2:1 pixel mapping (often called high density, hiDPI, or retina) display, it helps to actually see some pixels. Let's take a look at an icon where it's important that the content is sharp, because any blurriness is going to be obvious to the viewer:

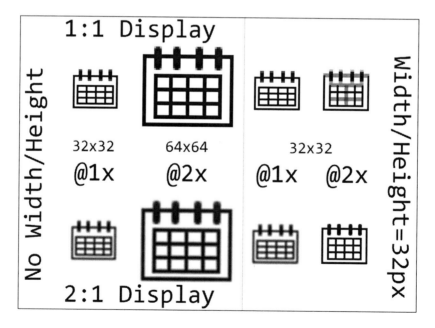

The top half of the image is a screenshot from a 1:1 display. The bottom half is from a 2:1 display. The left-hand side is rendered when we include an `img` tag with no `width` or `height` attribute. Because the low-density version is 32 x 32 pixels and the high-density version is 64 x 64 pixels, they render using two different sizes. On the right-hand side, the same icons are rendered, but each has a specified `width` and `height` of `32px`. We should also point out that the two icons being rendered are not identical: the **@1x** version is optimized for a low-density display using 32 x 32 pixels and the **@2x** version is optimized for a high-density display using 64 x 64 pixels. The *why* should be very apparent: we want the icon to look as sharp as possible on as many screen densities as possible.

It should be pretty obvious why we should care about up and down sampling now. The two images at the top left of the image are nice and sharp, but the two images at the bottom left are blurry. This is because the browser is up sampling these images so that they appear to be roughly the same size regardless of the screen's resolution. Unfortunately, this up sampling necessarily loses information and, to compensate, the browser applies some mathematical transformations to the image to avoid pixelization. This is far from perfect and it takes processing time as well. So, we would like to avoid this whenever we can.

The icon in the top right corner is a pretty good example of why it's best to avoid down sampling everything from the high-density version: it isn't nearly as sharp as the low-density version on a 1:1 display. This is because the browser must now fit four times the number of pixels in a quarter of the space, and some information is necessarily *lost*. Sometimes, this works out okay—some of the lines in the icon are still sharp, for example—but other times, this creates blurry lines.

The two icons in the lower right corner represent the same images, but on a 2:1 display. The second icon is nice and sharp. The first icon, on the other hand, is again very blurry. This is because the low-density version has to be up-sampled to the 2:1 display so that it appears to be of the same size.

At this point, it should be obvious that there is a disconnect between the actual resolution of each icon and the sizes we use when we tell HTML or CSS how big the image is. The low-density version is 32 x 32 pixels and the high-density version is 64 x 64 pixels. But in both the cases, we need to tell the browser that the icon is 32 x 32 pixels. But this does mean that in order to get the very best results, we need to supply the correct version of the icon to the browser or we'll get substandard results. It also means that we need to create versions that are optimized for the density on which the icon will appear—simply up or down sampling in Photoshop will generate the same or similar suboptimal results.

For this reason, it is suggested that you design your assets using vector graphics rather than raster images. Vector graphics can be easily resized and tweaked as needed to get the desired output, but a raster image can only be scaled, which may lead to blurry results.

There are various mechanisms you can use in order to ensure that the browser displays the appropriate version of the icon, though which one you use will often depend upon the context.

If you're using an `img` tag, you can request the appropriate version using the `srcset` attribute. There are different ways you can use this attribute, but we're worried about pixel density. The following handles 1:1, 2:1, and 3:1-density displays:

```
<img src="calendar.png" srcset="calendar.png 1x,
calendar@2x.png 2x, calendar@3x.png 3x" />
```

You can include as many versions of the icon as you need; the browser will attempt to choose the best option. Of course, for the best display, it's best to provide versions targeting each display density your app might run on.

If you're using `background-image` in your CSS, however, you need a different mechanism: media queries. Consider the following example:

```
.icon {
    width: 32px; height: 32px;
    background: url('./calendar.png') no-repeat center center
                / 32px 32px;
}
@media only screen and (-webkit-min-device-pixel-ratio: 1.01),
    only screen and (min-resolution: 1.01dppx),
    only screen and (min-resolution: 193dpi) {
    .icon {
        background-image: url('./calendar@2x.png');
    }
}
@media only screen and (-webkit-min-device-pixel-ratio: 2.01),
    only screen and (min-resolution: 2.01dppx),
    only screen and (min-resolution: 289dpi) {
    .icon {
        background-image: url('./calendar@3x.png');
    }
}
```

In the preceding example, you may be wondering why we are using fractional bounds for the pixel ratios. If we specified `min-resolution: 1dppx`, we'd be telling the browser to render the 2:1 version on a 1:1 display. This is something we want to avoid. However, if we specified `min-resolution: 2dppx`, any display that falls between 1:1 and 2:1 would end up *up-scaling* the 1:1 version rather than *down-scaling* the 2:1 version. Though neither is ideal, the 2:1 version will render better than the 1:1 version will on these kinds of displays. Technically, this is why the `dpi` version is much better; we don't have to worry about fractional numbers.

So, why `193dpi`? It's the closest analogue that matches with `1.01dppx`. The same is true for `289dpi` — it matches `2.01dppx` closely.

If you're lazy, you could simply just allow the browser to down-sample the densest version of the icon that you have. This *works*, but it's not perfect. For one, the best results will only occur on the displays that are a half (or a quarter, and so on) the density of the densest version. Secondly, the browser is forced to do more work than necessary. If it has to do this often, your app's rendering performance might suffer.

If you look at the code package of this book, there is an example you can run in your own browser or on your device that illustrates these different techniques. It is located in `snippets/04/ex2-responsive-icons/index.html`. If you are using the interactive snippet playground, select **4: Responsive Design** and **Example 2**.

Icons often require modifications to look their best on displays with different pixel densities. For example, some icons need to be simplified in their 1:1 version, while a 3:1 version may need slight adjustments to look best on a high-density display. When you design icons, it's always best to do it in a vector editor. Design for a high-density display first; then make the appropriate adjustments for any low-density displays.

Images that represent photographs fare much better than icons, but there's no reason for us to display blurry photographs on a high-density display. Thankfully, down sampling high-density images on a 1:1 display is much less obvious than down sampling icons. It's not ideal, since the browser has to do additional work to render high-density images on a low-density display. So, it's best to use an image editor to down-sample the image and supply the correct image to the browser.

When we know the image's size on the screen, it's easy to provide optimized versions for many different display densities. However, there are times when we won't be able to accommodate every possible size variation. This often occurs when we want an image to fill the width of the viewport but maintain the correct aspect ratio. Other times, we may want the image to fill the viewport as a background (or even foreground) image. Again, we want the aspect ratio to be maintained. Because of the number of screen densities and resolutions, there's no practical way we can create optimal versions of the image for all the variations we might encounter.

One common pattern is to render an image in a heading that fills the width of the device. This pattern looks something like the following image:

Typically, there is an upper bound on the height of the image, so it's always evident that there is text below the image. In this case, one would also be tempted to be lazy and simply downscale the densest image. But as we've already mentioned, this has a negative impact on performance. It would be good to determine whether all the pixels in the image can be rendered; if not, you can use a less dense image.

This type of pattern is pretty easy to achieve—the CSS is actually quite short:

```
.fancy-heading {
    background: #789 url('./header-1024.jpg') no-repeat right 33%
                / cover;
    width: 100%;
    height: 25vw; min-height: 250px;
    position: relative;
}
```

```
@media only screen and (min-width: 1025px),
  only screen and (min-width: 513px)
  and (-webkit-min-device-pixel-ratio: 1.5) {
    .fancy-heading {
        background-image: url('./header-2000.jpg');
    }
}
```

Even though the CSS is short, there's quite a bit going on here. You can see this if you view `snippets/04/ex3-responsive-header-images/index.html` from the code package in a browser and resize the width of the browser. The header will resize according to the size and the image will always fill the heading area. Likewise, you'll notice that the heading text will also change its size based upon the width of the browser window or the device, though this isn't shown in the preceding CSS.

 If you want, you can also view the example using the interactive snippet playground. Select **4: Responsive Design**, **Example 3**.

There are a couple of interesting features of this CSS:

- The value of `background-size` is set to `cover` (as shown after the slash in the `background` property shorthand). This instructs the browser to size the image such that it covers the entire area. The browser will also maintain the aspect ratio of the image.

- The value of `background-position` is set to `right 33%`. We can specify any position we need; it just depends upon the image we're using and whether there's anything important we want to try to keep visible.

- The `height` value is `25vw`. This ensures that the heading is always 25% of the width of the viewport. We also set `min-height` simply to keep the height from getting too small.

- By default, the image we are using is 1024 x 512 px wide. This is down-sampled from the original image, which is 2000 x 1000 wide. If the width of the browser is greater than 1024 logical pixels, we may as well automatically switch to the larger image. Otherwise, the browser will have to up-sample the smaller image.

- For pixel densities of 1.5:1 or higher, we display a larger image when the logical pixel width exceeds 512 px. We could have specified a 2:1 density; but if the pixel density is more than 1:1, it's better to down-sample than up-sample it. The ratio we've chosen here is fairly arbitrary.

The text that appears over this image is also responsive — the size changes based upon the width of the browser. However, there are cases when we might want to limit the font-size. In addition, since this example has text over an arbitrary image, it's helpful to add additional properties to make the text more readable. Here's the CSS:

```css
.fancy-heading h1 {
    box-sizing: border-box;
    font: normal 10vw Helvetica, sans-serif;
    text-align: right;
    color: white;
    text-shadow: 0 5px 5px black;
    background-image: linear-gradient(180deg, rgba(0, 0, 0, 0),
        rgba(0, 0, 0, 0.75));
    position: absolute;
    bottom: 0px;
    left: 0; right: 0;
    padding: 10px; margin: 0;
}
@media only screen and (min-width: 1024px) {
    .fancy-heading h1 {
        font-size: 77pt;
    }
}
```

Let's go over the interesting portions of the preceding code:

- The `text-shadow` property is used to separate the text from its background by rendering a shadow around the text. This is useful especially if the background image has near white areas.

- The `background-image` property specifies is a gradient that darkens the area behind the text. Again, this is intended to increase readability.

- The `font-size` value is `10vw` or 10% of the viewport's width. If the size gets too big, however, we cap the size at `77pt`. Note that this is arbitrary — a matter of whatever looks best to your eye.

Note that the shadow and gradient are performance-intensive; the browser has to calculate how the shadow and gradient should look and this takes additional time. Don't overuse these effects or your app may start to feel sluggish.

Another typical pattern is a fullscreen image. With the use of viewport units, this can be accomplished using only a small variation of the previous code:

```
.fancy-heading {
    ...
    width: 100vw;
    height: 100vh;
}
```

If you didn't want to use viewport units, the same can be accomplish by absolutely positioning the image and setting the top, left, right, and bottom properties to 0.

> This example is at snippets/04/ex4-responsive-fullscreen-images in the code package of this book. If you want, you can also view the example using the interactive snippet playground. Select **4: Responsive Design, Example 4**.

So far, we've been using cover, which is great unless you want to ensure that the entire image is always visible. If the latter is what you need, use contain instead. You'll need to have an appropriate background-color value though, since the image may not fill the element entirety. Instead, the browser fits the image within the element's area and finds the largest size it can use without cropping it.

Using flex-box layout

Complex layout in CSS has often been a source of frustration. Sometimes, it is possible to use the display: table-* variants to get the desired effect; but these are far from ideal for nontabular data.

The **Flexbox layout module** provides us with mechanisms to control the layout of our elements, even when the dimensions of the parent element or viewport may not be known. This makes it ideal for responsive mobile applications. Flexbox enjoys reasonably good support in modern browsers (see http://caniuse.com/#feat=flexbox). Unfortunately, the specification has gone through several iterations, and older browsers implemented the specification at those stages. Anything lower than iOS 6.1 and Android 4.4 uses an older version of the syntax. So, if you plan on supporting either of these, you would have to support multiple versions of the specification. Generally, this isn't difficult; but older versions don't always support the same features. In most browsers, you'll also have to use an appropriate prefix, such as -webkit-.

In this section, we'll be using the modern syntax for Flexbox. There are lots of other tools, however, that you can use to supply prefixes automatically, including Autoprefixer (`https://github.com/postcss/autoprefixer`), or you can even develop Sass mixins to do the same thing.

First, we need to get some terminology out of the way. Flexbox's layout rules can affect two different kinds of elements: containers and items. This should be obvious; but when we're dealing with HTML, we often think of elements in terms of parent-children relationships. In the Flexbox layout, the container is essentially the parent and the items are the direct descendants. Visually, the relationship is like the following image:

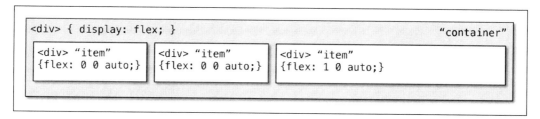

Notice that the container element receives a `display: flex` style rule. This instructs the container to lay its items out in a flexible manner. Relative to its parent, the container itself will be laid out as if it were styled with `display: block`. There is also an `inline-flex` option if you need it (equivalent to `inline-block`).

The items within will automatically be laid out flexibly; but you'll almost certainly want to specify how these items can grow or shrink. There are three rules to accomplish this:

- `flex-grow`: Determines whether the element can grow and how much it can in relation to other items. By default, growing is disabled, but setting this property to zero will also disable growth.

- `flex-shrink`: Determines whether the element can shrink. By default, shrinking is allowed, but setting this property to zero will also disable shrinking.

- `flex-basis`: Determines the default size of the element prior to growing or shrinking. If `auto` is specified, the browser adjusts the size based on `flex-grow`.

There is a shorthand property named `flex`, which is what you see in the prior image for each item. The order is `flex: <flex-grow><flex-shrink><flex-basis>`. The latter two numbers aren't required; if they aren't specified, the browser will intelligently figure them out.

In the preceding example, you can then see that we've prevented the two leftmost elements from growing. The rightmost element, however, is free to fill the remaining space, and it does.

`flex-grow` is more than simply a switch to enable or disable growth. It can also be used to determine relative growth between items. If all the items except the middle item received `flex-grow: 1` and the middle item received `flex-grow: 2`, it would be twice as wide as the others, as you can see in the following image:

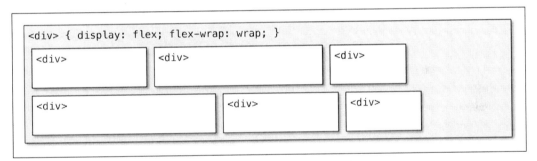

Flexbox can also wrap items that may not fit within the container using `flex-wrap`. The values you can supply to this property are `nowrap`, `wrap`, and `wrap-reverse`. The first two should be pretty obvious, but the last is interesting; it allows you to reverse the order of the layout.

Visually, wrapping looks like the following image:

Unfortunately, devices using the old Flexbox syntax will have problems with this—they don't support wrapping. This eliminates a lot of the flexibility of the module unfortunately, and there's no great workaround. For our purposes, we assume you are using a device with a reasonably modern browser (iOS 6.1+ or Android 4.4+).

Flexbox also allows us to determine how the spacing between elements is applied with a property named `justify-content`. Several values are permitted:

- `flex-start`: This aligns the items to the start of the container
- `flex-end`: This aligns the items to the end of the container
- `center`: This aligns the items to the center of the container
- `space-between`: This adds space as necessary between the items, but it doesn't add space at the start or end
- `space-around`: This adds space as necessary around the items, including the items at the start or end

The following image demonstrates `space-between`:

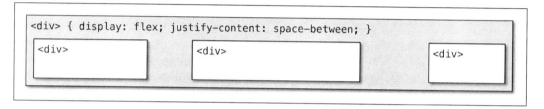

You may have noticed that we've tried to avoid mentioning width, left, or right with regards to these properties. There's a good reason: Flexbox permits both horizontal layouts (`row`) and vertical layouts (`column`). The same properties can be used in each orientation, so it makes more sense to talk in terms of the start or end of a container than it does to say the left or right of the container.

To change the direction of the layout, the `flex-direction` property can be used. It accepts four values:

- `row`: This orders the items horizontally, as one would text (left to right or right to left depending upon the language). This is the default.
- `row-reverse`: This orders the items out horizontally, but in the reverse order.
- `column`: This orders the items vertically.
- `column-reverse`: This orders the items vertically, but in the reverse order.

Let's see an example of a vertical layout:

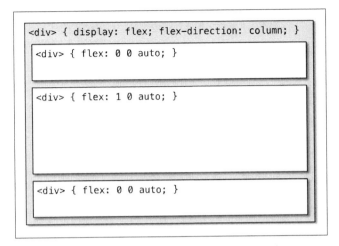

As you can see, Flexbox gives us a lot of options when it comes to layout. There are many more properties that you can use. We can't cover everything in this chapter, unfortunately. A great reference is at `https://css-tricks.com/snippets/css/a-guide-to-flexbox/`. Bookmark it; you'll probably need it while working with this layout module (I sure did!).

So, how would we put all this together in order to create a complex layout? Say, like the following one?

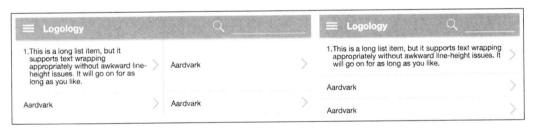

There's quite a bit going on in the preceding layout. On the left-hand side, you can see the layout as if it were on a wide device. On the right-hand side, the layout is on a narrow device. In fact, if the device were even narrower, the navigation bar's height would grow as needed to avoid truncating the search widget.

We can achieve this layout very easily. We'll leave out the colors, the fonts, and the like, and focus solely on the Flexbox properties we used. The following image shows how this layout is achieved:

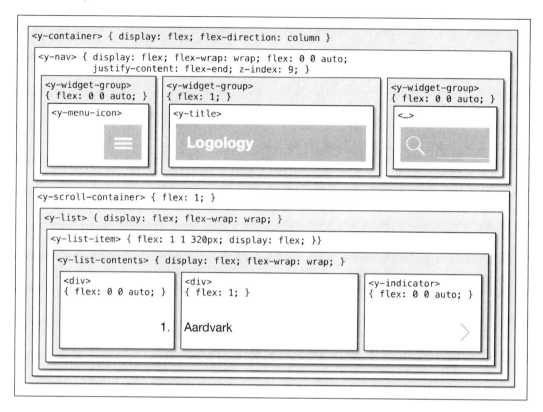

 If you want to see a functioning example, visit `snippets/04/ex5-flexbox-ui/index.html` in the code package of this book. If you're using the interactive snippet playground, select **4: Responsive Design** and **Example 5**.

Now, there's quite a bit going on there, and it shows how one can achieve a complex layout using the Flexbox module. Let's go over some of the more interesting details:

- It's worth noting that `y-container` is absolutely positioned in this example and anchored to the viewport's corners.

- The outer container, `y-container`, is oriented vertically using `flex-direction: column`. This lets us include a navigation bar that isn't absolutely positioned. While there's nothing wrong with absolutely positioning the navigation bar, if the bar can grow, it becomes very difficult to ensure that it doesn't obscure other content that may not be able to move out of its way. You can, of course, require that the navigation bar always be a certain height, but this isn't always ideal. In our example, we allowed the navigation bar to expand if the items don't all fit. This would definitely overlay the items below it if we were positioned absolutely.

- The navigation bar, `y-nav` isn't allowed to flex using `flex: 0 0 auto`. This is because we don't want the navigation bar to take up any more (or less) space than it really needs.

- The scroll container, `y-scroll-container`, on the other hand, is allowed to flex using `flex: 1`. It will fill up whatever space is left over from the navigation bar.

- Inside the navigation bar, there are three `y-widget-group` elements. Except for the middle item, these aren't allowed to flex either. The middle item, however, can take up the remaining space. The rightmost item actually has `width: 25vw` on it in our example code. So, this element does resize, but according to the viewport width, not the Flexbox container.

- The navigation bar also permits wrapping. If the navigation bar is too narrow, each widget group can wrap to the next line. This allows each one to remain visible and usable without resorting to truncation or hiding.

- Within the scroll container, we have a list, `y-list`. As you can see from the example image, this list can split itself up into columns as needed. This is accomplished by placing `flex-wrap: wrap` on the `y-list` element and then `flex: 1 1 20rem` on the items. This sets `flex-basis` to `20rem`, which means that the browser will base the size of each item on this value rather than their intrinsic size (that would be a lot smaller). It also means that the browser will grow the size of the element until it can fit two (or more) elements of `20rem` on the same line. This means that our list items will usually be `20rem` or wider. However, we also allow them to shrink (`flex-shrink: 1`). So, if the browser has less space available, it'll reduce the width of the items as necessary.

Once you start thinking about layout in terms of the Flexbox module, a lot of complex layouts become possible and even easy. While we could always generate reasonably complex layouts before, it often required out-of-the-box thinking and absolute positioning. Sometimes, these methods were very fragile; an element that was too large might break the entire layout.

All of this flexibility does come at a cost: the browser has to do a lot more work to figure out where all your elements go. This means that you have to decide whether the increased flexibility is worth the reduction in performance. If you have a lot of items using Flexbox, you might notice some sluggishness in your user interface. So, you need to use only as appropriate.

As we've mentioned before, you also need to be aware that only the devices using fairly modern browsers engines will work well with this type of layout. Our example assumes iOS 6.1 or higher and Android 4.4 or higher. Older browsers that support the older syntax for Flexbox can still participate, but the wrapping feature isn't supported, which can severely hamper complex layouts. You can often provide fallbacks or other workarounds for those browsers if you try hard enough. But only you can make the decision as to whether or not it is worth your time and effort.

Summary

We covered a lot in this chapter, all having to do with responsive design. We will never know what device size our app might face, and we want to ensure that it looks as best as it possibly can in just about any environment. In this chapter, we covered the differences between logical and physical pixels, how to render images responsively, and how to use the Flexbox module for complex user interfaces.

In the next chapter, you'll learn about making our app accessible for users who may have issues with their sight.

5
Hybrid Application Accessibility

Accessibility is incredibly important for your mobile application, even though it's often overlooked. It's easily as important (if not more so) than localization and globalization, especially since making an app accessible doesn't require one to know multiple languages well or pay others to create translations.

Yet application accessibility is often overlooked, even in native applications. This is unfortunate, especially with regard to native applications, since it's easy to add accessibility features using the native SDK.

Hybrid applications also have good support for accessibility features on modern devices. As such, hybrid app developers really have no excuse for not implementing accessibility features in their applications.

It's easy to overlook this if you don't need any of the accessibility features. If your eyesight is 20/20, your hearing is excellent, or you don't experience any dexterity issues, it's easy to forget that other individuals who wish to use your app may not be able to utilize your app in the same way you do.

In this chapter, we'll cover some ways that you can create apps that are accessible to your users. Here's what we'll cover in this chapter:

- Types of accessibility features
- Accessibility for free
- What is WAI-ARIA?
- WAI-ARIA roles

- Accessibility examples
  - Separation of presentation and content
  - Accessible icon buttons
  - Accessible navigation
  - Accessible lists
  - Accessible alerts and dialogs
- Fitting in with native accessibility features
  - Installing the PhoneGap mobile accessibility plugin
  - Detecting the user's preferred text size
  - Detecting a screen reader
  - Speaking custom text
  - Useful tools

Getting started

Several of the examples in this chapter are also available using the interactive snippet playground that accompanies the code package of this book. Instructions to launch the playground are in the README.md file in the code package. Once it starts, select **5: Accessibility** and then select the first example.

Types of accessibility features

There are many different categories of accessibility features you may need to consider while making your app accessible. You'll need to consider whether your app really needs to account for these categories, of course. But it's important to be aware of the various needs your users may have. Let's go over the various forms.

You'll want to check out http://webaim.org/articles/ that has a lot of information on the various kinds of disabilities and how best to help your users. We've summarized some of the information available from this fantastic resource in the following sections, but you really should review this site in its entirety.

Color vision deficient

Many of your users may be color vision deficient (otherwise known as *color blind*). See https://en.m.wikipedia.org/wiki/Color_blindness for some statistics on prevalence.

The term color blindness is an unfortunate one; it's not that affected individuals don't see color — many of them do. It's that they may have difficulty distinguishing certain colors from other colors. Achromacy (seeing no color) is *extremely* rare; most individuals do see many different colors.

There are several different deficiencies: red, green, blue, and achromacy. The deficiency is a result of the cones in the individual's eye not being sensitive to certain wavelengths. For example, an individual's eye with a red deficiency has cones that aren't very sensitive to red light.

There's an easy way to help any of your users who have color vision deficiencies: don't rely on color alone to convey information. For example, if your app identifies an error state with a red color but identifies a normal state with a green color, a red deficient user may not be able to tell the difference.

There's another reason you should avoid using colors to convey information: colors may mean something different based upon your user's location. Green doesn't always mean *go,* and red doesn't always mean *stop.*

For many apps, color vision deficiency doesn't usually have much of an impact. This said, any app that relies upon the user distinguishing colors from other colors (perhaps, a bubble popping game or a painting app) should provide some alternative means of conveying important color information (perhaps, by using other iconography).

Low vision

Low vision refers to visual deficiencies that cannot be corrected by eye glasses or contacts. There are many different kinds of low vision, such as macular degeneration, glaucoma, cataracts, and so on. But in general, users with low vision will have problems distinguishing anything that is very small or lacking in contrast.

This type of disability definitely has an impact upon the application's user interface design. It's very common to see websites and apps that have very small point sizes for text and a foreground and background color with low contrast. These can sometimes be difficult for people with perfect vision to read, but an individual with low vision is definitely going to have a lot of problems with this type of content.

There are a couple of ways you can help these users. They are as follows:

- Increase the font size
- Increase the contrast

This doesn't necessarily mean that your app must do both by default. Perhaps, you like a certain color scheme that has low contrast. You can always provide a setting that allows your users to switch to a higher contrast color scheme should they need it. The same goes for font sizes; allowing the user to change the font size to something comfortable may be preferable to starting out with a large font size *just in case*.

 It should be noted that both iOS and Android support setting larger font sizes in each platform's Settings app. Unfortunately, hybrid apps don't inherit this setting automatically, but there is a plugin available that handles this for us. We'll discuss this plugin later in the chapter.

Blindness

Up to this section, we could rely on users being able to perceive some visual cues. For example, a user might not be able to tell certain colors apart, but they can see how the information is grouped together.

With a blind user, however, we can't rely on *any* visual cue to help the user navigate through our app. This means that our typical expectations of a user being able to tap a button or scroll a long piece of text go right out the window.

Thankfully, there is a lot of software that translates web content into a more useable form for blind users. Furthermore, mobile devices have extensive accessibility features built into the operating system that provide assistance for blind individuals. Apps can get some of this for free, but our app can also improve the experience by providing more specific cues so that the assistive technology can better understand our app's intentions.

It's important to recognize several key points while making the app accessible to blind individuals:

- Images are unusable. Whenever possible, provide textual representations. Keep in mind that these alternative representations don't need to be literal. If you have an image that represents a stop sign, you don't necessarily need to describe it like an eight-sided object painted red with white lettering and so on when the salient information is simply *stop*.

- Context matters. Those who have good vision can infer a lot of context visually. For those who don't, the only context is the information just conveyed. The order in which the items are presented to users is often the source or DOM order. So, if your DOM is out of order, your app won't make any sense.

- Navigation occurs from link to link. Instead of scrolling and tapping directly where the user wants to go, links are navigated sequentially. This means that if your navigable items are out of order, the user may become confused.

- The app should provide ways to skip repetitive, long, or tedious content.

- What's on the screen isn't *visible* in its entirety immediately. The user needs to wait until their assistive technology has provided the information to them. This may take considerable time depending upon the assistive technology and content.

Auditory disabilities

Apps that don't generate sound needn't worry about auditory disabilities. But if your app plays video or music, or your app is a game that plays sound effects and the like, you should definitely provide accessibility features for your users.

We won't go over the various types of hearing disabilities, since the solution is the same: provide captions and transcripts of the audio material. For a game, you could provide an onscreen representation of a sound whenever it occurs in relation to the in-game entity that caused said sound.

Motor disabilities

Motor disabilities mean that your user may not be able to interact with the device in the way people with full control of their hands and fingers can. A user may not be able to directly touch the screen or they may have problems performing gestures (like pinch to zoom). In these scenarios, providing fallback methods for gestures is wise. It's also important to provide ways of skipping long or tedious material for those who need to interact with your app sequentially. This also means that your content needs to be in an order that makes sense and provides correct context.

Dyslexia

Dyslexia is an extremely common cognitive disability that impairs language or visual processing. For long passages of text, some individuals with dyslexia find that specially crafted fonts can help. One such font is OpenDyslexic. It's available at `http://opendyslexic.org`. While this shouldn't necessarily be the default font in your app, if your app displays a lot of text (say, an e-book app), you may want to consider making it an option your dyslexic users can enable.

Seizures

For most productivity or enterprise applications, this isn't a big deal; but it's important to be aware of it, especially if you're developing games or you are tempted to flash something quickly in order to get your user's attention.

In short, unless you provide an appropriate warning and mechanism to disable the feature, don't strobe or flash items quickly. These can cause your users to feel nauseated and dizzy; even worse, some users can experience seizures.

Games are an obvious place where you might not be able to avoid this; the game might depend upon it. Super Hexagon would be a classic example; the game's difficulty depends upon the flashing, strobing, and rotating playfield. In these cases, it would be wise to place a warning that those prone to dizziness, nausea, and/or seizures from onscreen content should avoid the app.

Accessibility for free

In the previous chapter, we mentioned that HTML and CSS was largely responsive by design. It actually takes some work to prevent HTML from being responsive.

The same is somewhat true for accessibility. This isn't because HTML was really originally built with accessibility in mind (it wasn't), but because many of the assistive technologies that have been developed had to cope with the web content that wasn't accessible. In these cases, the assistive technology had to glean as much information as possible from the markup. Some HTML elements, such as `a`, `input`, `select`, `option`, and so on, provide a lot of useful information. Screen readers have developed an understanding of how these are often used and how to interact with them over the years.

HTML 2.0 brought about the famous `alt` attribute. Here were the first glimmerings of accessibility on the web, but it wasn't added solely for accessibility. The `alt` attribute is meant to render when the original content can't be rendered. It's since been used as a simple way of describing images when these images can't be rendered by a screen reader or Braille device.

HTML 4.0, however, really started to take accessibility seriously. In addition to requiring `alt` on all `img` tags, it also allowed `title` and `lang` attributes on all tags. Furthermore, HTML 4.0 encouraged the separation of presentation styling and content. This made it much easier for assistive technologies to render the web in a form understandable to the user.

Along with this support in HTML, the W3C (World Wide Web Consortium) released WCAG (Web Content Accessibility Guidelines), a set of guidelines web developers should follow in order to ensure an accessible design. The second version of these guidelines was published in 2008 and is available at `http://www.w3.org/WAI/intro/wcag.php`.

All of this doesn't mean that our apps become completely accessible for free—far from it, but it does mean that if an HTML element or attribute works for our needs, we should use it. Conversely, it means that we shouldn't coopt an HTML element and use it in an unexpected way.

Let's look at a few simple examples where we can gain accessibility nearly for free by simply using HTML elements and attributes. Consider the following snippet:

```
<img src="dog.jpg" />
```

Take a moment to consider how users with various disabilities might encounter difficulties with the preceding content when it is rendered in a browser. From the source code, it's fairly obvious that this will be an image of a dog. But your users won't have immediate access to the source code and filenames aren't guaranteed to be this descriptive.

We can immediately improve the usability and accessibility of this image by doing the following:

```
<img src="dog.jpg" alt="Image of my dog, Shelley." />
```

Immediately we can see that an assistive technology would be able to describe the image to the end user. This would be important for any user with low or no vision.

> The `alt` attribute isn't really an accessibility feature, although we can use it like one. If a browser fails to load the image or can't render it (for example, a text-only web browser), the `alt` attribute content is also displayed.

The `alt` attribute is only permissible on the `img` and `area` elements. For other elements, the `title` attribute should be used instead. The `title` attributes are usually rendered as tooltips on the desktop; but they are also spoken by screen readers, usually after a few seconds of initially navigating to the item. For example:

```
<button title="Share this page with your friends">Share</button>
```

Some assistive technologies will initially render this as "Share, button" when the user navigates to the element. Should the reader wait for a few more seconds, the `title` attribute will be usually rendered as well. Other technologies may render both at the same time. Either way, having a `title` attribute certainly provides additional and useful context for your users.

Most assistive technologies will infer quite a bit from your app's use of HTML elements. In the previous example, using the `button` tag provided additional information that could be used to provide the user with additional information. We could have used a `div` tag, of course. This, if appropriately styled, would have worked visually as well. But `div` provides no additional information to an assistive technology, and as such, should be avoided when alternatives exist.

This means that whenever there is an HTML element that matches our app's semantics, we should utilize it. For example, where there are tap-able elements, we should use `button` or `<input type="button|submit|reset" />` instead of `div`.

Conversely, it is very unwise to use HTML elements whose semantics don't match our app's intent. For example:

```
<h1 onclick="doSomething();">Add Item</h1>
```

Although extremely contrived, this example is going to be confusing to an end user, because a screen reader already has a pretty good notion of what `h1` is and how to represent it (a top-level header). If our app decided that it was, instead, a button, the screen reader would have no way of knowing this and would mislead our users.

HTML5 brought about a lot of new elements with new semantics. We can use `nav` instead of `<div class="navigation">` or `aside` instead of `<div class="sidebar">`. Assistive technologies that understand HTML5 can use these new elements to provide additional context to our users.

What is WAI-ARIA?

Even with built-in accessibility for HTML elements and some accessibility features such as `alt` and `title`, it's clear that web applications need to convey much more information to assistive technologies. Quite often, hybrid applications render elements for which there is no HTML equivalent. Furthermore, the semantics of a web app simply don't always align well with the existing accessibility features of websites. Enter the WAI-ARIA specification.

 WAI-ARIA is short for the **Accessible Rich Internet Applications** specification from the **Web Accessibility Initiative** at W3C.

This specification allows you to specify additional semantics for your HTML elements so that you can more clearly indicate what the element is doing. There are two main categories of semantics:

- **Roles**: This indicates the semantic role the element is performing in the application. For example, a navigation bar would be given the `role="navigation"` HTML attribute. There are generally two types of roles: **landmark** and **widget**. Landmark roles mark the sections of a page: banners, groups, content, asides, and so on, while widgets mark specific user interface controls.

- **Attributes**: These are the `aria-` prefixed attributes on the element that represent data values or other states. WAI-ARIA maintains a distinction between *states* and *properties*. States typically are more dynamic in nature (that is, they change more often), but it's practically simpler to reference these as attributes.

As we mentioned at the end of the previous section, WAI-ARIA does have some overlap with HTML5. As an example, a `nav` element automatically receives `role="navigation"`. When possible, you should prefer the HTML5 element so that you don't have to write a lot of supporting code for the WAI-ARIA roles and attributes. If you're targeting a browser that *doesn't* understand HTML5, you'll want to include both for maximum compatibility (for example, `<nav role="navigation">`).

 WAI-ARIA roles and attributes do not change the functionality of the element in question, nor do they alter the appearance. They are only used as hints for assistive technologies.

All modern mobile browsers (except Blackberry) support WAI-ARIA. However, some platform support has been very recent. Android, for example, only supports WAI-ARIA since Android 4.4. Furthermore, except for Mobile IE, the remaining browsers that support WAI-ARIA tend to do so partially. In other words, if you must target older platforms, you shouldn't rely solely upon WAI-ARIA to create accessible apps — that is, don't use a lot of `div` elements with the `role` and `aria-` attributes, unless there's no other way to accomplish what you need to do.

There are a lot of useful articles online that discuss WAI-ARIA. Unfortunately, covering this subject completely is beyond the scope of this chapter. This isn't necessarily a problem, since there are many cases where using HTML5's new elements (such as `nav`) will get you improved accessibility for free. Even so, it would be wise to read upon WAI-ARIA for the future. These links are very useful:

- `https://developer.mozilla.org/en-US/docs/Web/Accessibility/ARIA`
- `http://caniuse.com/#feat=wai-aria`
- `http://www.html5accessibility.com`
- `http://w3c.github.io/aria-in-html/`
- `http://oaa-accessibility.org/examples/`
- `https://www.marcozehe.de/2014/03/27/what-is-wai-aria-what-does-it-do-for-me-and-what-not/`
- `http://www.w3.org/TR/wai-aria-practices/`

The WAI-ARIA roles

Although we can't cover everything that WAI-ARIA covers, we can quickly go over the landmark roles and widgets that would be apt to use in a hybrid application. There are more roles available, but they aren't apt to be the roles you'll need in most apps.

 Where an HTML5 element has the same semantics, we've listed them in parentheses. You should favor using these elements over the WAI-ARIA roles, unless you are targeting devices that don't have good HTML5 or WAI-ARIA support.

A useful reference is at `http://www.karlgroves-sandbox.com/CheatSheets/ARIA-Cheatsheet.html`, which also served as the basis for the following reference.

- `article` (`<article>`): Content (such as a blog post, and so on).
- `banner` (`<header>`):It is typically used to mark a site's heading.
- `complementary` (`<aside>`): It is used to mark related content that can be separated from the primary content. For example, a *see also* or *more about...* section.
- `contentinfo` (`<footer>`): A container that includes information about the document; typically, a footer.
- `form` (`<form>`): Indicates a collection of labels and the corresponding input elements.

- main (<main>): Main document content.
- navigation (<nav>): A navigation element containing links to other documents
- search: A collection of elements that allow the user to perform a search operation.

There are a large number of widget roles that should cover just about any user interface element you need. We won't list all the widget roles that are available; we'll just list the ones you are more apt to use grouped by category. Pay attention to those that have HTML5 equivalents. You should prefer these HTML5 elements over WAI-ARIA roles if you can:

- Content-related: Text, images, and so on
    - heading (<h#>): A text heading
    - img (<img>): An image
    - link (<a href="...">): A link to another resource
    - separator (<hr>): Separates groups of items

- General
    - group (<div>, <optgroup>, <fieldset>): Used to group widgets
    - presentation: The assistive technology will not attempt to interact with this element

- Messages:
    - alert (alert()): An important message that is often time-sensitive
    - log: An element that receives information updates that may remove old updates
    - marquee: A region where information is updated frequently, but where the information isn't essential
    - status (<output>): A message that contains advisory information (but may not represent a serious error)

- Dialogs and alerts
    - alertdialog: A dialog that contains an alert message
    - dialog: This indicates a dialog that the application displays in order to receive additional input from the user
    - toolbar: A condensed list of actions, usually horizontal

- Form elements
  - button (`<button>`, `<input type="button|submit|reset">`): A button that can be tapped
  - checkbox (`<input type="checkbox">`): A checkbox
  - radio (`<input type="radio">`): An individual radio item; part of a group where only one can be checked at a time
  - radiogroup: A group of radio elements
  - slider (`<input type="range">`): A widget that allows the user to select from a range of values using a slider
  - textbox (`<input type="text|...">`, `<textarea>`): This describes a text input element

- Select lists
  - combobox (`<select>`): This is often used to represent a widget where the user can type to select information
  - listbox (`<select>`, `<datalist>`): A widget that allows the user to select an item from the list
  - option (`<option>`): An item in a select or data list

- Grids and tables
  - columnheader (`<th scope="col">`): A column header within a table or grid
  - grid (`<table>`): A table or grid
  - gridcell (`<td>`): A cell in a table or grid
  - row (`<tr>`): A row of cells in a grid or table
  - rowgroup (`<thead>`, `<tfoot>`, `<tbody>`): A group of rows in a grid or table

- Lists
  - list (`<ul>`, `<ol>`): A static list
  - listitem (`<li>`): An item in a list or a directory

- Menus
  - menu (`<menu>`): A list of items that the user can select from
  - menubar: This usually represents a horizontal, persistent menu that contains drop-down menus
  - menuitem: An item within a menu or a menu bar

- ○ `menuitemcheckbox`: A menu item that is a checkbox
- ○ `menuitemradio`: A menu item that is one of a group of items, only one of which can be selected

- Trees
  - ○ `tree`: A hierarchical list that allows subtrees to be collapsed or expanded
  - ○ `treegrid`: A grid that allows the collapsing and expanding of its rows (like a tree)
  - ○ `treeitem`: An item in a tree

Accessibility examples

There are a lot of examples of using the WAI-ARIA and HTML Accessibility features, but there aren't many that concentrate solely on mobile hybrid apps. In this section, we'll go over a few examples that should give you a good idea of how you can create accessible widgets in your app.

Separation of presentation and content

If you are new to this concept, it's time to get very familiar with separating your app's presentation and content. This will make it much easier for assistive technologies to properly render your app to your end user. Of course, with the web technologies at our disposal, this is actually very easy to accomplish; *visual* presentation should reside in your CSS (or Sass) and the content should reside in your HTML. If you're saying "well, of course!" right now, you're probably wondering why I even brought it up—it seems pretty obvious. But sometimes, it isn't always immediately obvious as to what constitutes *content* and what constitutes *presentation*.

 For dynamically-generated content, the same applies: your code should generate HTML elements for the *content* and use the existing CSS classes for the *presentation*.

We could, for example, make a really simple (and wrong) rule: all images should be included in your HTML, because images are content. If you think for a few seconds, however, you'll quickly realize that this isn't true: icons on buttons are images, but they aren't content, especially for users who can't see them. Instead, they'll care more about what the button is supposed to do; they aren't likely to care about what icon you may use for those who can see them.

What will be content and what will be presentation will largely depend upon your app, so there's no hard and fast rule that we can use to determine which is which. Generally, the dividing line is between the elements that form the *chrome* of your app (navigation bars, tool bars, and so on) and the data the app displays or operates on. The former is generally presentation, and the latter is content.

Accessible icon buttons

Since we mentioned icon buttons in the previous section, let's cover how you might create an accessible icon button. Because we need to separate the presentation from the content, we'll need to use CSS and HTML to accomplish this:

```
<button class="icon-bookmark"
title="Bookmark this word">Bookmark</button>
```

So far, this isn't terribly exciting. But it's already very accessible; a screen reader might read this Bookmark button as "Bookmark this word". For those who do have good vision, let's style it appropriately:

```
.icon-bookmark {
  -webkit-appearance: none;
  -moz-appearance: none;
  border: 0;
  margin: 0; padding: 0;
  background: transparent url('bookmark.png') no-repeat
              center center / 32px 32px;
  width: 32px; height: 32px;
  color: currentColor;
}
/* don't forget to use media queries to deal with
high-resolution displays! */
```

In most apps, you'd want to have even more styling for this icon, but the earlier mentioned styles are sufficient to get the point across. The visual appearance of the icon isn't content, it is presentation, so it belongs in our CSS. For users who don't care about the presentation, they don't need to worry about the styling. By separating the icon's image into the CSS, assistive technologies won't erroneously indicate to the end user that there was an image present.

Note also that we didn't have to use any WAI-ARIA attributes in the preceding HTML code. This is because the assistive technologies that understand HTML5 and WAI-ARIA will automatically assign the `button` role to the element. If, however, you are targeting older platforms that may not automatically do this, you could use the following instead:

```
<button role="button" class="icon-bookmark"
title="Bookmark this word">Bookmark</button>
```

Should you want to render an icon with no text while still remaining accessible, applying a `font-size: 0` style is the easiest method. This prevents the text from rendering on the screen, but the assistive technology can still render the button's text to the end user.

Accessible navigation

Most views in mobile applications have the concept of a navigation bar at the top of the view. These bars can range from very simple bars containing only a view's title to very complex bars containing buttons and input elements.

In general, these aren't difficult to make accessible. Consider the following example:

```
<nav class="y-nav" >
  <div class="y-widget-group">
    <button class="y-menu-glyph"
            title="Tap to open sidebar">Menu</button>
  </div>
  <div class="y-widget-group y-flex">
    <h1 class="y-title">Logology</h1>
  </div>
  <div class="y-widget-group y-group-align-right">
    <form method="POST">
      <label role="search">
        <div role="presentation"
             class="y-search-glyph">Search</div>
        <input type="text" />
      </label>
    </form>
  </div>
</nav>
```

We're not going to worry about presentation in these (or most) examples, because it really doesn't matter very much from the perspective of any assistive technology. This isn't to say that assistive technologies ignore CSS entirely; they will often detect `display:none` and ignore those elements, but most other styles are ignored.

Notice that we're not free of the `div` elements in this example. But semantically, they are the closest match (although you could make a good argument for `span` as well). Even without the class names, we can get a pretty good idea that the `div` elements exist primarily to group related items in the navigation bar.

So, how will this render using a screen reader? The `nav` element automatically receives a `navigation` role, so the user will know that they are within a navigation bar. If the users select the `Menu` button using their assistive technology, they'll hear "Menu, button (longer pause) Tap to open sidebar". If they advance through the navigation bar, they'll hear the name of the app (`Logology`) and then hear that they are focused on an input element ("Search, text field… double tap to edit").

This example also illustrates the importance of how the order of your code affects the results. If we place the title prior to the `Menu` button, the user will hear the information in that order. In this example, it's not a huge deal; the context is easily inferred. But for other elements, it is extremely critical that you get the order correct. Remember that your user may not be able to see your app's visual hierarchy in order to infer the context.

Also, note that there are only two instances of a WAI-ARIA role present, and it's only to properly handle the search widget. First, the `label` element that wraps around the icon and associated input element receives the role of `search`; the icon itself is also marked with a `presentation` role. This type of role tells the screen reader to ignore the element completely for accessibility purposes, which is just fine; the icon really has no real purpose other than as a visual cue. In general, if we didn't supply this second role, nothing bad would happen: `div` elements are generally ignored by assistive technologies, unless a role is specified.

If you're worried about compatibility, the following version will spell out the WAI-ARIA roles:

```
<nav role="navigation" class="y-nav" >
  <div role="group" class="y-widget-group">
    <button role="button" class="y-menu-glyph"
            title="Tap to open sidebar">Menu</button>
  </div>
  <div role="group" class="y-widget-group y-flex">
    <h1 role="heading" aria-level="1"
```

```
        class="y-title">Logology</h1>
    </div>
    <div role="group" class="y-widget-group y-group-align-right">
      <form method="POST" role="form">
        <label role="search">
          <div role="presentation"
                class="y-search-glyph">Search</div>
          <input role="textbox" type="text" />
        </label>
      </form>
    </div>
  </nav>
```

Accessible lists

A common design pattern in mobile applications is the list view. Each list item can be selected to drill it down and get more information. This is usually marked visually with a chevron or another icon. Generally, these map quite well to the existing HTML tags such as ul and li. Let's see an example:

```
<ul class="y-list" >
  <li class="y-list-item">
    <button class="y-list-contents">
      <div>1.</div>
      <div class="y-flex">A list item.</div>
      <div class="y-indicator"></div>
    </button>
    <div class="y-list-actions" >
      <button class="y-fav-glyph"
              title="Save this item as a favorite.">
              Favorite</button>
      <button class="y-share-glyph"
              title="Share this item with a friend.">
              Share</button>
    </div>
  </li>
    ...
</ul>
```

Again, the styling doesn't really matter here, except for one important detail: in the preceding example, we've also included list actions. On some platforms, these might be exposed by a swipe on the list item; on others, they might be displayed next to the list item. Swiping is a potentially problematic gesture, so you should ensure that there are other ways of accessing the functionality if these items aren't always visible. Furthermore, if they aren't visible on the screen, they should be marked with an `aria-hidden="true"` HTML attribute, otherwise they can still be selected by assistive technologies.

> If you try this using VoiceOver or similar technologies, you may find that this doesn't react as it might natively. On iOS, a list item with additional actions receives the additional prompt like "swipe up or down to select a custom action, then double tap to activate." Unfortunately, there's no way to simulate this exactly using WAI-ARIA.

Note that we've surrounded our list content with `button`. This is because the entire list item is selectable (not simply the elements internal to the list item), and we need to convey this to the end user.

Accessible alerts and dialogs

Most apps will need to display an alert or a dialog to the user at some point during the app's operation. Although you can do so simply by modifying the DOM and styles appropriately, this doesn't alert any assistive technology that something really important may have occurred. A simple alert structure might be as follows:

```
<div class="y-alert-container">
 <div class="y-alert-dialog">
  <h1>Important!</h1>
  <p>An important message!</p>
  <button>OK</button>
 </div>
</div>
```

> This structure is just representative; typically, this will be added programmatically when the alert dialog needs to be displayed.

In order to alert the user of the new alert dialog, we need to add a few attributes:

```
<div class="y-alert-container">
 <div class="y-alert-dialog" role="alertdialog">
  <h1>Important!</h1>
  <p role="alert">An important message!</p>
```

```
    <button>OK</button>
  </div>
</div>
```

Notice the two new `role` attributes. The `alertdialog` role marks which container will contain the message and the `alert` role indicates the element that will contain the message itself.

This will work, except that the underlying content is still visible to the assistive technology. Most alert dialogs don't fill the entire screen, but *are* modal. So, we don't want the user to be confused as to which widgets are usable and which ones aren't. To fix this, we can add `aria-hidden="true"` to any content that we need to hide from the assistive technology and then remove the attribute whenever the dialog is dismissed.

There's another thing: once the dialog is displayed, the first button needs to be focused on programmatically. If we don't focus on an element within the alert, the assistive technology will still think that the user is on the previously selected item.

Typically, all of this is accomplished using JavaScript. Here's an example: note that we assume the app's main content is contained with an element having `mainWindow` as the `id` attribute:

```
function simpleAlert() {
    let outerDiv = document.createElement("div"),
        innerDiv = document.createElement("div"),
        titleEl  = document.createElement("h1"),
        messageEl =  document.createElement("p"),
        buttonEl = document.createElement("button"),
        mainWindow = document.getElementById("mainWindow");

    outerDiv.className = "y-alert-container";
    innerDiv.className = "y-alert-dialog";

    //content
    titleEl.textContent = "Important!";
    messageEl.textContent = "This is an important message.";
    buttonEl.textContent = "OK";

    // accessibility
    innerDiv.setAttribute("role", "alertdialog");
    messageEl.setAttribute("role", "alert");

    // create the dom structure
    outerDiv.appendChild(innerDiv);
```

```
innerDiv.appendChild(titleEl);
innerDiv.appendChild(messageEl);
innerDiv.appendChild(buttonEl);

document.body.appendChild(outerDiv);
setTimeout(function () {
  // show the dialog visually;
  // inside a setTimeout for animations
  outerDiv.classList.add("visible");
  // hide the underlying content from the Accessibility API
  mainWindow.setAttribute("aria-hidden", true);
  // focus the button
  buttonEl.focus();
}, 0);

buttonEl.addEventListener("click", function() {
    // hide the dialog visually
    outerDiv.classList.remove("visible");
    // wait for animations to finish before removing it form
    // the DOM
    setTimeout(function() {
      // let the underlying content become visible to
      // assistive technologies
      mainWindow.removeAttribute("aria-hidden");
      document.body.removeChild(outerDiv);
    }, 400);
}, false);
}
```

Fitting in with native accessibility features

One issue with hybrid apps has been the difficulty of fitting in with the user's accessibility settings. Both, iOS and Android have numerous settings that provide accessibility assistance. The native SDKs usually respond to these settings nearly by default—that is, native apps can respond to the user's settings almost for free. And where work is necessary on the part of a native app, it's usually just a matter of reading a preference setting and responding accordingly (for example, increasing the font size).

Hybrid apps don't receive these benefits automatically, which means that they often operate in a vacuum where they aren't responding to the user's accessibility settings. This clearly marks the app as *ill-behaved* when most of the user's native apps respond to their changes in text size, captions, or what not, but your hybrid app does not.

Technically, because of Cordova's ability to use plugins, all of these settings could be presented to our hybrid application. There is a plugin that accomplishes quite a bit of this, though it doesn't expose *every* possible setting. For most apps, however, the settings this plugin exposes are more than sufficient for most needs.

The plugin (called the Mobile Accessibility Plugin) is available at `https://github. com/phonegap/phonegap-mobile-accessibility`, and has excellent documentation. It exposes whether or not certain accessibility features are enabled or disabled, and it also exposes the users' preferred text size. This plugin allows our app to immediately adapt to the user's preferences rather than appear to be the odd app out.

Installing the Mobile Accessibility Plugin

If you're using the Cordova CLI, installing the plugin is simple:

```
cordova plugin add https://github.com/phonegap/phonegap-mobile-
accessibility
```

The Gulp workflow is also pretty easy to add if you're using it, but the plugin needs to be added to our `package.json` file. Find the `cordova.plugins` array and add the repository to it, as follows:

```
{
  cordova: {
    ...,
    "plugins": [
      ...,
      "https://github.com/phonegap/phonegap-mobile-accessibility"
    ]
  },...
}
```

Once added, you can reinitialize the build artifacts by executing the following:

```
$ gulp init
```

```
$ gulp copy
```

Detecting the user's preferred text size

Both, iOS and Android allow the user to override the default text size used in the body text to something that's more comfortable. We can hook into this setting and scale our user interface appropriately.

Doing so is very simple once the plugin is installed. After the `deviceready` event is received, we can execute the following:

```
MobileAccessibility.usePreferredTextZoom(true);
```

This will cause the plugin to determine what the user's preferred font size is, and will adjust the size of the text (but not any images or icons) accordingly. This is done very quickly; although if your layout is complex, it might be noticeable for a very short time. If this is disturbing, you may wish to keep your app's splash screen visible for a short time while until the browser is done adjusting its content.

Technically, you don't have to call this method every time; this setting is actually stored in `localStorage` and the app will continue to adjust the app's text size. This makes this method useful for a settings view, where you may wish to allow the user to toggle whether or not the application respects the system's font size setting.

If `false` is passed, the plugin will no longer manage font scaling.

> On iOS, there's an alternative to using this plugin to manage the font size. You can learn more at http://mir.aculo.us/2013/09/16/how-to-create-a-web-app-that-looks-like-a-ios7-native-app-part-1/, but be aware that this is not cross-platform compatible.

Detecting a screen reader

Ideally, our app shouldn't care whether a screen reader is active or not. But sometimes, it can be useful to know, as the app might wish to change the way it processes gestures or change the way it renders its views. In order to detect whether a screen reader is active, we can do as follows:

```
MobileAccessibility.isScreenReaderRunning( isActive => console.
log(`Screen reader is active? ${isActive ? "yes":
"no"}.`));
```

If your app does care whether or not the screen reader is active, chances are good you'll also want to be notified if this changes. To do this, we need to listen for a special event that is fired whenever the screen reader is turned on or off:

```
function screenReaderHandler( features ) {
  if (features !== undefined &&
      features.isScreenReaderRunning !== undefined) {
    if (features.isScreenReaderRunning) {
      // screen reader is running, act accordingly
    } else {
      // screen reader isn't running, act accordingly
    }
  }
}
window.addEventListener(

MobileAccessibilityNotifications.SCREEN_READER_STATUS_CHANGED,

screenReaderHandler, false);
```

Both of these methods are generic: on iOS, they will check whether VoiceOver is active, and on Android, they will check whether TalkBack is enabled. There are methods that check these specifically. If you wish to do so, check the documentation for the plugin.

Speaking custom text

Sometimes, it can be handy to speak text to the user programmatically. This plugin provides two methods to control speech through the screen reader just for this purpose.

To speak a custom line of text, you can do as follows:

```
MobileAccessibility.speak("Word added to your favorites.");
```

If you need to stop the speech, you can do as follows:

```
MobileAccessibility.stop();
```

Useful tools

There are many different tools that can be used to help check your app's accessibility. Some can be run in a browser, while others require use in an emulator or on a physical device:

- Accessibility Inspector, available on OS X and iOS
- VoiceOver, available on OS X and iOS
- TalkBack, available on Android
- Accessibility DevTools for Chrome at `https://chrome.google.com/webstore/detail/accessibility-developer-t/fpkknkljclfencbdbgkenhalefipecmb`
- Accessibility panel in Safari/WebKit (right-click on **An Element** and then on **Inspect Element**. It will show the node details in the sidebar. Then. you have to expand the **Accessibility** panel)

 Although the earlier mentioned tools are incredibly useful to test your app's accessibility, your users will be the best source of information regarding your app's usability. Always test your app with your users to see how the accessibility fares in real life scenarios.

Summary

We went through quite a bit in this chapter. If you really want to serve your accessible users well, you'll want to read over all the content we've linked in this chapter. If it seems daunting, that's because it is. This isn't something you can pick up in just a couple of hours. You'll need to test your app with users to see how it gets used in a real-world situation, and then iterate accordingly.

In the next chapter, we'll cover methods we can use to test our application's functionality, both from a code perspective and from the perspective of user interface automation.

6
Testing and UI Automation

Ensuring that your app functions as it should is absolutely critical. When your app is small, it's tempting to leave the testing as an afterthought. After all, it's a small app and it is reasonably easy to test by hand, right? Unfortunately, even a small app that targets more than one device is immensely complicated to test, simply because you wouldn't have all the devices available for testing. Furthermore, it's incredibly boring to test your app by hand after each change on every platform; you will make mistakes doing so. Thankfully, there's a better way.

It's unfortunate that testing often gets left as an afterthought, because it's an incredibly important part of the development process. Unfortunately, it's easy to overlook it when you're first learning a language, since you're usually assumed to be working with small, easily verifiable portions of code and not a large multi-thousand-line codebase. Why write a test when a simple twenty-line program can easily be proved to be correct, right? However, a 500-line program isn't so easy to test. A 5,000-line program is even worse, and a 100,000-line program is impossible without either a lot of assistance or automation.

Automation testing simplifies our testing process dramatically. Instead of running a lot of manual tests, we can tell the automation tool how to run the test for us and what results the test should produce if everything is working as it should. The automation tool can then execute all our defined tests for many different platforms and perform tests much faster than we ourselves can do, which means that it is much more likely to be executed after every code change. This lets us feel pretty confident that our app works as designed—as long as we've provided sufficient test cases to the automation tool. If one doesn't supply enough test cases to the tool, the automation tool won't catch all the problems. And, of course, you'll still need to have real users test your app; it's unlikely you'll think of every possible scenario. Once your testers identify a potential issue, you can write a test that ensures it will be checked continuously in the future.

In this chapter, we'll cover the following:

- An introduction to assertions
- Writing tests using Chai
- Running test suites using Mocha
- Writing UI automation tests
- Running UI automation tests using Appium and Mocha
- Integrating our tests with Gulp

Getting started

Several of the snippets in this chapter are available using the interactive snippet playground that accompanies the code package of this book. Instructions to launch the playground are in the README.md file in the code package. Once it starts, select **6: Testing and UI Automation** and then browse and experiment with the examples. Where applicable, each section and snippet will indicate which chapter and example you should select.

An introduction to assertions

Automated testing relies on the concept of assertions. Assertions themselves are quite simple: they are simply a statement of fact. If the statement is factually true, the test will pass (or will continue to the next step); but if the statement is false, the test will fail and report an error.

 The snippets in this section are located at snippets/06/ex1-basic-assertions/a in the code package of this book. When using the interactive snippet playground, select **6: Testing and UI Automation** and Example **1a**.

Consider the following short snippet:

```
let x = 5;
let y = x * 2;
```

We can make several assertions about this code after it has been executed:

- x will contain the value 5
- y will contain the value 10

Testing this manually isn't terribly difficult. We can open up a JavaScript REPL or a browser's debugging console and determine the truth of these assertions pretty easily. However, that's tedious to do on a continuous basis. We can do better than this. Let's add some code to our snippet:

```
if (x !== 5) {
    throw new Error("x is not 5!");
}
if (y !== 10) {
    throw new Error("y is not 10!");
}
```

It's obvious, however, that there are some boilerplate to this code. Also, it would be nice to write the assertion as a positive statement, instead of a negative one. Let's write a simple method to help us:

```
/**
 * Throws an error with `msg` if `expr` is false.
 */
function assert(expr, msg) {
  if (!expr) {
    throw new Error (msg);
  }
}
```

Now, let's consider the following examples:

```
let x = 5;
assert (x === 5);                    // [1]
x = 4;
assert (x === 5);                    // [2]
assert (x === 5, "X isn't 5")        // [3]
```

The first assertion [1] does nothing; the assertion is in fact true. However, if we redefine the value of x and try again, an error will be thrown at assertion [2]. This error won't be terribly useful; it'll be a generic error, so it's wise to use the form in [3] instead. This will throw an error with the message X isn't 5.

Actual assertion libraries usually offer more features, such as testing for specific values (rather than simple true or false checks), property inspection, whether or not a block throws an error, and so on. However, they all build upon a very simple concept: if a fact isn't true, throw an error.

Writing tests using Chai

Chai is an assertion library. Instead of needing to write several variations of `assert`, Chai provides several different methods that we can use to create tests that are easy to read. Chai also uses method chaining to create a more English-like version of the test, so they are both easy to read and write.

 For more information on Chai, visit `http://www.chaijs.com`.

Chai is useful because it allows us to write expressive tests without a lot of work. It also caters to you, the developer, by letting you choose one of several provided interfaces. There are three:

- `assert`: Tests use an assert-styled interface, akin to what we used in the prior section. There are a lot of utility methods that you can use, such as `assert.typeOf`, `assert.equal`, and more. One can also just use `assert(expression, message)` as we did in the previous section.

- `expect`: Tests use `expect` and method chaining to form an English-like statement. For example, `expect(x).to.equal(5)` or `expect(a).to.have.property('b')`.

- `should`: Tests use a `should` property on objects and method chaining to form an English-like statement. For example, `x.should.equal(5)` or `a.should.have.property('b')`. If there is a chance the expression one is testing will evaluate to `null` or `undefined`, use the `expect` interface instead.

It's really up to you which interface you prefer; there is no right or wrong answer here. Personally, I prefer `should`, but you can use any of them and create perfectly fine test suites.

 For more on the differences between the various interfaces, see `http://chaijs.com/guide/styles/`.

In order to use Chai, you'll need to install it as a development dependency in your project:

```
npm install --save-dev chai@3.2.0
```

Before using a Chai method, our test needs to require the module and request the desired interface, as follows:

```
let assert = require("chai").assert;      // assert interface, or
let expect = require("chai").expect;      // expect interface, or
let should = require("chai").should();    // should interface
```

Chai also has the ability to use plugins, which can expand the functionality of Chai itself. A lot of the Cordova code is asynchronous and, typically, we would use promises to abstract it away. To use promises with Chai, we need to add a plugin called `chai-as-promised` (available at `http://chaijs.com/plugins/chai-as-promised`):

```
npm install --save-dev chai-as-promised@5.1.0
```

Using the plugin requires a little different boilerplate code. Thus, instead of `require`, the code looks more as follows:

```
let chai = require("chai");
chai.use(require("chai-as-promised"));
let should = chai.should();              // or .expect or .assert
```

Now, while working with promises, we can write a test like `promise.should. eventually.equal(5)`. `Chai-as-promised` will handle the asynchronous nature of promises on its own.

There's one other detail when it comes to writing tests with any assertion library. No one wants the test code to be in the same file as the app's code. If our testing code was inline alongside our app's code, we'd end up generating testing code in our production app, which would slow things down. It would also make it difficult to test different scenarios. Instead, tests are always written in files separate from the code that they are testing.

In the case of simple code tests, they are typically placed in a `test` subdirectory. This is where you'll find your code tests in the code package for this book. If you've built your project directory manually, you should add this folder now:

```
cd /your/project/directory/root
mkdir test
cd test
```

Typically, you'll have many files within this directory, each testing for specific things. As such, we don't want to write a lot of boilerplate code. Instead, it is better to create some helper utilities so that we don't need to write a lot of boilerplate. Let's create a `helper` directory within the `test` directory, which we'll use to build helper utilities:

mkdir helper

cd helper

Now, we will create a file called `setup.js`. It should look as follows:

```
"use strict";

var chai = require("chai");
var chaiAsPromised = require("chai-as-promised");
chai.use(chaiAsPromised);

var should = chai.should();
exports.should = should;     // or assert or expect
```

With the boilerplate out of the way, how do we separate our code from the test? Let's start by writing some code that will do something to an object. We'll call it `code.js` (be sure to place it in the `test` directory) and it should have the following:

```
"use strict";

exports.doSomething = function (obj) {
    obj.x = 5;
}

exports.doSomethingElse = function (obj) {
    obj.x = 4;
}
```

Note that this doesn't do anything useful; but keep in mind that this could be any file from our project that performs some function. You'll typically need to return an object or a function so that the test code can drive it. But your app usually has the same requirements, so this isn't difficult.

Now, let's write a test file called `test.js`:

```
"use strict";

let should = require("./helpers/setup").should;
let code = require("./code.js");

let anObject = {
```

```
    x:0
}

code.doSomething(anObject);
anObject.x.should.be.equal(5);                    // [1]

code.doSomethingElse(anObject);
anObject.x.should.be.equal(5);                    // [2]
```

Notice how we require `should` using our `setup.js` file. Because we're using our `setup.js` file this way, we can write promise-based tests as well (although this example doesn't require promises). In short, any boilerplate that you repeat to set up the assertion library can go into `setup.js`, since it will apply to all your tests.

Take a moment and figure out what the results of the test will be before continuing with this section.

 A similar snippet to the one in this section is located at `snippets/06/ex1-basic-assertions/b` in the code package of this book. When using the interactive snippet playground, select 06 and Example 1b.

Assertion [1] in the previous code will pass, because `anObject.x` will be set to 5. However, assertion [2] will fail; `anObject.x` will be set to 4, which isn't equal to 5. It's fairly easy to see this just from the code, but we need a way to actually run the test.

We can do this pretty easily: use `node` itself. Unfortunately, until `node` understands the same ES2015 that Babel uses, we need to actually use a wrapper around `node` called `babel-node`. It's easy to install; although we won't use it for long in this section, it's a good idea to install it anyway. It's very useful for playing around with the ES2015 syntax:

npm install -g babel-node

Now we can run our test:

babel-node test.js

Initially, you might think things have gone horribly wrong. But take a moment to look at the output. It should look something like the following:

```
logology-v06/node_modules/chai/lib/chai/assertion.js:107
        throw new AssertionError(msg, {     [1]
            ^

AssertionError: expected 4 to equal 5     [2]
```

```
    at Object.<anonymous> (logology-v06/test/test.js:15:22)    [3]
    at Module._compile (module.js:460:26)
    at normalLoader (/usr/local/lib/node_modules/babel/node_modules/
babel-core/lib/api/register/node.js:199:5)
    at Object.require.extensions.(anonymous function) [as .js] (/usr/
local/lib/node_modules/babel/node_modules/babel-core/lib/api/register/
node.js:216:7)
    at Module.load (module.js:355:32)
    at Function.Module._load (module.js:310:12)
    at Function.Module.runMain (module.js:501:10)
    at Object.<anonymous> (/usr/local/lib/node_modules/babel/lib/_
babel-node.js:144:25)
    at Module._compile (module.js:460:26)
    at Object.Module._extensions..js (module.js:478:10)
```

If you don't see an error that looks like it, something did go wrong; you've probably messed up the paths a little bit. But if you do see it, you've done it right.

So what does the error tell us?

1. An assertion failed (the error type is `AssertionError`).

2. The assertion that failed was 4 `===` 5. Do note that the line number at [3] is incorrect, because Babel is transpiling our ES2015 code and passing it on to Node.js.

Of course, none of this is pretty. It's hard to tell exactly which assertion failed (was it the first or the second?) and it's hard to pull the important information out of all that mess. Furthermore, there's another difficulty: running multiple tests at once. Thankfully, there's a better way and it's called a test runner, which we'll cover in a moment.

Writing tests using Chai is pretty simple, but there's not sufficient space in this chapter to fully document what you can do. Instead, let's go over some common examples. If you want to know more, see the documentation at `http://chaijs.com/api/`. Note also that we're using the `should` interface in all the following examples. The `expect` interface is the same (except for the `expect()` portion), but the `assert` interface uses different methods.

Language chains

Language chains make it easy to write your test case in typical English. You've already seen an example: `be`. On its own, `be` doesn't do anything; it's just there for readability. `x.should.be.equal(5)` is equivalent to `x.should.equal(5)`, which is also equivalent to `x.should.be.be.be.be.equal(5)`. You are not likely to write the latter, but this ability to chain certain words makes for very expressive test cases.

> The examples in this section are located at `snippets/06/ex2-language-chains` in the code package of this book. When using the interactive snippet playground, select **6: Testing and UI Automation** and Example **2**.

Not every word is valid, so you do need to know what words you can chain: `to`, `be`, `been`, `is`, `that`, `which`, `and`, `has`, `have`, `with`, `at`, `of`, and `same` are all chainable. `a` and `an` are also chainable, but they have another feature: type checking, which we'll cover in a moment.

This means that you can write a phrase like `x.should.have.property("apple").which.is.equal(5)` and Chai knows what you mean (`x.apple===5`).

Logical words

These are words that test for logical conditions:

> The examples in this section are located at `snippets/06/ex3-logical-words` in the code package of this book. When using the interactive snippet playground, select **6: Testing and UI Automation** and Example **3**.

- `not`: This negates the assertion; equivalent to `!`.
- `true`: This asserts that the value is `true`. For example, `(1===1).should.be.true`.
- `false`: This asserts that the value is `false`. For example, `(1===2).should.be.false`.
- `ok`: This asserts that the value is truthy. For example, `(1).should.be.ok`, `"hello".should.be.ok` but `(false).should.not.be.ok`.

Testing existence and types

The following lets you test for the existence of variables as well as their type:

The examples in this section are located at `snippets/06/ex4-testing-existence-types` in the code package of this book. When using the interactive snippet playground, select **6: Testing and UI Automation** and Example **4**.

- `null`: This asserts that the value is `null`. For example, `expect(x).to.be.null` or `expect(x).to.not.be.null`. Note that it only works with `expect` or `assert`.

- `undefined`: This asserts that the value is undefined. For example, `expect(x).to.be.undefined`. Note that it only works with `expect` or `assert`.

- `exist`: This asserts that the value is neither `null` nor `undefined`. For example, `let x=5; x.should.exist;` is a true statement, but you should really use the `expect(x).to.exist` form in case x is `null` or `undefined`.

- `a`, `an`, `instanceOf`: This asserts that the value is of the specified type. For example, `"hello".should.be.a("string")`. Make sure to check for the existence of the item you're testing first.

Testing equality

You've already seen one way to check equality: `equal`. However, there are several other methods you can use depending on the context, as follows.

The examples in this section are located at `snippets/06/ex5-testing-equality` in the code package of this book. When using the interactive snippet playground, select **6: Testing and UI Automation** and Example **5**.

- `equal`, `equals`, `eq`: This tests for strict equality; equivalent to the `===` operator. For example, `(5).should.equal(5)` is true, but `[1].should.equal([1])` is not, even though it appears to be true from a visual standpoint. From a JavaScript standpoint, however, each array is a separate instance, so they are not strictly equal. To avoid this, you can use `equal` in conjunction with `deep`: `[1].should.deep.equal([1])` is true. Note that if there's a chance the item you're testing will be `null` or `undefined`, use the `should.equal(x,5)` or `expect(x).to.be.equal(5)` forms.

- `eql`, `eqls`: This is an alias for `.deep.equal`.

- `above, gt, greaterThan`: This asserts that the value is above the provided threshold; equivalent to the > operator. For example, `[1,2,3].should. have.length.above(1)` and `(5).should.be.above(4)`.

- `below, lt, lessThan`: This asserts that the value is below the provided threshold; equivalent to the < operator. For example, `[1,2,3].should. have.length.below(4)`.

- `least, gte`: This asserts that the value is above the provided threshold or is equal; equivalent to the >= operator. For example, `[1,2,3].should.have. length.at.least(3)` and `(10).should.be.gte(5)`.

- `most, lte`: This asserts that the value is below the provided threshold or is equal; equivalent to the <= operator. For example, `[1,2,3].should.have. length.at.most(3)`.

- `within`: This asserts that the value is between the two provided values. For example, `"hello".should.have.length.within(4,6)`.

- `closeTo`: This asserts that the value is close to the provided value within a provided precision. For example, `(5.75).should.be.closeTo(6, 0.5)`.

- `match`: This asserts that the string matches the given regular expression. For example, `"hello".should.match(/.*/)`.

- `string`: This asserts that the string contains the given substring. For example, `"hello".should.have.string("lo")`.

Testing collections

When it comes to testing what an array, object, or string might contain, there are several very useful methods as well, as follows:

The examples in this section are located at `snippets/06/ ex5-testing-collections` in the code package of this book. When using the interactive snippet playground, select **6: Testing and UI Automation** and Example **6**.

- `length, lengthOf`: This asserts that the array or string is of the specified length. For example, `[1, 2].should.be.length(2)`.

- `contain, contains, include, includes`: This asserts that the array or string contains the provided item. Equivalent to `indexOf`. For example: `"hello". should.contain("lo")` and `[1, 2, 3].should.contain(2)`.

- `empty`: This asserts that the collection is empty. Checks for `length ===` 0 for strings and arrays. An object is considered to be empty if it has no enumerable properties.

- property: This asserts that the item has the specified property, and optionally, a specified value. If used with deep, one can use dot and bracket notation to drill deeper into an object. For example, ({x:5}). should.have.property("x") and ({x:{y:2}}).should.have.deep. property("x.y", 2). Arrays work as well: ({x:[1,2]}).should.have. deep.property("x[0]", 1).

- ownProperty, haveOwnProperty: This asserts that the item has the specified property and that the property is the item's own—that is, not inherited via the prototype chain.

- respondTo: This asserts that the item has the specified method. For example, x.should.respondTo("aMethodName").

- key, keys: This asserts that the item has the specified keys. Whether the object should have all of the provided keys or not depends upon the various modifiers in the prior language chain.

  - any: If this is used in the chain, the item only needs to have one of the provided keys for the assertion to be true. For example, ({x:5,y:10}).should.contain.any.keys("a", "b", "x") passes, because the object contains x as a key.

  - all: If this is used in the chain, the item needs to contain all of the provided keys for the assertion to be true. Whether or not the item can have more keys is determined if have or contain is used in the language chain. For example, ({x:5,y:10,z:20}).should. contain.all.keys("x", "y") passes, because it has all of the specified keys. ({x:5,y:10,z:20}).should.have.all.keys("x", "y") fails, because it has more keys that are specified.

Running test suites using Mocha

Since it's vital that we quickly identify which of our tests are failing, we need a utility that aggregates all our tests together and presents the results in a readable format. There are lots of fantastic test runners out there (Karma, Chutzpah, Jasmine, and so on). But in this section, we'll use Mocha. Mocha is pretty simple: it will execute each test we provide, identify which ones pass, and then proceed to call out any errors in an obvious manner.

 You can find more documentation on Mocha at http://mochajs.org.

First, we need to install Mocha:

```
npm install -g mocha
```

Next, we need to write some test suites that Mocha understands. Go ahead and get rid of the `code.js` and `test.js` files we created earlier. It's time for some real tests now! In fact, let's test our app's `AbstractDictionary` class.

Here's a really simple test that I wrote to verify that the dictionary could, in fact, create a new `Dictionary` object:

```
"use strict";
let should = require("./helpers/setup").should;
import Dictionary from "../src/www/js/app/models/Dictionary";

describe("Dictionary Tests", () => {
    let dictionary = new Dictionary();
    it("should be able to create a new instance", () => {
        return dictionary.should.exist;
    });
});
```

Note that the preamble is the same as what we used in our prior test file besides importing our `Dictionary` object. The part that is new is what starts with `describe`.

`describe` is simply used to group one or more tests together. `describe` can be nested at as many levels as you need (although if you nest very deep, you should probably split your test suites into separate files). In the output, the tests that are executed within the group are displayed with a nice header, allowing easy reference.

A test case is defined using the `it` method. There can be as many of these as necessary to fully test your code. In fact, as you think of the tests, you should put pending tests into your test suite; these are defined as the `it` methods without a function body:

```
it("should be able to jump up and down");
// will be marked as PENDING in the output
```

This lets you come back and define the actual test later, while also tracking the tests that still need an actual implementation.

Each test can be fully self-contained or it can be dependent upon previous execution. It's really up to you and the code you are testing. In our case, we wanted each test to build on the prior results so as to reduce code repetition. For example, here's how we verify that a newly created dictionary is truly empty (and won't throw an error if we search the empty dictionary):

```
describe("Dictionary Tests", () => {
    let dictionary = new Dictionary();
    describe ("#Create", () => {
        it("should be able to create a new instance", () => {
            return dictionary.should.exist;
        });
    });
    describe ("#Empty", () => {
        it("should return an empty sorted index", () => {
            return dictionary.sortedIndex.should.have.lengthOf(0);
        });
        describe ("#find", () => {
            it("searching on an empty dictionary by
              lemma should not error", () => {
                return dictionary.getEntries({lemma:"cat"}).
                  should.eventually.have.lengthOf(0);
            });
            it("searching on an empty dictionary by wordnetref
              should not error", () => {
                return dictionary.getEntries({wordNetRef:0}).
                  should.eventually.have.lengthOf(0);
            });
        });
    });
});
```

Because we now have several tests, we've introduced additional `describe` statements. This allows us to categorize our tests. The first test simply verifies that we can create a new dictionary, so it gets the `#Create` category. The next several tests verify the emptiness of this dictionary, so they collectively get the `#Empty` category. The last two tests, however, search within the dictionary, so we give them a subcategory of `#find`. In Mocha's output, each `describe` statement creates a new indentation level, so each test's category is easily visible.

Notice the `eventually` in the preceding code? This is how `chai-as-promised` waits for promises to resolve themselves.

So far, these tests are pretty simple. Let's look at one more example with some more complicated tests:

```
describe ("#AddApple", () => {
    it("should be able to add an entry.", () => {
        let definition = new Definition({
            wordNetRef: 1,
            lemmas: ["apple"],
            partOfSpeech: "noun",
            gloss: "A tasty fruit"
        });
        return dictionary._addDefinition(definition).should.exist;
    });
    it("should now return a single sorted index", () => {
        return dictionary.sortedIndex.should.have.lengthOf(1);
    });
    it("... that contains the word Apple", () => {
        return dictionary.sortedIndex.
          should.deep.equal(["apple"]);
    });
    describe ("#find", () => {
        it("should be able to find the entry for Apple via lemma",
          () => {
            return dictionary.getEntries({lemma:"apple"}).should.
                    eventually.have.lengthOf(1).and.
                    deep.property("[0].gloss","A tasty fruit");
        });
        it("should be able to find the entry for Apple via
          wordnetref", () => {
            return dictionary.getEntries({wordNetRef:1}).should.
                    eventually.have.lengthOf(1).and.
                    deep.property("[0].gloss","A tasty fruit");
        });
    });
});
```

All of these tests should be pretty self-explanatory. The most complicated tests are in the #find category. In these, we are testing for lengthOf (to ensure the return result only contains one item), and to ensure that we received the correct definition.

After we've defined some tests, we can run them using Mocha:

```
mocha --require "babel/register" .
```

If you aren't using ES2015, you don't need the `--require "babel/register"` portion.

The dot indicates to Mocha that it should run all the tests it can find in the current working directory. You can specify the files you want, or even multiple paths and files. However, one will usually want to run all the tests in a specific directory.

The output should look as follows:

```
Dictionary Tests
  #Create
  √ should be able to create a new instance
  #Empty
  √ should return an empty sorted index
    #find
    √ searching on an empty dictionary by lemma should not error
    √ searching on an empty dictionary by wordnetref should not error
  #AddApple
  √ should be able to add an entry.
  √ should now return a single sorted index
  √ ... that contains the word Apple
    #find
    √ should be able to find the entry for Apple via lemma
    √ should be able to find the entry for Apple via
wordnetref
... [snip] ...


  27 passing (47ms)
```

The preceding result is typically what you're hoping for: each test listed has passed (indicated by the checkmark) and there are no errors at all. Although this is a great thing, it is still important to remember that this doesn't ensure that your code is necessarily bug-free: Mocha can only test for cases that you have explicitly defined.

However, you'll often see something like the following:

```
Dictionary Tests

... [snip] ...

  #AddRock/Stone
  √ should be able to add a fourth entry with two lemmas.
```

```
    √ should return a sorted index of length 4
        1) ... that is [apple, cat, rock, stone]


  ... [snip] ...


  26 passing (61ms)
  1 failing


  1) Dictionary Tests #AddRock/Stone ... that is
[apple, cat, rock, stone] :


      AssertionError: expected ['apple', 'cat', 'rock', 'stone' ]
to deeply equal ['apple', 'cat', 'rock', 'stones' ]
      + expected - actual
      [
        "apple"
        "cat"
        "rock"
      -   "stone"
      +   "stones"
      ]


  ... [snipped out stack trace] ...
```

First, note that the errors are initially listed alongside the passing tests. Instead of a checkmark, they are listed with a number. This number is like a footnote; it can be used to refer to the actual errors that are listed later. It also means that the error messages themselves (that are quite long and verbose) don't muddy up the list of tests, meaning that it is still easy to determine which tests are passing and failing.

The errors themselves come at the end. They are labeled with the same number displayed in the test list, and also include every `describe` and `it` description so that the tests are easy to locate in your code. The message indicates the failed assertion and then it goes on to indicate the differences. This is extremely useful, since it lets you see what portions of the result were correct and what portions weren't. Finally, the stack trace is listed. It would normally lead you directly to the error in your code, except that, for the ES2015 transpiled code, the line number will almost always be incorrect (this is why I've snipped it from the previous example). You should instead ensure that your test cases are well labeled so that you can locate the issue easily without relying on the line number.

Sometimes, your test cases fail simply because of a typo or a misunderstanding of what the results should look like. In the preceding case, we had a typo in the test case. As such, don't assume that a failing test means that your code has a bug. It might mean instead that your *test case* has a bug. Always be sure to test your test cases too, and be sure that they themselves are accurate.

There are several important things that you should know with regard to code testing your Cordova app:

- The code tests occur in a Node JavaScript environment, not in a browser or on your device.

- If you need to verify that your app creates DOM elements correctly, you can simulate certain facets using various modules, such as jsdom (`https://www.npmjs.com/package/jsdom`).

- The code tests cannot verify plugin behavior. It would be best to provide alternative behavior that can simulate the plugin behavior so that you can test the other facets of your app.

These are, of course, extremely limiting when it comes to verifying the correctness of your application. Thus, we need some additional tools that we can use to test our apps on our devices.

Writing UI automation tests

To verify the correctness of our application on physical devices, we need to delve into user interface automation. These tests focus more on the interaction with your app and the verification of correct results rather than verifying the internal logic of the application. A test looks more like a collection of interactions with the app's widgets instead of it directly dealing with models, views, controllers, and the like. Checking for the proper result looks more like ensuring whether certain widgets are displayed on the screen rather than if an object has a specific property.

Although the goals of automation testing are the same as code testing, you do have to approach the tests from a different perspective. While testing your code directly, you have access to the objects that your code creates and you can interact with them easily. While testing your app via automation, you have to approach your app from the perspective of the user: what buttons should be pressed and what should the visual results be? In some ways, it can be useful to view your internal code testing as white-box testing and your application testing as black-box testing.

The analogy isn't perfect because black-box testing usually implies that you don't know or have no access to the internals of the application. Most automation tools will provide some level of introspection in your app; thus, it is usually possible to verify the internal state, which in some ways violates the black box analogy. Even so, it's a good way to think about it: the black box forces you to interact with the visible interface, not with the internal code.

There are many different tools that perform user interface automation, but one has to verify that the tools can work with mobile devices as targets. Furthermore, although the automation tools might work with native code, we also need a tool that allows us to use cross-platform code. After all, we don't want to have to write multiple versions of our tests for each platform we target, unless we absolutely have to (and there are cases where that is required).

There are, unfortunately, very few tools that meet all these requirements. The best (in terms of reliability, stability, and community support), as of this writing, is Appium. Appium can run automation tests on iOS and Android devices, as well as the iOS simulator and the Android emulator. Appium uses JavaScript for test case definitions and integrates well with Mocha, a test runner we're already familiar with. As such, it makes an excellent choice for our needs.

 To test iOS apps, you'll need a Mac. To test Android apps, you can use Windows, Linux, or Mac OS X.

Installing Appium

Installing Appium is pretty simple:

```
npm install -g appium@1.4.16
```

This installs a global utility named `appium`. This utility serves as the bridge between your automation test and your device. Thus, it needs to be running before you run any automation tests that use it. We'll cover how to start it up in a moment.

Now, make sure your environment is properly set up for Appium:

```
$ appium-doctor
```

If everything that Appium needs is set up correctly, you should see the following notice:

```
√ All Checks were successful
```

However, there are several other tools we need to install if we're going to test iOS apps. This is due to the way iOS handles remote debugging. Android is much more permissive and doesn't require nearly as much initial setup.

First, for iOS, we need to install a tool that assists Appium with the deployment of your app to the device. Although Cordova uses a tool called `ios-deploy`, Appium uses a different tool called `ideviceinstaller`. This tool is easy to install, assuming that you already have the `brew` package manager installed:

```
brew install --HEAD ideviceinstaller
```

Next, we need to install a proxy that allows Appium to interact with the app on a physical device:

```
brew install ios-webkit-debug-proxy
```

While we're testing our app on a physical iOS device, this proxy needs to be running as well. We'll cover how to start this proxy up in a moment.

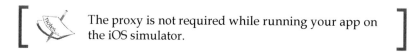

The proxy is not required while running your app on the iOS simulator.

To interact with the web components in our application, we need to install one more tool. This step applies to both iOS and Android:

```
npm install --save-dev wd@0.3.12
```

`wd` is web driver. It lets Appium interact with the system's web view that Cordova uses. Our application itself won't use this driver, but our test cases will; hence, the `--save-dev` flag.

Technically, you don't need to install anything else, but there's one more thing you should install: the Appium desktop application. This isn't required to run your app tests, but it is invaluable for exploring your app while writing tests. This is because you won't be using only web technologies to interact with the app. Instead, you have to know how the app is represented from an automation perspective to locate the widgets that you want to interact with. Being able to click around in your app and discover the internal structure is much simpler and faster than guessing it.

To do this, you can download the desktop application at `http://appium.io`. Just click on the **Download Now** button and then install the application.

Exploring your app with Appium

Now that we have everything installed, let's explore how our app appears to Appium. Go ahead and launch the Appium desktop app that we just downloaded. It should look as follows:

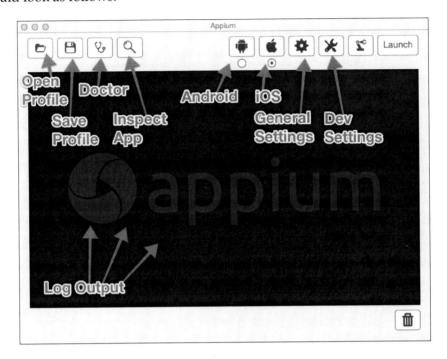

Let's go over the various areas of the app:

- Profile Management is useful while testing many different apps and configurations
    - **Open Profile** will open a previously saved Appium profile
    - **Save Profile** will save the current settings as a new Appium profile
    - **Doctor** will run `appium-doctor` for you to verify that your environment is properly configured
    - **Inspect App** will open the **Appium App Inspector** dialog. We'll cover this window in more detail shortly

- Platform configuration and selection is necessary for configuration of of Android and iOS SDKs
  - ○ The **Android** button will display a configuration dialog that lets you specify where the Android SDK is located, where your app's package is located, and what additional settings it provides. The radio button below the Android icon indicates which platform will be used when you click on **Launch**.
  - ○ The **iOS** button will display a configuration dialog that lets you specify where your app's package is located, what version of iOS Appium should you use, and more. The radio button below the Apple icon indicates which platform will be used when you click on **Launch**.

- Settings
  - ○ **General Settings** contains general configuration options. These settings aren't platform-specific, unlike the Android and iOS settings.
  - ○ **Dev Settings** contains additional developer settings. We won't be using this in this chapter, but you may wish to explore the settings on your own.

- **Launch** will start your app on the selected platform. While the app is running, this will read **Stop**. Clicking on it again will stop the app.

- The **Log Output** area will display Appium's output as your app runs. This is often quite verbose, but is useful when you want to explore the low level results.

Before we can actually explore our app, there are a few settings that we need to configure. Click on the **General Settings** button to display the global configuration settings. Here's our configuration:

Your settings don't need to be exact. Here are a few that we've found useful:

1. **Server Address** and **Port**: You normally won't need to change these. But if you have another service running on this port, you will need to change it to an unused port.

2. **Prelaunch Application**: This ensures that the app is started on the device or simulator automatically.

3. **Kill Processes Using Server Port Before Launch**: This makes sure that any previously existing processes are terminated before you launch your app.

4. **Use Colors**: This simply makes the log file more readable.

5. **Force Scroll Log to Bottom**: This also makes the log file easier to track. When new items are logged, the log file itself will automatically scroll to the new information.

To test our app, we need know where our app packages are located. You should already have versions that function on a simulator, but you may or may not have built one that functions on a real device. Let's go ahead and do this:

```
# Using Gulp

  gulp build --for ios --mode debug --target device

  gulp build --for android --mode debug --target device


# Using Cordova

  cordova build ios --device

  cordova build android --device
```

 You can use `emulator` in place of `device` to build for the emulator/simulator, although the emulator/simulator target is the default build target.

Next, we need to determine where the app packages are. Cordova follows a pattern, so it's not terribly hard to figure out, thankfully. The paths are as follows:

- iOS Device build: `<project root>/build/platforms/ios/device/<app-name>.ipa`

- iOS Simulator build: `project root>/build/platforms/ios/emulator/<app-name>.app`

- Android (Device & Emulator): `<project root>/build/platforms/android/build/outputs/apk/android-debug.apk`

These paths are important, because Appium uses them to deploy and launch our application. Now, click on either the Android robot icon or the iOS Apple icon in the Appium app. This will let you specify where your app will live on your computer and what device settings should be used.

For iOS, our configuration looks as follows:

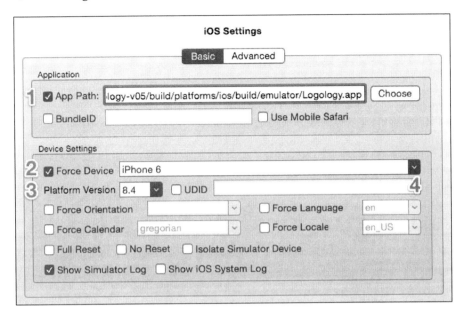

Let's go over the various settings:

1. **App Path**: This specifies the location of our app package. In our example, we're using the iOS simulator, so we will use the iOS Simulator build.

2. **Force Device**: This lets us determine which device emulator will be launched.

3. **Platform Version**: This lets us launch the device emulator with a specific iOS version. While testing on a real device, this should match the iOS version of the physical device.

4. **UDID**: To test on a physical device, Appium needs to know the device's UDID. While using the simulator, you can leave this blank.

> If you want to test on a physical device, you need to know the device's UDID. You can find it by executing `xcrun instruments -s devices`. Assuming your device is attached to your machine, it should appear alongside all the simulators you have installed. Your device's UDID is listed in brackets. You also need to have the webkit debug proxy running, as follows: `ios_webkit_debug_proxy -u <your device UDID>:27753 -d &`.

For Android, our configuration looks as follows:

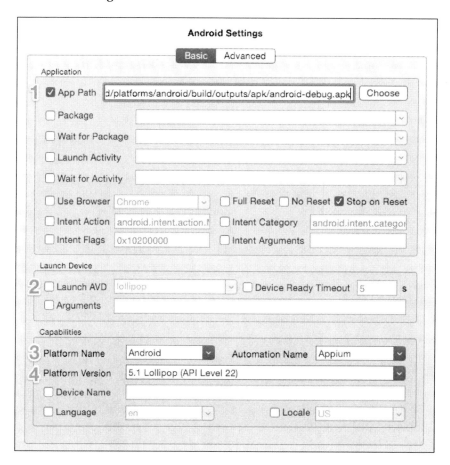

These settings are as follows:

1. **App Path**: This specifies the location of our app package. Android doesn't care if we're using an emulator or a physical device, so this usually doesn't need to change, unless you're testing on devices with different chipsets (Intel versus ARM, for example).

2. **Launch AVD**: If checked, Appium will launch the specified emulator. The emulators listed come from the `android avd` command. You may see other emulators listed if you have Genymotion installed, but you can't launch Genymotion using this tool. If you want to use Genymotion, you must launch the virtual device prior to any testing and leave this setting unchecked.

3. **Platform Name**: You'll want to select **Android** for this setting.

4. **Platform Version**: You need to match this to the version of Android running on your physical or emulated device.

You'll also need to specify the location of your Android SDK; click on the **Advanced** tab and enter the path of your SDK in **2**:

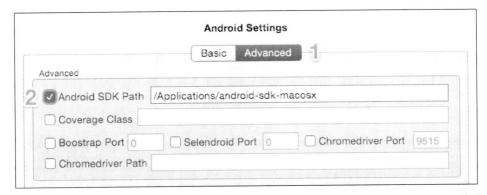

For both Android and iOS, you will need to match the configurations to the emulator/device you are using. For example, if your device is running Android 5.1, you should ensure the Android settings refer to Android 5.1. If your iOS device is running 8.4, make sure the version for the iOS configuration is set to 8.4.

To start your app, you can select the platform you want to use by clicking on the radio button below the Android or Apple icon and then clicking on the **Launch** button.

If you are testing on a device, be sure to plug your device in to your computer prior to launching your app with Appium. If you're using Genymotion, launch your virtual device prior to launching your app with Appium.

Your app should launch in your simulator or on your attached device and a lot of information should be displayed in the log window. Once your app has started, click on the **Inspect App** button (it has a magnifying glass icon). You should see something that looks similar to the following screenshot:

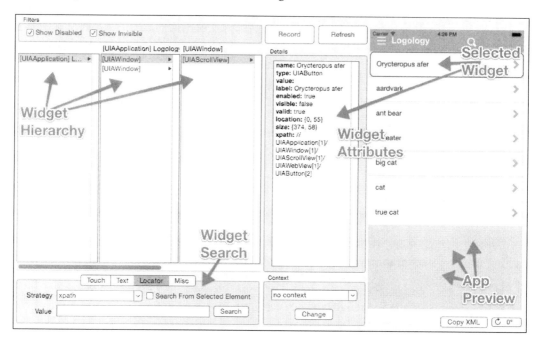

There are several areas of interest on this screen, but we're most interested in four of them. These areas give us everything we need to write proper tests for our app, as follows:

1. The **Widget Hierarchy** is displayed in the multiple column area in the middle of the dialog. As you click on the widgets, the widget's children will appear in the adjacent column.

2. The **App Preview** is displayed on the far right-hand side of the dialog. Selected widgets should appear with a red border in the preview.

3. The **Widget Attributes** area displays information about the selected widget. These attributes can be used while programmatically searching for widgets.

4. The **Widget Search** tab sheet in the lower left corner is useful while testing search strings before you bake them into your test case. It's not displayed by default, so you'll have to display it manually.

As you interact with your app in the emulator or on your physical device, the preview won't automatically refresh. To get a fresh preview, click on the **Refresh** button.

If you were testing an app that used only native components, you could start finding your elements pretty easily. Since our app is a hybrid app, we first need to find the web view that corresponds to our Cordova app. You'll recognize it by the widget class. On iOS, it's labeled **UIAWebView**, and on Android, it's the second widget that is labeled **android.webkit.WebView** (there are two for some reason).

Once you locate the Cordova web view, you can continue drilling down into the widget hierarchy. You should start recognizing your own app's elements. The hierarchy and attributes of one our app's views is similar to the following screenshot:

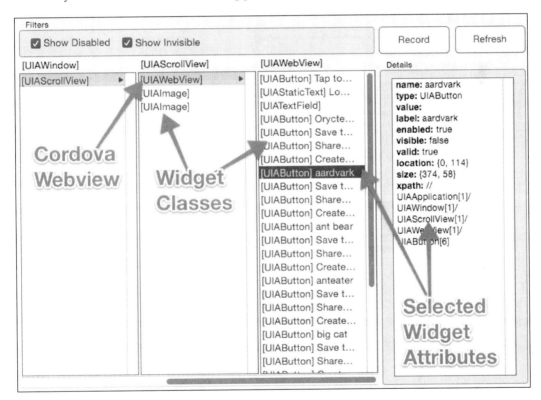

 The text within brackets in the hierarchy is the **Widget Class**. This describes the widget's type. It can be used to programmatically locate widgets, but it is platform-specific; thus, you should use it only as a last resort.

You might notice that the hierarchy only vaguely resembles your app's DOM structure. Both iOS and Android take liberties with regards to this and both use different hierarchies. Thus, while building your tests, you'll want to look at your app on both platforms so that you can know where the elements you need to work with are actually located. To craft good cross-platform test cases, you'll then want to look for commonalities that work on both iOS and Android so that you can still create a simple test case that works on both platforms.

Let's take a look at our app's hierarchy on iOS after we've swiped a row to reveal some actions:

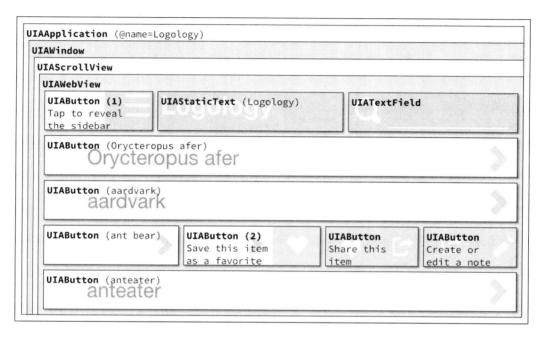

If you compare this hierarchy to the previous screenshot, you can see that the elements don't show much structure at all. We've arranged them nicely so that they correspond visually with the app's preview. But as far as Appium is concerned, they are simply a linear list of widgets.

We've mentioned that the hierarchy is different for each platform. Let's see the same layout on Android:

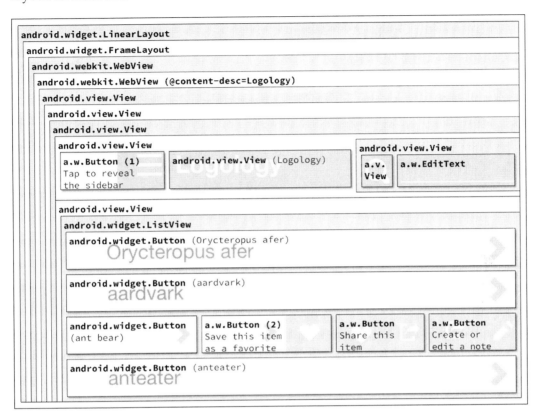

In some ways, Android's hierarchy is a lot closer to our DOM layout. For example, the navigation bar has its own container and the search widget also has a container. Yet, in other ways, it is similar to the iOS hierarchy. That is, the list itself has no depth, even though it does have depth in the DOM.

As you explore your app's hierarchy, you might notice something important: the hierarchy and properties are similar to the *accessibility* hierarchy that your app presents. In short, all the work you put into making your app accessible for your end users also pays off dividends in testing, since you can use that same information to test your apps!

Let's say we want to tap the hamburger icon to reveal the sidebar. We've marked this in both the diagrams as **(1)**. We can't just write something like `tap({x:50, y:50})`, where `x` and `y` are coordinates simply because the widget at that location might be very different depending on the device, the platform, the orientation, and more. So, we need to locate the widget via other means. We will do this with **Location Strategies**. Typically, we'll use the **XPath** strategy, which is a way to search through XML documents. Appium can convert the app's widget hierarchy to XML, and XPath works across multiple platforms, thus making it a good choice.

First, let's go over some basic XPath syntaxes. Let's say we had an XML document of the following form:

```
<UIAWebView id="w1">
  <UIAButton id="btn1" name="button 1" />
  <UIAButton id="btn2" name="button 2" />
  <UIAList id="lst1">
    <UIAButton id="btn3" name="button 3" />
  </UIAList>
</UIAWebView>
```

To directly reference a specific node, say `button 3`, we can use the following XPath query:

```
/UIAWebView/UIAList/UIAButton
```

Now, this looks a lot like a file or URI path, right? This is by design: XPath uses some of the conventions you are already familiar with and expands upon them to enable more complex searches through the tree.

Let's see some more examples. Try to work out what they match before you continue further:

1. `/UIAWebView/UIAButton`
2. `/UIAWebView/UIAButton[2]`
3. `/UIAWebView/*`
4. `//UIAButton`
5. `//UIAButton[3]`
6. `//*[@name="button 3"]`
7. `//*[@name="button 2" or @name="button3"]`
8. `//*[@name|@id="button 1"]`

So, most of these should be pretty easy; but it's possible that a few of the answers may surprise you. Let's see which nodes these XPaths match:

1. Matches #btn1 and #btn2, because they are direct descendants to UIAWebView, which is the root element.

2. Matches #btn2. It is the second UIAButton that is a direct descendant of UIAWebView.

3. Matches #btn1, #btn2, and lst1. * can be used as a wildcard to match any element type.

4. Matches #btn1, #btn2, and #btn3. By using //, the search is no longer fixed to the root element.

5. Matches nothing. Surprised? Well, it turns out that even though #4 returned three elements, [3] isn't like an array index. Instead, it's matching any UIAButton that is third in relation to its parent, of which we have none.

6. Matches #btn3. We're using an attribute search (@name). The value is case-sensitive.

7. Matches #btn2 and #btn3. We can use or and and in order to create more complicated search strings.

8. Matches @btn1. The | operator is a union: it will look at two attributes, name and id.

We can also use functions so that we don't have to search for the exact text. For an example, let's look at the search string that can find our hamburger icon programmatically:

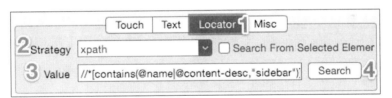

To see this particular tab sheet, you'll need to click on the **Locator** tab first. **Strategy** should already be set to **xpath**; but if it isn't, change it accordingly. Next, you need to enter your search string into the **Value** field and click on **Search**.

The full search string we've built is //*[contains(@name|@content-desc,"sidebar")]. If you click on the **Search** button, the hamburger icon that reveals the sidebar should be highlighted in red.

If an item can't be found or more than one item is found, Appium will notify you with an alert dialog.

This search string looks for any widget that contains the text sidebar. If the sidebar is open, this search would be actually too vague; it'll find two buttons. But if the sidebar is not visible, the search will find the hamburger icon as we desired. In this case, we'd actually want to search for an exact match to Tap to reveal the sidebar.

Let's try a more complicated example. Let's say we wanted to locate the **Favorite** icon marked by **(2)** in our hierarchy. This button would add `ant bear` to the user's favorite definitions.

We could be very specific, of course (it's the third button with **Save this item as a favorite** in the `name|content-desc` union):

```
//*[@content-desc|@name="Save this item as a favorite"][3]
```

However, we usually need to be more generic. After all, if there were more rows or the rows were arranged in a different order, the location of the button would change. To do this, we first need to locate the particular row we need:

```
//*[@content-desc|@name="ant bear"]
```

Once we've found the row, we need to drill into it and find the associated **Favorite** button. Again, we could be fairly specific; it just happens that the button is the definition's immediate sibling:

```
//*[@content-desc|@name="ant bear"]/following-sibling::*[1]
```

If our app's DOM structure were to change, this test would stop working. Thus, we need to look for specific content; in this case, **Save this item as a favorite**:

```
//*[@content-desc|@name="ant bear"]/following-sibling::*[@content-
desc|@name="Save this item as a favorite"]
```

If you were to execute this, you'd find out that the search actually locates several more items; namely, all the **Favorite** buttons that follow our favorite definition. Thus, we need to restrict the return set to the first item. Here's what the final query looks like:

```
//*[@content-desc|@name="ant bear"]/following-sibling::*[@content-
desc|@name="Save this item as a favorite"][5]
```

Unfortunately, describing XPath fully is beyond the scope of this chapter. You'll want to check out the examples in the code package of this book (our tests are under the `logology-v06/test-ui` directory). You can also find lots of good resources online, such as:

- `https://en.wikipedia.org/wiki/XPath`
- `https://developer.mozilla.org/en-US/docs/Web/XPath`
- `https://msdn.microsoft.com/en-us/library/ms256086(v=vs.110).aspx`
- `http://www.w3.org/TR/xpath20/` (specification)
- `http://chris.photobooks.com/xml/` is an excellent XPath tester that highlights the matched nodes. Be sure to select XPath in the upper-left corner. You can then enter an XML document and an XPath search, and then click on **Render** to highlight the matched nodes.

Now the benefit of the Appium desktop app should be clear: it's a great way to test your XPath search strings against your app itself while exploring how your app's hierarchy appears to Appium.

Creating test cases

For this section of the chapter, you'll want to take a look at the `logology-v06/test-ui` directory in the code package of this book to simplify the test setup. You don't have to use it if you don't want to, but you'll then need to do the Appium configuration manually.

Inside `test-ui/helpers`, we have several items:

- `servers/`: This directory contains two scripts that define where the Appium server is running. SauceLabs offers a mechanism to run your tests remotely; if you want to use it, you can. Just update `sauce.js` in this directory with your access information. We'll use the `local.js` server settings, which defaults to `localhost:4723` (note that, if you need to change the port number that Appium runs on, you'll have to update this file).

- `profiles/`: Appium determines which device to use on the basis of specified capabilities. When you only have a single physical device attached, what you want to test with would be pretty obvious; but you'll usually have several simulators and multiple platforms available simultaneously. Thus, Appium needs to be able to figure out what to use. The settings that are specified match those that we used in the Appium desktop app. We've defined several profiles within this directory, but you'll need to adapt them to your own environment. A profile looks as follows:

```
exports.profile = {
    browserName: "",
    platformName: "Android",
    platformVersion: "5.1.1",
    deviceName: "Android Emulator",
    app: __dirname + "/../../../build/platforms/android/build/
outputs/apk/android-debug.apk"
}
```

- `util.js`: This contains the utilities and the initialization code. It contains the boilerplate code used to select the appropriate capability based on the environment variables. It also returns an instance of a web driver that we can use to *drive* the application.

- `should.js`: Requires `chai` and `chai-as-promised`. It contains the boilerplate code very similar to our code tests.

Let's look at a simple test case:

```
"use strict";

var util = require("./helpers/util");
var should = util.should;

describe("Test", function() {
    this.timeout(300000);
    it("should have a rootContainer", () => {
        return util.driver.elementByCss("#rootContainer")
                            .should.eventually.exist;
    });
})
```

The test itself should be pretty simple. We're checking for the existence of a particular DOM element. Because the startup takes a while, we've added `timeout`, and we have used `eventually.exist`, because `elementByCss` returns a promise.

Wait! I hear you saying: we can use CSS selectors to locate elements in our app? Why did we just go over this complicated thing called XPath?

The sad answer is this: while you can indeed determine whether certain DOM elements are present in the DOM and more (you can verify their contents and the like), there's one key thing you *can't* do: touch them.

Oh, a lot of documentation will tell you that you can and you're welcome to *try*. It usually goes along these lines:

```
return util.driver.waitForElementByCss
("main.SearchViewController nav button.menu-icon")
.click();
```

Unfortunately, *nothing happens*. If you were verifying that `click` actually worked by checking the visibility of another element, the test would eventually fail, because `click` never occurs. If you fare better, congratulations! But the only reliable method of interaction for me was to switch to the native context and find the desired element via XPath, as follows:

```
util.switchToNativeContext()
    .waitForElementByXPath
    ("//*[@content-desc|@name='Tap to reveal the sidebar']")
    .click()
    .then(util.switchToWebViewContext)
    .waitForElementByCss
    ("main.MenuViewController.default-displayed", 2000)
    .isDisplayed().should.eventually.equal(true);
```

 If you only want to simulate a click, you could use `.safeExecute()` and execute some arbitrary JavaScript code in our app's context. For example, we could send a notification that would open the sidebar. While this works, it's definitely quite a bit removed from the way a user would interact with the device: they don't send a notification, they touch a button.

There are two contexts in a hybrid app and each context provides various search mechanisms. The contexts are as follows:

- The native context treats the app as a native application. This means that we have to search through the visible hierarchy using XPath; but it also means that we can interact with other native controls. If we were testing a plugin that presented a native user interface, we'd need to switch to the native context for it as well.

- The web context, on the other hand, refers to the web view that Cordova is using to wrap our app's code. Within the web context, we can look elements up by the CSS selectors, execute arbitrary JavaScript code, and more. We can't actually *touch* anything.

> There is a convoluted way to tap elements using only CSS To locate them; check the code package for specifics. Unfortunately, on iOS this makes The tests run very slowly.

We can't cover every available method you can use for automation in detail, but here are some very useful commands that you can execute on the driver or the elements found by the driver:

- Working with contexts
  - `contexts()` returns an array containing all the available contexts. The native context will have the substring `NATIVE` in it and the web view context will have `WEBVIEW`. Other than these, the complete string may be anything, but it will usually have an underscore and a number included.
  - `currentContext()` returns a string containing the current context.
  - `context(someContext)` switches to the specified context or the default context if no value is provided.

- Finding elements
  - `elementByXPath(xpath)` finds an element by the specified XPath search string. Use the plural form (`elementsByXPath`) if you need to get multiple elements. You can check whether an element exists using `hasElementByXPath`. If you want the element if it does exist or `undefined` if it doesn't, you can use `elementByXPathIfExists`.
  - `elementByCss(selector)` finds an element using the specified CSS selector string. This works only if you are in the web context. As seen earlier, there are multiple variations: `elementsByCss`, `hasElementByCss`, and `elementByCssIfExists`.
  - `elementByAccessibilityId(id)` finds an element using the specified accessibility ID. This doesn't work very well in the web context, since we can't set this value directly. But when you are working with native widgets, such as the ones you might find in a plugin, it can come in handy.

- Element properties
  - ° `clear()` will wipe out a `textarea` or `input` element's value.
  - ° `isSelected()` indicates if the element is selected. This is used for the `option` elements or the checkboxes and radio buttons.
  - ° `isEnabled()` indicates if the element is enabled.
  - ° `isDisplayed()` indicates if the item is displayed on the screen.
  - ° `getComputedCss(property)` returns the computed CSS property for the element.

- Navigating browser history
  - ° `back()` will navigate to the previous page in the history. It's useful while testing routers.
  - ° `forward()` will navigate to the next page in the history.
  - ° `refresh()` will reload the current page.

- Executing code
  - ° `safeExecute(javascriptCode)` executes the arbitrary code within your app. You can use this to inspect the state of your app, much like you might do manually in a browser console.
  - ° `safeEval(expression)` evaluates an arbitrary JavaScript expression within your app and returns the result.

- Touch interaction
  - ° `shake()` will simulate the shaking of the device. For example, on iOS, this might be used to trigger an undo operation.
  - ° `click()` will simulate the clicking on an element once it has been located.
  - ° `scroll(xOffset, yOffset)` will simulate a scrolling gesture in the specified directions.

- Keyboard interaction
  - ° `deviceKeyEvent(keyCodeToSend)` simulates the pressing of the specified key. You can use `util.wd.SPECIAL_KEYS` for special keys, such as Home and the like. A full list is available at `https://github.com/admc/wd/blob/master/lib/special-keys.js`.
  - ° `hideKeyboard()` hides the soft keyboard.
  - ° `submit()` will submit the form associated with the element.

- Miscellaneous

  - ○ `setImplicitWaitTimeout(ms)` defines how long Appium will wait while searching for elements

  - ○ `lock()` will lock the device's screen

  - ○ `backgroundApp()` will send the app to the background

  - ○ `startActivity({appPackage:, appActivity:})` can be used to launch an activity on an Android device

  - ○ `openNotifications()` will open the notifications shade, only on Android

  - ○ `takeScreenshot()` will take a screenshot

For much more documentation, you should refer to the following sites:

- `http://appium.io/slate/en/master/?javascript`

- `https://github.com/admc/wd/blob/master/doc/api.md`

For more examples on automation tests, see the code package of this chapter.

Running UI Automation tests using Appium and Mocha

Now that we've got our tests defined, how do we start them? First, we need to ensure Appium is running. You should do this in its own session, since once started, you can't do anything else unless you stop the server:

```
appium
```

 You can run `appium &` to put Appium in the background on Linux and Mac OS X. The output still generates on the screen, so if you do put it in the background, you'll probably want to log the output, as follows: `appium > output.log & 2>&1`.

Once Appium starts, it will wait for an automation test to be run. If we're using emulators or physical Android devices, we could start these tests now. However, for iOS, we need to start the WebKit Proxy (again, in another session) if testing on a physical device:

```
ios_webkit_debug_proxy -u <your device's UDID>:27753 -d
```

For our code tests, we'll use Mocha to run the tests themselves. However, we need to set some environment variables first:

```
# if using sh or bash
UIA_PROFILE=device-profile UIA_UDID=device-udid UIA_LOGGING=enabled UIA_
SERVER=local mocha . --require "babel/register"
# if using fish
env UIA_PROFILE=device-profile UIA_UDID=device-udid UIA_LOGGING=enabled
UIA_SERVER=local mocha . --require "babel/register"
% on Windows
set UIA_PROFILE=device-profile
set UIA_LOGGING=enabled
set UIA_SERVER=local
mocha . --require "babel/register"
```

 These environment variables are arbitrary; they are just the variables we used in `test-ui/helpers/util.js`.

Of all these environment variables, only UIA_PROFILE is required. If UIA_LOGGING is omitted, our test scripts will assume that no verbose logging should be generated. If UIA_SERVER is omitted, local will be assumed. UIA_UDID is only for testing on a real iOS device; otherwise, it can be omitted as well.

Thus, if we wanted to start a test using an Android simulator, we might type the following command:

```
UIA_PROFILE=android-5-1-1 UIA_LOGGING=enabled mocha ./test-ui/test.js
--require "babel/register"
```

If you've turned logging on, you'll probably be quickly overwhelmed with the output that is generated. This is useful for verifying the accuracy of your tests. However, once you're sure that your tests are working as you want, you can disable logging and you'll be returned to the typical Mocha output: a list of tests and whether they passed or failed.

Integrating our tests with Gulp

So far, we've executed our tests manually using environment variables and `mocha`. It would be nice if we could use `gulp` to execute our tests instead, right?

Thankfully, that's really pretty simple. First, we need to install a plugin that integrates Gulp and Mocha:

```
npm install --save-dev gulp-mocha@2.1.3
```

Then, we need to add a line to the top of `gulpfile.js`, if you haven't already done so:

```
require("babel/register"); // enable ES2015 in our tests
```

We also need to add a few configuration settings to the `config` object in `gulp/config.js`:

```
var config = {
    ...
    test: {
        code: "test/*.js",
        ui: "test-ui/*.js"
    },
}
```

These configuration settings will be used in our testing tasks to indicate the JavaScript files that should be considered as tests. Notice that our code and UI automation tests live in different directories.

Next, we need to add a new task executes our code tests. Let's call it `gulp/tasks/test.js`:

```
"use strict";

var gulp = require("gulp"),
    notify = require("gulp-notify"),
    config = require("../config"),
    paths = require("../utils/paths"),
    mocha = require("gulp-mocha");

function test() {
    return gulp.src(paths.makeFullPath(config.test.code),
                {read: false})
            .pipe(mocha({reporter: "spec"}))
            .once("error", notify.onError(
            "TEST: <%= error.message %>\n <%= error.stack %>"))
            .once("error", function () {
                process.exit(1);
            })
            .once("end", function () {
                process.exit();
```

```
                  });
    }
    module.exports = {
        task: test
    }
```

This should be fairly straightforward; most of it is error handling and notifications. In fact, the `process.exit` methods are there to ensure a clean exit from the test. Otherwise, this is equivalent to executing `mocha . --reporter=spec`. Because we've required Babel at the top of `gulpfile.js`, all our tests automatically get transpiled by Babel.

Our automation tests aren't more complex. The only additional code is in handling the environment variables:

```
    "use strict";

var gulp = require("gulp"),
    gutil = require("gulp-util"),
    notify = require("gulp-notify"),
    config = require("../config"),
    settings = require("../settings"),
    paths = require("../utils/paths"),
    mocha = require("gulp-mocha");

function testUI() {
    var iosUDID = gutil.env.udid;
    var profile = gutil.env.profile;
    var server = gutil.env.server || "local";

    process.env["UIA_PROFILE"] = profile;
    process.env["UIA_SERVER"] = server;
    if (settings.VERBOSE) {
        process.env["UIA_LOGGING"] = "enabled";
    }
    if (iosUDID) {
        process.env["UIA_UDID"] = iosUDID;
    }

    return gulp.src(paths.makeFullPath(config.test.ui),
                {read: false})
            .pipe(mocha({reporter: "spec"}))
            .on("error", notify.onError(
                "TEST-UI: <%= error.message %>"))
            .once("error", function () {
                process.exit(1);
            })
            .once("end", function () {
                process.exit();
            });
```

```
    }

module.exports = {
    deps: ["build"],
    task: testUI,
}
```

Other than the section dealing with the environment variables, the only other change is that of `config.test.ui` as the configuration setting that indicates where the tests are stored.

 Also note that `test-ui` is dependent upon the `build` step. We make this a dependency, because we need the built app packages for testing. If you want, you can remove the dependency; but you'll need to remember to rebuild your app manually every time something changes.

Alternatively, you can create a setting that allows you to skip the build step whenever you need (which might be useful when you are simply changing your test code). Check the code package for this book for an example. Note that the change is actually in gulp/tasks/cordova-build.js, not test-ui.js.

Now, to run code tests, you should just be able to execute the following:

```
gulp test
```

To run the automation tests, the command gets a little more complicated, but not terribly so:

```
gulp test-ui --target=device|emulator --profile=appium-profile
          --udid=ios-udid --verbose=yes|no --server=local|sauce
```

Your target should line up with the profile you are using for testing. If you are testing on an emulator, specify `emulator` for the target. If you're testing on a device, specify `device`. The `udid` switch is only required to test on physical iOS devices. Logging is controlled by `verbose`; if omitted, it no logging occurs. `server` is also optional; if omitted, it will default to `local`.

There's no reason why you couldn't chain several of these commands together such that one Gulp command kicks them all off, but we'll leave it as an exercise for you.

Summary

Wow! We dealt with a lot of complicated stuff in this chapter. We installed Mocha and Appium. We also covered creating code tests and user interface automation tests. Finally, we integrated our processes into Gulp.

In the next chapter, we'll delve into IndexedDB, which is a persistent object store. We'll use this to store data for our app.

7
IndexedDB

There are many different kinds of persistent storage that Cordova apps can use. Which storage mechanism you use depends largely upon the storage needs of your application. Furthermore, your app isn't restricted to a single type of storage. It might make the most sense to store user preferences in `localStorage` and larger files using the File API. On the other hand, neither `localStorage` nor the File API provides a simple mechanism for storing, retrieving, and searching structured data. You can use them for these purposes, of course, but you'll have to do most of the hard work yourself. Two storage mechanisms come to our rescue so that we don't have to reinvent the wheel. The older (and now deprecated) standard, Web SQL Database, uses a relational data model typical of databases such as Oracle, PostgreSQL, Microsoft SQL, and so on. A newer standard called IndexedDB (short for Indexed Database) uses key-object storage. This is particularly useful with JavaScript, because we're most often working with objects. So, persisting these objects becomes very simple.

Neither IndexedDB nor Web SQL Database is specific to Cordova; you can use them on desktop browsers as well. This is a nice feature, because you can test your app's storage on a desktop browser for faster iteration and easier debugging. If you've written a website application for desktops, you could also potentially reuse your storage code (and probably a lot of other code as well). There's a catch though (there always is!): IndexedDB support is hit and miss; to use it without encountering a lot of painful issues, you'll probably need to use a polyfill or other wrapper. Thankfully, there are several available that are excellent.

In this chapter, we'll cover the following:

- IndexedDB support and polyfills
- Differences between relational and key-object storage
- Creating a database
- Creating an object store within the database

- Handling database upgrades
- Transactions
- Storing objects
- Getting objects
- Deleting objects
- Using cursors and indexes
- Closing the database

Getting started

This chapter focuses mostly on the basics of using IndexedDB. If you want to see a real-life example, we've implemented IndexedDB into our demonstration app in the code package of this book located at `logology-v07/`.

Several of the snippets in this chapter are also available using the interactive snippet playground that accompanies the code package of this book. Instructions to launch the playground are in the `README.md` file in the code package. Once it starts, select **7: IndexedDB** and then browse and experiment with the examples. Where applicable, each section and snippet will indicate which chapter and example you should select.

IndexedDB support and polyfills

Before we go further, it's important to discuss the support situation for IndexedDB. As it is a more recent specification than Web SQL Database, it has much less support. On some platforms that support it, is can also be extremely limited and/or buggy.

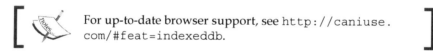

> For up-to-date browser support, see `http://caniuse.com/#feat=indexeddb`.

As of this writing, IndexedDB had the following mobile browser support:

- iOS: No support on iOS 7.x; extremely buggy behavior on iOS 8.x as well as iOS 9.x
- Android: no support for versions less than 4.4; full support on Android 4.4 and higher

Desktop support fares quite a bit better; Chrome and Firefox has supported a full IndexedDB implementation for several versions now, while Safari on Oave has a buggy implementation (which should be no surprise, given that iOS also has a buggy implementation). On the desktop, Internet Explorer has had a partial implementation since version 10.

All of this means that if you're going to support different platforms and OS versions, you're almost certainly going to need a polyfill or wrapper that works around the various issues you're likely to encounter. There are many different options available:

- IndexedDBShim (`https://github.com/axemclion/IndexedDBShim`): This uses Web SQL Storage if IndexedDB isn't available.

- Cordova-IndexedDB (`https://github.com/DickvdBrink/cordova-indexeddb`): This wraps IndexedDBShim in a Cordova plugin for simpler installation

- Cordova-Plugin-IndexedDB (`https://github.com/MSOpenTech/cordova-plugin-indexedDB`): This is another Cordova plugin that wraps IndexedDBShim

- Treo (`https://github.com/treojs/treo/`): This module takes another approach and provides a lightweight wrapper around IndexedDB that is a bit easier to use (it supports promises, easy version changes, and more). It can also fallback to Web SQL Database using IndexedDBShim if the platform doesn't support IndexedDB natively.

All of the above options are perfectly viable and acceptable for applications (and there are doubtless other libraries out there as well that work). The first three follow the specification exactly, so there's no change in your existing IndexedDB code. Treo is a wrapper around the specification that aims to provide a simpler syntax, so there's a little bit of code change necessary. But as you'll see through the chapter, it's actually worth it to get more readable code.

Differences between relational and key-object storage

Let's cover some of the differences between a relational storage model and a key-object storage model, because although both the storage models seem similar initially, they are, in reality, very different. As such, you may choose to use both in your application if some of your data is better stored and queried using the relational model while other data more closely fits the key-object model.

The relational storage model simply describes relationships between data described at the schema level. A **schema** describes the fields in a data structure. In relational storage models, schemas are also often called tables.

Tables store data as a series of rows and columns, somewhat like a spreadsheet, except that the rows and columns aren't numbered in the same way (for example, a spreadsheet typically names columns with sequential letters and rows with sequential numbers). The relational component itself describes how one data in one table relates to data in nother table.

These types of databases are great at storing very structured data that have a lot of relationships with other data. These databases also typically use **SQL** (**structured query language**) as the language one uses to manipulate and retrieve data. Chances are pretty good that you've seen some SQL code in your development experience at some point. That said, since we'll cover the relational storage model more in the next chapter, we won't go into much detail just yet.

The key-object storage model is another way to store structure although, here, the data structure itself tends to be more flexible. Each object is stored and later referenced using a unique identifier. This unique ID might be autogenerated or it might be a property on a given object that is guaranteed to be unique. Objects can also be indexed by other properties that may or may not be unique to make finding objects even easier.

The key difference between this and the eldifferentiator is that there is no described relationship between object stores. Technically, one still has a schema (although more flexible than a relational model), since often there are properties that one expects to exist on all the persisted objects. Beyond this, however, there's no specified relationship between two stores.

For example, in the relational storage model, the relationship between an `order` and `customer` schema is directly described in the database. For example, an `order` schema might have a `customer_id` field, and a relationship specifies that this `customer_id` field directly relates to the `customer` schema (via the `customer_id` field). This provides powerful mechanisms for both query optimization and data consistency, and they can be enforced at the database level.

Visually, this kind of relational storage model might look as follows:

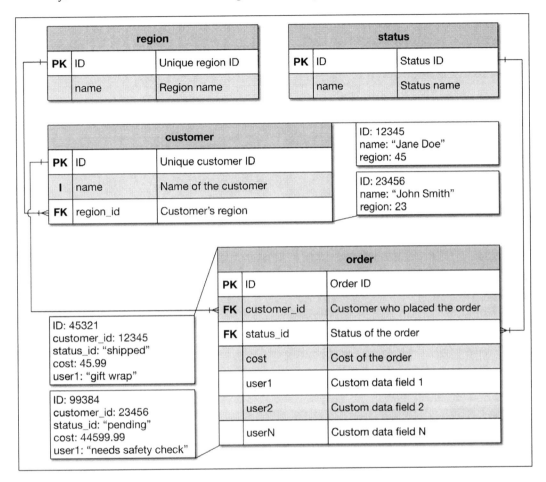

It should be pretty obvious that the relational storage model, while being highly structured, is not always ready to handle any kind of data that might come its way. Many times, one adds "user" or custom fields to a table (as used in the order table above) so that there is a way to provide custom data for specific objects. Of course, this becomes a nightmare over time to develop with and to manage. Frighteningly, I've seen databases with two-hundred-plus fields labeled only with a generic column name and a number. Developing with and reporting on that data was next to impossible.

In a key-object storage model, the relationship itself still exists: if we wanted to obtain information about a customer given an order, we'd need to look up the customer given the customer ID. There is, however, no way to describe these relationships within the database itself, and there's no mechanism to provide query optimizations or data consistency at the database level. Instead, these must be managed at the application level.

Visually, the key-object storage model might look as follows:

As you can see, structured data is still being stored, but the store itself can be more flexible as to what data it accepts. This isn't to say that the relationships are gone— not at all; they're just now in your code. Additional custom data will not be handled automatically by the app either. The app has to be built to expect additional data and understand what to do with it when it sees it. Even so, the store itself will not balk at additional fields that weren't initially anticipated when the when it sees it.

In many ways, the key-object storage model is quite a bit simpler than the relational model. Assuming you have a key or an index, you can find an object very quickly. You could also make an argument that you could then obtain related data quicker than a relational database might simply because you don't have to worry about complex SQL parsing and the various query optimizations that most relational databases make in order to generate performant queries. On the other hand, you can argue that the relational model incurs less of a mental and development cost. The relational model makes it very simple to all the related data at once (rather than in a series of steps), and most relational databases do a good job of optimizing queries (at the expense of more complex internal code).

Where you fall on this spectrum will vary. Both storage models have their pros and cons. If you need highly flexible data, a relational database is probably not the best way, since chances are good you'll end up having to store data in a lot of binary or character blobs, and querying these is rarely fun. If you need to write very complex queries that rely on a lot of related data, you may find that the relational model is far simpler to use. It really depends on your data structures.

Creating a database

Before we can store any objects in our database, we need to create the database first. This isn't as simple as `createDatabase` or even an `openDatabase` operation. Due to the asynchronous nature of IndexedDB and the fact that various browsers and platforms have used prefixed versions of IndexedDB, the process is actually a bit more complex.

 The snippets in this section are located at `snippets/07/ex1-create-database/*` in the code package of this book. When using the interactive snippet playgroundselect **7: IndexedDB** and the examples from **1a** to **1c**.

Here's an example:

```
// Example Snippet 1a
// IndexedDB has been prefixed, so we need to get the prefixed
// version if the non-prefixed versionis not available. from:
// https://developer.mozilla.org/en-
//          US/docs/Web/API/IndexedDB_API/Using_IndexedDB
let indexedDB = window.indexedDB || window.mozIndexedDB ||
    window.webkitIndexedDB || window.msIndexedDB;   //[1]

function openDatabase({name, version, onopen, onerror} = {}) {
    //[2]
```

```
    let req = indexedDB.open(name, version);
    req.onerror = function(evt) {
      console.log("[DB] Encountered an error opening the database:",
                  evt.target.error);
    };
    req.onsuccess = function(evt) {
      let db = this.result; //[3]
      db.onerror = onerror || function(dbEvent) { //[4]
          console.log("[DB] Encountered a database error:",
                      dbEvent.target.error);
      };
      onopen(db); //[5]
    };
}

function gotADatabase(db) { //[6]
  console.log(db);
}

openDatabase({ //[7]
  name: "StarterDictionary",
  version: 1,
  onopen: gotADatabase});
```

If that looks a little bit scary, don't worry; it's not really as bad as it looks. Part of the complexity is simply due to the fact that IndexedDB does everything asynchronously and uses events to communicate the status of each request. It's a bit like XMLHttpRequest or the File API without promises.

Because browsers have used prefixed versions, we have to determine which property the browser is using to represent the interface to IndexedDB. This is what we're doing in [1] in the first line of the previous example. Thankfully, if you use IndexedDBShim, this goes away, so you can always reference indexedDB.

The openDatabase function ([2]) does the hard work of opening a database. First, it calls indexedDB.open, which looks pretty self-explanatory. The first parameter, name, specifies the name of the database, and version specifies the version number. The version number will be useful a little later.

 The version must be a non-floating-point number. 1.3 or "one" won't work.

The open method returns a request object; we've called it req in our example. When the request encounters an error or completes successfully, it will fire the appropriate event, so we have to attach event handlers (onerror and onsuccess, respectively) to the request. Because the open operation is asynchronous, we can get away with assigning the event handlers after making the actual request to open the database, as the request won't be executed immediately.

When the database opens successfully, you can obtain a handle to the database itself by copying the value in this.result to a more descriptive variable name (like db) as seen in [3]. In our example, the very next thing we do ([4]) is assign a global error handler that simply logs any errors that occur to the console. (A production app would need something more robust here.) Once we do this, we will send our database handle to a callback ([5]).

The last line section of the example ([7]) actually illustrates the use of our openDatabase function. We want to open or create a database called StarterDictionary; it's at version 1. When it is open, it will call gotADatabase with the handle ([6]). This function is really simple; it just logs the database to the console at the moment.

This is probably not how you would want to create or open databases. So, we will convert it to use promises instead, as seen in the following example:

```
// Example Snippet 1b
let indexedDB = window.indexedDB || window.mozIndexedDB ||
    window.webkitIndexedDB || window.msIndexedDB;

function openDatabase({name, version, onerror}) {
  return new Promise((resolve, reject) => {
    let req = indexedDB.open(name, version);
    req.onerror = function(evt) {
      reject(evt.target.error);
    };
    req.onsuccess = function() {
      let db = this.result;
      db.onerror = onerror || function(dbEvent) {
          console.log("[DB] Encountered a database error:",
                    dbEvent.target.error);
      };
      resolve(db);
    };
  });
}

openDatabase({
```

```
    name: "StarterDictionary",
    version: 1
}).then(db => console.log(db))
  .catch(err => console.log(
        "Encountered an error opening the database:", err));
```

Ah, that's much better. But it's far from perfect, since you're responsible for wrapping IndexedDB with promises. What if there was a a library that did this for us? Turns It turns out, there is and it's called Treo.

We've mentioned Treo already, so you might want to check out the website we mentioned earlier. If we want to add it to our project along with a fallback to the Web SQL Database if the browser doesn't natively support IndexedDB, we can do it pretty simply:

```
$ npm install --save treo treo-websql
```

Once we've installed it in our project, it's easy to open or create a database (albeit one we can't do much with yet, because we have no schema):

```
// Example Snippet 1c
let treo = require("treo"),
    promise = require("treo/plugins/treo-promise"),
    webSQL = require("treo-websql");

let schema = treo.schema()
                 .version(1);

let db = treo("StarterDictionary", schema);
db.use(webSQL());   // [1]

db.use(promise());      // [2]

console.log(db);
```

A couple of notes here: the `db.use` commands in [1] and [2] enable Treo plugins. The first enables the Web SQL Database as a fallback if IndexedDB isn't supported natively. The second enables the use of promises.

 The order of these two commands is very important. Flip them around at your own peril.

I don't know about you, but I much prefer this kind of code! As such, for the remainder of this chapter, we'll show the *vanilla* code that doesn't use Promises or Treo and then we'll show the Treo version. If you want to make your own promise wrapper around IndexedDB, I'll leave that to you as an exercise.

 If you're looking at the snippet code in the code package, you'll notice that it doesn't use `require`. Instead, the snippets use the browser versions of these files. You can use Treo either way, but I prefer to use `require` and NPM when I can.

So far, our database doesn't do anything useful. We've not defined any schemas to store objects. Let's see how we can do that in the next section.

Creating an object store within the database

So far, our database can't store anything because we've not created an object store. If you're familiar with tables or schemas from relational databases, these are somewhat similar. And, of course, before we can store any objects in them, we have to first create a place for them to be stored.

The only time you can modify the structure of your database is in the `onupgradeneeded` handler. This handler is called whenever the database needs to be upgraded, which makes sense, but it's also called when the database is brand new.

In order to create an object store, we need to determine at least some of the properties we'll expect most objects to have. Although you can store any kind of objects you want with any number of properties, one does need a way of finding objects in the store without having to iterate over every stored object.

The primary mechanism for looking up an object is the object's **key**. This key can be a property that exists on all the objects that will be stored and is unique across the set, or it can be automatically generated by the database itself. Which method you use is important: there's no simple way to change to the other method.

Objects are rarely located solely by their key, so one needs other ways to locate an object. In IndexedDB, these are called indexes. An **index** is a reference to the location of one or more objects – much like a mailing address or the locatixes, appropriately enough. These indexes don't have to be unique and they don't have to exist as properties on all of the objects in the store (these objects just won't be in the index). Combined, the object's key and the various indexes provide a way to access data quickly, while also remaining extremely flexible.

An object store is created by calling `createObjectStore` on the database handle. It takes at least one parameter, but typically you'll pass two: the name of the store (or schema or table) and whether or not the store will use a specific property as a key or an automatically generated ID.

Once a store is created, additional indexes are created by calling `createIndex` on the resulting object store. Here, three parameters are typically used: the name of the index, the object property to index, and any additional options (such as whether or not the values are required to be unique across the index).

Aside from the key used to locate the object, all the indexes are technically optional for any object that is stored. Furthermore, the object can have any number of additional properties, so the store's schema is open-ended. This is very unlike a typical relational database, but this also provides a lot of power and flexibility when it comes to storing JavaScript objects.

Let's imagine an object store for our demonstration app, Logology. We need to store definitions in a way we can quickly retrieve. Consider the following schema:

		definition		
K	wordNetRef	Unique ID; points to the definition in WordNet	02124272
I []	lemmas	Array of words that have this definition	["cat", "true cat"]
	gloss	Definition	feline mammal…
	partOfSpeech	Noun, Adjective, etc.	Noun

This schema doesn't necessarily describe every property that might go along with a definition, but it represents what we'd typically expect to find for a `definition` object. The first field, `wordNetRef`, is marked with a K, which is just our way of indicating that this property is the key for the object store.

 If you're not familiar with WordNet, it's a free English dictionary put out by Princeton University (more information is available at `http://wordnet.princeton.edu/`).

Each WordNet definition has a database location. Since this is unique, it makes sense to use it for our definitions as well (we'll get our definitions from their dictionary. It's free after all, assuming one abides by their license).

The next field, `lemmas`, is an array representing the base forms (that is, not pluralized or otherwise inflected or conjugated) of the word to which this definition applies. One definition may apply to many different lemmas; in this sense, these lemmas are synonyms of each other (consider pop versus soda). Likewise, one lemma may apply to multiple definitions (consider pop: does it mean a soda or a sound, or maybe even one's father?).

`gloss` is simply the definition itself. WordNet's definitions are pretty short and sparse, but they'll do for our purposes. One could write additional content themselves or license other dictionary content.

Finally, `partOfSpeech` represents whether or not the word is a noun, verb, and so on.

Of course, there are all sorts of other properties one could imagine; perhaps, a list of antonyms or a link to an image if the definition is about an object. What's critical is that these don't have to be specified in the object store's schema.

> The snippets in this section are located at `snippets/07/ex2-create-store/*` in the code package of this book. When using the interactive snippet playground, select **7: IndexedD** and the examples **2a** and **2b**.

With this in mind, let's look at a simple example of creating this store using IndexedDB:

```
// Example Snippet 2a
function openDatabase({name, version, onopen, onerror, onupgrade}
                        = {}) {
    let req = indexedDB.open(name, version);
    ...
    req.onupgradeneeded = function(evt) {
        onupgrade(evt.target.result);
    };
}
...
function schemaV1(db) {
    // schema definition has a primary key based on property
    // wordNetRef
    let definitionStore = db.createObjectStore("definition",
                            {keyPath: "wordNetRef"});
```

```
            definitionStore.createIndex("lemmas", "lemmas",
                                    {unique: false, multiEntry: true});
}


    openDatabase({name: "StarterDictionary", version: 1,
              onopen: gotADatababase, onupgrade: schemaV1});
```

Note that we don't list every field that might be present. You only need to include fields that you might use to gain access to the object later. In our case, the `wordNetRef` and the `lemmas` properties are the only ways to find a word.

 Indexes can be unique (`unique: true`) or nonunique (`unique: false`). Furthermore, if `multiEntry: true` is passed, all the items in the corresponding object property will be added to the index. For example, in the previous image, both `cat` and `true cat` would be in the index pointing at the same definition.

In Treo, however, this is quite different (and a lot easier to follow):

```
// Example Snippet 2b
let schema = treo.schema1()
                .version(1)
                .addStore("definition", {key: "wordNetRef"})
                .addIndex("lemmas", "lemmas",
                            {unique: false, multiEntry:true});


let db = treo("StarterDictionary", schema);
db.use(webSQL());
db.use(promise());
```

Handling database upgrades

As it may be already apparent, IndexedDB databases are tagged with a version number. Whenever the app requests a database version that is newer than the one the user actually has, `onupgradeneeded` will be called so that the app has a chance to modify the database.

 The snippets in this section are located at `snippets/07/ex3-upgrade-database/*` in the code package of this book. When using the interactive snippet playground, select **7: IndexedDB** and examples **3a** to **3b**

Thankfully, onupgradeneeded is provided with the old version number of the database and the desired version number of the database, otherwise we'd have difficulty deciding what needed to be changed. With this information, we can upgrade our database pretty simply. First, let's modify our openDatabase function slightly to the following:

```
// Example Snippet 3a
function openDatabase({name, version, onopen, onerror, onupgrade}) {
    let req = indexedDB.open(name, version);
    req.onerror = function(evt) {
        console.log("[DB] Encountered an error opening the database:"
+ evt.target.error);
    };
    req.onsuccess = function() {
        let db = this.result;
        db.onerror = onerror || function(dbEvent) {
            console.log("[DB] Encountered a database error:" +
dbEvent.target.error);
        };
        onopen(db);
    };
    req.onupgradeneeded = function(evt) {
        let oldVersion = evt.oldVersion;
        // Safari returns a really silly value for newly created
databases.
        // From https://github.com/treojs/idb-schema/blob/master/lib/
index.js
        onupgrade(evt.target.result, oldVersion > 4294967295 ? 0 :
oldVersion);
    };
}
```

All we've done is modified the onupgradeneeded event handler to store the old version (attached on to evt) and then passed it on to our upgrade handler (which we specify when we call openDatabase). If you're wondering about the comparison against that large number in [1], it's because Safari returns an absurdly high number if the database has just been created rather than a more sensible 0 like every other browser does.

Now we can construct an upgrade function:

```
// Example Snippet 3a, continued
function upgradeDatabase(db, oldVersion) {
  for (let curVersion = oldVersion; curVersion < db.version;
         curVersion++) {
    switch (curVersion) {
      case 0:
        let definitionStore = db.createObjectStore("definition", {
            keyPath: "wordNetRef"
```

```
          });
        definitionStore.createIndex("lemmas", "lemmas", {
            unique: false,
            multiEntry: true
          });
        break;
      case 1:
        db.createObjectStore("notes", {
            autoIncrement: true
          });
        db.createObjectStore("favorites", {
            autoIncrement: true
          });
        break;
      default:
        console.log("No upgrade steps available");
    }
  }
}
```

Now, let's say our app wants to open version 2 of the database. If the database newly created, `oldVersion` will be equal zero. So, both `case 0` and `case 1` will be executed. If the database was already at the first version, only `case 1` would be executed (because it's being upgraded from version 1 to version 2).

Now, let's see it the Treo way. By now, you're probably guessing it's a lot simpler and it is:

```
// Example Snippet 3b
let schema = treo.schema()
                .version(1)
                  .addStore("definition", {key: "wordNetRef"})
                  .addIndex("lemmas", "lemmas",
                            {unique: false, multiEntry:true})
                .version(2)
                  .addStore("favorites", {autoIncrement: true})
                  .addStore("notes", {autoIncrement: true});
let db = treo("StarterDictionary", schema);
db.use(webSQL());
db.use(promise());
```

If you're paying attention or if you've done even simple version migrations in the past, you will know that database schema upgrades are rarely this simple. If you just need to remove some stores or indexes, it's pretty simple. You can call `deleteObjectStore` and `deleteIndex` (vanilla) or call `dropStore` and `dropIndex` (Treo). On the other hand, your data might also need restructuring. Unfortunately, there's no easy way to do this. You'd need to copy the data in the store, change it to a temporary store, delete and recreate the store, and then copy the data from the temporary store back.

Transactions

All the interactions that read from or write to an object store must be performed within the context of a transaction are a mechanism that ensures data consistency. If any part of a transaction fails, all the actions that occurred during the transaction are reverted.

You can request a transaction from the database as follows:

```
let transaction = db.transaction(["store", ...], mode);
```

The first parameter to transact is the list of stores that you are going to use in the `transaction`. You have to specify these in advance to actually query or modify the data within.

The second parameter is optional. It specifies whether or not the transaction is simply reading data (`readonly`) or if the transaction needs to write data (`readwrite`). There is also a `versionchange` mode that you can use to make changes to `store` schemas, but you should only do this kind of operation during a database upgrade. If this parameter isn't supplied, `readonly` will be assumed.

A transaction will generate events, so you can track what's going on with respect to the transaction. There are three event types that a transaction might generate:

- `error`: An error occurred during the transaction. Unless you do something to avoid it, the data changes within the transaction will be automatically rolled back. You can handle the error differently by first calling `preventDefault` on the error and then handling the error appropriately.
- `abort`: The transaction will be aborted and all the changes will be rolled back.
- `complete`: The transaction will be completed and all the changes will be persisted.

 It is very important to recognize that there is no guarantee that any data you save is actually persisted when you receive the `complete` event. In fact, there is no real mechanism you can use to ensure that the data has been persisted to the store at all. As such, if the data is extremely critical, you may not want to use IndexedDB.

Once you have a transaction, you can obtain access to the object stores you specified when you created the transaction by calling `objectStore` with the name of the store.

If, for whatever reason, you need to terminate the transaction, you can call `abort()`. But you'll lose any changes you made during the transaction, since they will be rolled back.

Transactions only remain active for as long as there are requests which are pending in the transaction. Once there are no more requests, the transaction becomes inactive and can no longer be used to generate requests.

So, how does Treo handle transactions? Very, very differently. In fact, if you just need to get or store a single item, Treo will handle the transaction for you automatically. If you need to perform several operasingle transaction, Treo supplies a `batch` method that will perform the operations in a single transaction. We'll come back to this method a little later.

Storing objects

Storing objects is pretty simple, assuming you have appropriate error handlers at the database and transaction level. You can track events for each object you store; but this is a quick way to become overwhelmed if you're storing a lot of data.

 The snippets in this section are located at `snippets/07/ex4-store-objects/*` in the code package of this book. When using the interactive snippet playground, select **7: IndexedDB** and the examples from **4a** to **4b**.

There are two ways you can store an object: you can add it or you can put it. Here are the differences between both methods:

- `add`: This will store an object. The object must not already exist in the store. The object must satisfy any unique keys and indexes or an error will be generated.

- `put`: This will store an object if the object doesn't exist and it will update an object if the object is already present in the store. The object must satisfy any unique keys and indexes or an error will be generated.

Once you have a `readwrite` transaction, you can use either of the earlier mentioned methods to store an object. Let's take a look at an example:

```
// Example Snippet 4a
function gotADatabase(db) {
  // Definitions from WordNet. See wordnet/LICENSE-WordNet.md in
  // code package.
  let definitions = [
    {
      wordNetRef: "02124272",
      lemmas: ["cat", "true cat"],
```

```
        partOfSpeech: "noun",
        gloss: "feline mammal usually having thick soft fur and no
                ability to roar: domestic cats; wildcats"
      },
      {
        wordNetRef: "02130460",
        lemmas: ["cat", "big cat"],
        partOfSpeech: "noun",
        gloss: "any of several large cats typically able to roar and
                living in the wild"
      },
      {
        wordNetRef: "02085443",
        lemmas: ["aardvark", "ant bear",
                 "anteater", "Orycteropus afer"],
        partOfSpeech: "noun",
        gloss: "nocturnal burrowing mammal of the grasslands of
                Africa that feeds on termites; sole extant
                representative of the order Tubulidentata"
      }
    ];
    let transaction = db.transaction(["definition"], "readwrite");
    transaction.onerror = function(evt) {
      console.log("[DB] Transaction got an error: " +
        evt.target.error);
    };
    transaction.oncomplete = function() {
      console.log("[DB] All entries added.");
    };
  let definitionStore = transaction.objectStore("definition");
  definitions.forEach(definition => definitionStore.put(definition));
  }
```

Note that, even though IndexedDB does everything asynchronously, we can still persist a lot of data into a store as a mostly synchronous operation. It's not really synchronous though. Each request to store data will simply be queued until it can be processed. The data can't actually be retrieved until after the `complete` event is fired.

Treo supports adding data as well, but only provides a `put` method, since one typically doesn't want an error if trying to create an object that already exists — instead most developers want the object to be updated. For multiple objects or operations, Treo supports a `batch` method as well.

But first, one needs to obtain the object store. This is done by calling `store` with the object store name. Then put or batch can be called as desired. Let's look at an example:

```
// Example Snippet 4b
// assuming the same definitions as in the previous example
let definitionStore = db.store("definition");
definitionStore.batch(definitions)
  .then(() => console.log("All entries added"))
  .catch((err) => console.log("[DB] An error was encountered " +
    err));
```

At this point, the amount of code isn't substantially different, except that Treo lets us use promises in this case rather than the event handling mechanism in the vanilla example.

Getting objects

Retrieving an object that you've previously stored is pretty easy, provided you know the key. If you only know a value that is from an index, things become a little bit harder (though not terribly so). We'll discuss the latter case later.

 The snippets in this section are located at `snippets/07/ex5-get-objects/*` in the code package of this book. When using the interactive snippet playground, select **7: IndexedDB** and examples **5a** and **5b**.

As with storing objects, you first need to obtain a transaction. However, since we only need a read-only transaction, it becomes much easier to do. Take a look at the following example:

```
// Example Snippet 5a
let req = db.transaction(["definition"]).objectStore("definition")
          .get("02124272");
```

The value passed to `get` is the `wordNetRef` number, which is the key for the object. If you are using autogenerated keys, you'd specify them instead (though you might not know the key it off-hand, of course).

Once the object is located, a `success` event will be called. In fact, this event will also be called if no object exists for the specified key, so this is a condition you will need to check for yourself. If some other error occurs, `error` will be fired.

Let's finish the example:

```
// Example Snippet 5a, continued
req.onerror = function (evt) {
  console.log("[DB] An error occurred: ", evt.target.error);
};
req.onsuccess = function (evt) {
  let definition = evt.target.result;
  if (!definition) {
    console.log("Couldn't find the desired entry.");
  } else {
    console.log(JSON.stringify(definition, null, 2));
  }
};
```

When `success` is fired, the actual object is stored in `evt.target.result`. If this is `undefined`, IndexedDB wasn't able to find an object for the requested key. If it isn't `undefined`, then you can go on to do whatever you need with the object, such as display it to the user or perform additional computations.

In Treo, the process is pretty similar:

```
// Example Snippet 5b
let definitionStore = db.store("definition");
definitionStore.get("02124272")
  .then((result) =>
    console.log(result ? JSON.stringify(result, null, 2)
                       : "Couldn't find entry."))
  .catch((err) => {
    console.log("[DB] An error was encountered "+ err);
});
```

Again, like in the vanilla version, an `undefined` result means that the object couldn't be found.

Deleting objects

Deleting objects is pretty similar to retrieving them using `get`, only we use `delete` instead.

> The snippets in this section are located at `snippets/07/ex6-delete-objects/*` in the code package of this book. When using the interactive snippet playground, select **7: IndexedDB** and examples **6a** and **6b**.

Let's take a look at an example:

```
// Example Snippet 6a
let req = db.transaction(["definition"],"readwrite")
            .objectStore("definition")
            .delete("02124272");
req.onerror = function (evt) {
  console.log("[DB] An error occurred: ", evt.target.error);
};
req.onsuccess = function () {
  console.log("Deleted the entry.");
};
```

It's important to note that the `success` event will be called even if the object couldn't be found in order to be deleted. If some other error does occur, `error` will be fired instead.

Let's see Treo's version:

```
// Example Snippet 6b
let definitionStore = db.store("definition");
definitionStore.del("02124272")
  .then(() => console.log("Entry deleted."))
  .catch((err) => {
    console.log("[DB] An error was encountered "+ err);
});
```

Instead of `delete`, Treo uses `del` to delete entries, otherwise it's very similar to retrieving an object.

Using cursors and indexes

So far, we've only retrieved data with the unique key it was stored with. But we can also use the indexes we've created to locate an object without knowing the object's unique key.

The snippets in this section are located at `snippets/07/ex7-cursors-indexes/*` in the code package of this book. When using the interactive snippet playground, select **7: IndexedDB** and examples **7a** and **7b**.

In order to do so, we request an `index` from the object store after we've created a transaction. Once we have an index, we can call `get` to retrieve an object that is in the index. Let's see an example:

```
// Example Snippet 7a
let req = db.transaction(["definition"]).objectStore("definition")
            .index("lemmas").get("cat");
req.onerror = ...;
req.onsuccess = function (evt) {
  let definition = evt.target.result;
  if (definition) {
    console.log(JSON.stringify(definition, null, 2));
  } else {
    console.log("Couldn't find entry.");
  }
};
```

If you take a look at our `definitions` array several sections ago, you'll notice a problem: what if there is more than one object for an index value? The answer is that `get` doesn't care: it returns the first one found. As long as the index is unique, this is okay; but if the index is not unique, you'll have trouble retrieving all your objects. Cursors are a way around this. They let you iterate over multiple values. You can obtain a cursor by calling `getCursor` on an index or an object store. The cursor will then call `success` for each item in the index or object store as long as your `success` handler calls `continue` on the cursor. For example:

```
// Example Snippet 7a, continued
let req = db.transaction(["definition"]).objectStore("definition")
            .index("lemmas").openCursor();
req.onerror = ...;
req.onsuccess = function (evt) {
  let cursor = evt.target.result;
  if (cursor) {
    console.log(`key: ${cursor.key}, value:
              ${JSON.stringify(cursor.value, null, 2)}`);
    cursor.continue(); // get next object
  } else {
    console.log("No more entries.");
  }
};
```

The previous example will now list every definition for every object in the `lemmas` index. As long as there is a matching object, `cursor` will be defined. The key and value can be obtained by referencing the `key` and `value` properties, respectively. Once there are no more items, however, `cursor` will be `undefined`. This also means that if there weren't any entries in the index, `cursor` would start out as `undefined`.

While iterating over every item in an index or store can be useful, usually it's not quite what we want. Typically, we need to filter the results. In order to do this, we need to create a range that will limit the result.

`IDBKeyRange` provides several methods you can use to create ranges. You have several options available, depending on your needs:

- `only(key)`: The cursor will only return values that match the key exactly.
- `lowerBound(key [,exclusive=false])`: The cursor will return all the values, including and beyond the key. If `exclusive` is `true`, the key itself will be excluded.
- `upperBound(key [,exclusive=false])`: The cursor will return all the values up to the key. If `exclusive` is `true`, the key itself will be excluded.
- `bound(lowerKey, upperKey[,lowerExclusive=false [,upperExclusive=false]])`: This is a combination of both `lowerBound` and `upperBound`.

The returned range can then be passed to the `openCursor` method, as follows:

```
let IDBKeyRange = window.IDBKeyRange || window.webkitIDBKeyRange
                                     || window.msIDBKeyRange;
let range = IDBKeyRange.only("cat");
let req = db.transaction(["definition"]).objectStore("definition")
               .index("lemmas").openCursor(range);
```

Cursors will iterate in ascending order by default. If you want to change that order, you can do that as well. For example, the following would iterate in descending order:

```
let req = db.transaction(["definition"]).objectStore("definition")
               .index("lemmas").openCursor(range, "prev");
```

Treo dispatches with the notion of cursors entirely, and just does what you're most likely to want: it returns all the matching items. Let's look at an example:

```
let definitionStore = db.store("definition");
definitionStore.index("lemmas").get("cat")
  .then((result) =>
          console.log(result ? JSON.stringify(result, null, 2)
```

```
                            : "Couldn't find entry."))
    .catch((err) => {
      console.log("[DB] An error was encountered "+ err);
  });
```

Unless the index is unique (meaning that only one value can ever be returned), an array will be passed in to `result` instead. This array contains all the items in the index that match the key specified by `get`.

Treo supports native `IDBKeyRange` ranges if you want to use those, but it also supports a more expressive and easier-to-read version. For example:

```
definitionStore.index("lemmas").get({gte: "cat", lt:"dog"})...;
```

This does the same thing as `IDBKeyRange.bound("cat", "dog", false, true)`. All the objects matching `cat` and beyond would be returned, but only up to (and not including) `dog`.

Closing the database

Whenever your application is closed or terminated, the database will be closed automatically for you. If your need for the database is fleeting, you might seriously want to consider closing the database manually. You may also want to consider closing databases manually if you find yourself needing to open a lot of databases for short-lived transactions.

You can do so by calling `close`. Technically, you could monitor the status of the `close` operation by inspecting the returned request object. But usually, there's no need to do so. Do note that the database won't be immediately closed; the operation itself is still asynchronous, so if you need to immediately re-open the database, you'll definitely have to add a `success` handler (or a `then` handler while using Treo with promises).

Additional resources

There's quite a bit you can do with IndexedDB. We can't cover everything in this chapter. You may find these resources of use:

- Mozilla (MDN) documentation note that they use `errorCode` and `stopPropagation` thatwhich is incorrect)
    - https://developer.mozilla.org/en-US/docs/Web/API/IndexedDB_API/Using_IndexedDB
    - https://developer.mozilla.org/en-US/docs/Web/API/IndexedDB_API

- Microsoft's documentation: `https://msdn.microsoft.com/en-us/library/ie/hh673548(v=vs.85).aspx`
- The W3C specification: `http://www.w3.org/TR/IndexedDB/`
- Treo's repository: `https://github.com/alekseykulikov/treo`
- Browser support: `http://caniuse.com/indexeddb`
- Another wrapper (like Treo) called Dexie: `http://www.dexie.org`

Summary

In this chapter, we covered how to create an IndexedDB database, how to store and retrieve objects, as well as the differences between a relational and key-object storage mechanism. In the next chapter, we'll explore the relational side of the storage equation using the Web SQL Database.

8

Web SQL Database

Key-object stores are very useful, but sometimes we need a little more power. Web SQL Database lets us leverage **SQL** (Structured Query Language) in order to work with structured and relational data simply and efficiently, whereas IndexedDB often needs a lot of programming in order to combine the results from multiple tables or to perform full text searches. SQL makes it very simple to perform these tasks in only a few short lines of code.

As mentioned in the prior chapter, Web SQL Database uses a relational data model typical of databases such as Oracle, PostgreSQL, Microsoft SQL, and many others. This relational model is fantastic for heavily structured data, but isn't so great for data that has a flexible structure. The latter doesn't express relationships within the database schema itself, while the former does, so it can also enforce data integrity at the database level rather than at the code level.

There's one downside to using Web SQL Database: the standards body has essentially killed the specification. The browsers that implemented Web SQL Database used a single implementation: SQLite. The standards body didn't want to codify SQLite's brand of SQL as a part of the specification. That said, all the modern WebKit browsers support Web SQL Database, and this is true on desktops and mobile. So many sites now rely on it, that even though it is essentially a dead specification, it's unlikely to be removed anytime soon.

Since we're building apps with Cordova, we have access to the platform's browser implementation of the Web SQL Database. This does come with some significant limitations (notably storage space). As such, we'll be using a third-party plugin that uses the same API, but uses a separate SQLite database. This also means that even if the browsers start removing their Web SQL Database implementation, Cordova is still safe, because one can always add the plugin to regain the functionality.

Web SQL Database is essentially a wrapper around SQLite. SQLite is a lightweight and fast implementation of a relational database that has excellent support on mobile devices. To learn more about SQLite, you might want to visit their website: `http://www.sqlite.org`.

In this chapter, we'll cover the following:

- Web SQL database support
- Cordova SQLite plugin
- Creating and opening databases
- Using transactions
- Creating tables
- Inserting data and binding values
- Querying data
- Deleting data
- SQLite utilities

Getting started

This chapter focuses mostly on the basics of using Web SQL Database. If you want to see a real-life example, we've implemented Web SQL Database into our demonstration app in the code package of this book located at `logology-v08/`.

Several of the snippets in this chapter are also available using the interactive snippet playground that accompanies the code package of this book. Instructions to launch the playground are in the `README.md` file in the code package. Once started, select `8: Web SQL Database` and then browse and experiment with the examples. Where applicable, each section and snippet will indicate which chapter and example you should select.

Web SQL Database support

Web SQL Database is supported in all modern WebKit browsers. This includes Chrome and Mobile Safari on Android and iOS devices, respectively. Support on Android goes all the way back to Android 2.1, while support on iOS goes all the way back to iOS 3.2. On desktop browsers, support has been around for even longer.

Notably missing from this list is Internet Explorer and Firefox. These browsers only support IndexedDB (and IE only partially). There is no support for Web SQL Database to be found in either their desktop versions or their mobile versions. If you ever decide to eventually target Windows Phone or Firefox OS, you might want to be aware of this and plan accordingly.

When using browser-provided Web SQL Database support, we are constrained by storage limitations. In order to ensure that a website or an app won't just eat up all the space on a computer, browsers enforce quotas on the size of the database. This usually starts out at 5 MB. Most browsers will allow extensions up to 50 MB.

The Cordova SQLite plugin

The storage limitations enforced by the browser implementation of Web SQL Database is problematic for mobile apps, as 5 or even 50 MB may not be sufficient for the app's needs. Thankfully, there's a way around this limitation, and also around the fact that the standard is now dead and may be removed from browsers in the future: a third-party plugin.

There are several third-party plugins available that interface with SQLite, but the one we're going to use seeks to implement the same API as the specification used. This means that, in general, you can use the same code on desktop browsers and on mobile browsers. Some other plugins provide a very different API, which is fine, but it doesn't allow for as much reusability across platforms.

The plugin we'll be using is named *Cordova SQLite Storage* and is available from `https://github.com/litehelpers/Cordova-sqlite-storage`. You can add it to a Cordova project using the following command:

```
$ cordova plugin add io.litehelpers.cordova.sqlite
```

 If you need to distribute a pre-populated database, there is another version of this plugin that you can use at `https://github.com/litehelpers/cordova-sqlite-ext`.

Creating and opening databases

Creating and opening databases using Web SQL Database or the Cordova SQLite Storage plugin is easy, but there are a few differences between the two that you do need to be aware of. Before we cover these differences, let's go over the basics.

The snippets in this section are located at `snippets/08/ex1-create-database/` in the code package of this book. When using the interactive snippet playground, select `8: Web SQL Database` and Example **1**.

While using Web SQL Database, you can open a database with the following:

```
let db = window.openDatabase(name, version, description, quota);
```

Let's go over the parameters:

- `name`: This is the filename of the database. It usually ends in a `.db` extension. This parameter is required.

- `version`: Web SQL Database supports versioned databases. This is technically a string parameter, so you could use 1.0 or even `"one"`. My suggestion, however, is to always use 1 for a reason we're going to get to shortly.

- `description`: This is a short description of the database, but it's more for your use than anything else.

- `quota`: This parameter specifies how big you think the database will need to be, in bytes. Typically, one requests 1, 2, or 5 megabytes. If the size ever needs to be extended, opening the database with a larger quota will request additional space. Keep in mind that the quota is a *request*, not a guarantee; the user doesn't have to grant permission for any storage at all.

While using the Cordova SQLite Storage plugin, the preferred syntax is a little different:

```
window.sqlitePlugin.openDatabase(
    {name, location, createFromLocation,
     androidDatabaseImplementation, androidLockWorkaround});
```

Quite a bit different, right? *Technically*, you could use the first syntax (just add `sqlitePlugin`), but it's no longer the preferred syntax for the plugin. This is because the preferred syntax allows a lot of extra functionality, and also because the version, description, and quota aren't actually supported, which means there's no reason to use anything other than 1 as the database's version while working with the browser's implementation.

Most of the parameters are optional, but let's go over them all quickly:

- `name`: Like in the other version, this is the name of the database.

- `location`: This is an optional parameter, and it specifies where the database is actually stored. This only has an impact on iOS. The locations are as follows:
  - `0`: This stores the database in `Documents/`; it is visible to iTunes and is backed up by iCloud. This is also the default location.

- ○ 1: This stores the database in `Library/`. It is backed up by iCloud, but is not visible to iTunes.

  - ○ 2: This stores the database in `Library/LocalDatabase/`. It is not backed up by iCloud and is not visible to iTunes.

- `createFromLocation`: This lets you ship a prepopulated database along with your app. Whatever database is in your www folder with the exact same name is copied to the final location. If a database already exists there, it won't be copied again. This only works if using the plugin at `https://github.com/litehelpers/cordova-sqlite-ext`.

  - ○ 0: No pre populated database is used; the created database will be empty

  - ○ 1: The database is created using a prepopulated database

- `androidDatabaseImplementation`: Specifies which SQLite implementation should be used on Android. By default, the plugin will use its own implementation rather than the one provided by the system, but this does occasionally run into issues (especially while using the Crosswalk project or Ionic).

  - ○ 2: The database uses the system SQLite implementation rather than the plugin's own implementation. Use this for the best compatibility.

- `androidLockWorkaround`: By default, this isn't enabled, but some Android versions have issues with locking the database or losing data if the app is closed unexpectedly. This is only a problem if `androidDatabaseImplementation` is 2.

  - ○ 1: The database is closed after each transaction. This fixes the locking and data loss issue at the expense of performance. If you use `androidDatabaseImplementation` set to 2, you should probably include this setting as well.

Because of the differences between the standard and the plugin, it's usually best to abstract these differences away. Let's create a class that does just that:

```
// Example Snippet "WebSQLDB Class"; located at
// snippets/08/WebSQL/index.js
class WebSQLDB {
    constructor({name, version = "1", description,
                 quota = (5 * 1024 * 1024),
                 location = 0, createFromLocation = 0,
                 androidDatabaseImplementation = 2,
                 androidLockWorkaround = 1} = {}) {
        this.db = null;
        this.name = name;
```

```
        this.version = version;
        this.description = description;
        this.quota = quota;
        this.plugin = false;
        this.supportsReadOnlyTransactions = false;

        if (window.sqlitePlugin) {
            this.plugin = true;
            this.db = window.sqlitePlugin.openDatabase(
                {name, location, createFromLocation,
                 androidDatabaseImplementation,
                 androidLockWorkaround});
        } else {
            this.db = window.openDatabase(name, version,
                description, quota);
        }

        if (!this.db) { // [1]
            throw new Error("Could not instantiate a database.");
        }

        if (this.db.readTransaction) { // [2]
            this.supportsReadOnlyTransactions = true;
        }
    }
}
```

Note that the preceding code uses a lot of default parameters. These are the typical values that are suggested, so it makes sense to make them the default. If your app requires a different default, you can always make those the defaults instead.

Also, notice that we can tell whether or not opening the database was successful just by checking the return value [1]. If it's not set to an object, the action has failed, and we can complain appropriately. The last few lines [2] are just to check whether or not the environment supports read-only transactions, which we'll get into in the next section.

 Of course, it's a bit much to create a class just to open a database. But we'll be enhancing this class as the chapter continues.

In order to open a database using this class, we can do as follows:

```
let db = new WebSQLDB({name: "test.db"});
```

With this one class, we've abstracted away the differences between both the standard Web SQL Database and the plugin version. Now that we have an open database, let's look at how we can interact with the database.

Transactions

Before we go any further, we need to cover how Web SQL Database handles transactions. You *can* execute SQL commands against the database without using a transaction, but it's not recommended. Using a transaction gives you the opportunity to rollback any data you added, deleted, or changed in case of an error. In this way, transactions help maintain the consistency of the database.

 The snippets in this section are located at `snippets/08/ex2-transactions/` in the code package of this book. When using the interactive snippet playground, select **8: Web SQL Database** and Example **2**.

Transactions are easily initiated by calling `transaction` on the database object, as follows:

```
db.transaction( transactionCallback, error, success )
```

 Although it may appear from the first glance that Web SQL Database is asynchronous due to the use of callbacks, this isn't really the case. IndexedDB is the only local storage solution that is truly asynchronous.

Technically, the last two parameters to `transaction` are optional; most examples you find online won't use them. Even so, it's important to understand their purpose, so we'll go over each parameter:

- `transactionCallback`: This is (*and must be*) a callback function that accepts a single parameter. The parameter is an object that represents the transaction. The transaction is valid only for this time through the JavaScript execution run loop. This means that it won't be valid in `setTimeout` or a similar function.

- `error`: This function is called if an error occurs in the handling of the transaction. At this point, any changes in the transaction are rolled back. This parameter is *not* required.

- `success`: This function is called when the transaction is completed successfully. This is optional and is rarely provided in most examples, but it is quite important. Only upon this function being called can we be sure if the transaction completed successfully.

The most important parameter is `transactionCallback`. This must be a function that is tasked with actually carrying out the transaction, whether it be creating tables, adding data, or querying data. The function can perform as many commands against the transaction as it wants in a synchronous manner. If an error occurs at any point, the changes will be rolled back.

By default, the `transaction` method will assume that you are making changes to the database. If you're just executing the SELECT queries, you can call the `readTransaction` method instead, which will result in much better performance. While supported on most browsers, it is important to check for the existence of this function, because not all environments support it.

Let's look at an example of how all this works:

```
db.transaction(
    (tx) => {
        console.log("in transaction");
        // do queries, etc.
    },
    (err) => console.log(`Transaction error: ${err}`),
    () => console.log("Transaction completed successfully.")
);
```

Once inside the `transactionCallback` method, the transaction can be used to run queries and execute commands against the database. In our examples, we use `tx` to refer to this transaction simply because it's a short abbreviation and much easier to type.

 If you're familiar with the typical pattern of `success`, `error` callback methods, note that this method has them reversed.

This isn't quite ideal; wouldn't it be nice to be able to use promises with this? While it is indeed possible to use promises with Web SQL Database, one has to do it within the limitations imposed by the transaction itself: namely, that it is good only for this particular time through the JavaScript run loop.

Even so, let's add a transaction method to our class. It will look as follows:

```
transaction(cb, {readOnly = false} = {}) {
    return new Promise((resolve, reject) => {
        let r;
        this.db[(readOnly && this.supportsReadOnlyTransactions)
            ? "readTransaction" : "transaction"]((transaction) => {
            try {
                r = cb(transaction);
            } catch (err) {
                reject(err);
            }
        }, (err) => reject(err),
            () => resolve(r));
    });
}
```

Of particular importance is the fact that the *promisified* version still calls the transaction callback directly with the transaction object. This is due to the fact that promises work asynchronously and the transaction will be invalid by the time the next JavaScript run loop comes around. Instead we have to execute the callback immediately, and resolve when the transaction is completed successfully. This means that our promisified version isn't perfect, but it still lets us write the following:

```
db.transaction((tx) => {
    console.log("in promised transaction");
    // do queries, etc...
}).then(() => console.log(
            "Promise transaction completed successfully."))
    .catch((err) => console.log(`Promise transaction error:
                            ${err}`));
```

Note that we've not yet executed any queries against the database. Let's rectify this by creating some tables to store useful data.

Creating tables

Web SQL Database, as the name implies, relies upon SQL to create tables, store data, and retrieve that data. This means that you essentially need to know an additional language in order to use Web SQL Database; JavaScript isn't sufficient. That said, SQL is pretty easy to grasp. Even so, it's beyond the scope of this chapter to give you a complete understanding of the language. For SQLite's variant of SQL, `http://www.sqlite.org/lang.html` is a good resource.

 The snippets in this section are located at `snippets/08/ex3-create-table/` in the code package of this book. When using the interactive snippet playground, select **8: Web SQL Database** and Example **3**.

Creating a table is fairly straightforward. First, let's look at the SQL syntax you use to create tables, and then we'll move on to the JavaScript version using Web SQL Database. Note that in all our SQL examples, we're using SQLite's version of SQL:

```
CREATE TABLE [IF NOT EXISTS] tableName (
    columnName <TYPE> [<CONSTRAINT>] [, ...]
    [<TABLE CONSTRAINTS>]
)
```

SQL keywords are not case-sensitive. In our examples, keywords will typically be capitalized, but there is no requirement that they must be.

SQLite, the database used by all the Web SQL Database implementations, is not like most SQL databases in which the types are not static, but are rather more dynamic in nature (a bit like JavaScript, actually). This doesn't usually affect how we write SQL, but it can be important to recognize, because it does mean that SQLite is actually more flexible with regards to what can be stored. Here's how the various types you might see in SQL would be handled in SQLite:

Common SQL Types	SQLite Type Affinity	Description
CHAR, CHARACTER, VARCHAR, VARCHAR2, NCHAR, NVARCHAR, TEXT, CLOB	TEXT	The column will store data as text. Numerical data is converted into a text representation prior to being stored.
BLOB	None	Used for storing Binary Large Objects. Since the data is binary, there's no point in assigning a type affinity.
INT, INTEGER, TINYINT, SMALLINT, MEDIUMINT, BIGINT	INTEGER	Where possible, the numeric data will be stored using an integer rather than a floating point number. If a number outside of the signed 64-bit range is stored, it will be represented using floating point.
REAL, DOUBLE, FLOAT	REAL	Where possible, the numeric data will be stored using floating-point representation. If the number can be stored using an integer, it will be stored as an integer if doing so results in a space savings.
NUMERIC, DECIMAL, BOOLEAN, DATE, DATETIME	NUMERIC	Used to store numeric data. If text is inserted instead, an attempt is first made to convert the text to a number. If this fails, the text is stored as text.

As you can see, SQLite is pretty flexible when it comes to what can be stored with regards to types. As such, there's little point in being *too explicit* about the data you expect, unless you do so for purely self-documenting purposes.

With this in mind, we can start constructing some tables that would store the same definitions as we did in the previous chapter. First, let's look at the schema definition:

lemmas				
PK FK	wordNetRef	INTEGER	Unique ID; points to the definition in WordNet	02124272
PK	lemma	TEXT	Word that has the definition indicated	"cat"

definition				
PK	wordNetRef	INTEGER	Unique ID; points to the definition in WordNet	02124272
	partOfSpeech	TEXT	Noun, Adjective, etc.	Noun
	gloss	TEXT	Definition	feline mammal...

There's a little more detail here: namely, each column now has a type affinity. We also indicate which fields are primary keys (PK) and which fields are foreign keys (FK). The relationship is also defined with the line between the two tables; here, it indicates that one `definition` may have many associated `lemmas`.

Here's how we might define the definition table:

```
CREATE TABLE IF NOT EXISTS definition (
    wordNetRef INTEGER PRIMARY KEY,
    partOfSpeech TEXT,
    gloss TEXT
)
```

In this definition, we mark the `wordNetRef` field as `INTEGER PRIMARY KEY`. This means that the data stored within the field will be integers (and WordNet references are integers), and that these will also be the table's primary key. A key is simply a way to reference data within a table. The table's primary key is optimized for this purpose; it's the *primary* way you'll access data. It's automatically required to be unique across all the data within the table, and it automatically has an index created against it to make queries using it very fast.

The rest of the table uses the `TEXT` type affinity. You may often see `VARCHAR2` or other character types when SQL gets used; these would accomplish the same thing. Furthermore, you'll often see length specifications as well (such as `VARCHAR2(255)`). SQLite ignores these completely. If you do have limits on the length of text that you are working with, it's OK to include these limits in your table definitions, but SQLite won't actually honor such length limitations.

Our `lemmas` table is a bit more complex. Two fields are marked as the PRIMARY KEY, which means their values combined must be unique across the table. Furthermore, `wordNetRef` is marked as a FOREIGN KEY. Foreign keys reference keys on other tables (hence the term), and can be used to enforce these relationships. That said, SQLite doesn't enforce these relationships by default, but they are still very useful from a documentation point of view.

To create this table, we can use the following:

```
CREATE TABLE IF NOT EXISTS lemmas (
    wordNetRef INTEGER,
    lemma TEXT,
    PRIMARY KEY (wordNetRef, lemma)
    FOREIGN KEY (wordNetRef) REFERENCES definition (wordNetRef)
)
```

In SQL, it is considered an error if one tries to create a table that already exists. This can be useful knowledge; perhaps, the table that already exists is an older version and needs to be recreated. More often, though, we just want the table to be created as long as it doesn't already exist, and this is where the IF NOT EXISTS clause we've been using comes in. With this clause, if the tables exist, nothing will happen and no error will be thrown. If the tables don't exist, they'll be created normally.

This does raise the other side of the coin: if we can create tables, how do we destroy them? We can do this using the DROP command:

```
DROP TABLE [IF EXISTS] tableName
```

In fact, as long as the data can always be re-created, you can combine the DROP TABLE IF EXISTS and CREATE TABLE statements together and greatly simplify your transactions. Of course, if you need to transform saved data, this would be far from ideal, which is why it's also handy that DROP TABLE and CREATE TABLE can also generate errors when needed.

In order to use these SQL statements in our app, we need to call `executeSql` on a transaction object. The method accepts the SQL command we want to use, any additional bind values (we'll cover those in a moment), and a success and error callback, as follows:

```
tx.executeSql(sqlStatement, bindVariables, success, error);
```

All but the first are optional, so when we aren't worried about obtaining results from queries or determining whether a command fails (because the transaction error handler will be called instead), we can do the following to create our tables:

```
db.transaction((tx) => {
    tx.executeSql("DROP TABLE IF EXISTS definition");
    tx.executeSql("DROP TABLE IF EXISTS lemmas");
    tx.executeSql("CREATE TABLE definition ( wordNetRef INTEGER
        PRIMARY KEY, partOfSpeech TEXT, gloss TEXT)");
    tx.executeSql("CREATE TABLE lemmas ( wordNetRef INTEGER, lemma
        TEXT, PRIMARY KEY(wordNetRef, lemma) FOREIGN KEY
        (wordNetRef) REFERENCES definition (wordNetRef))");
    }).then(() => console.log("Tables created successfully."))
    .catch((err) => console.log(`Error: ${err.message}`));
```

 If you had a lot of statements to perform in your transaction, it'd be a good idea to place them in an array and then iterate over them. That way you don't have to type `tx.executeSql` a million times.

This is great if you or your team really understand SQL well, but if you want your code to feel more like JavaScript, you might want to wrap these types of commands with some utility functions. Furthermore, sometimes, it can be useful to execute these commands without having to continuously define a transaction (but this only makes sense when the entirety of the transaction would be a single command). To do this, we can define a method called `exec` on our class that looks as follows:

```
exec({transaction, sql, binds, readOnly = false} = {}) {
    if (!transaction) {
        return this.transaction((transaction) => {
            return this.exec({transaction, sql, binds, readOnly});
        }, {readOnly});
    } else {
        return transaction.executeSql(sql, binds);
    }
}
```

This isn't actually the entire method we use; we'll add more when we query data. However, it's good enough for our purposes at this point.

This method is actually two in one: if it's called without a `transaction` already established (passed in the `transaction` parameter), it will go ahead and instantiate a `transaction` on its own and return the promise. If a `transaction` has been established and passed in, the command will be directly executed. Notice that, in the latter case, there is no `success` or `error` handler. There's no `success` handler at this point, because we aren't currently interested in any results (which only make sense while working with queries); there is no `error` handler, because we'll let the `transaction` error handler deal with anything that arises.

> You can specify an error handler, but this handler is intended to be a recovery method. That is, the method must attempt to rectify the error encountered in some way, and it *must* return `false`. If not, an error will actually be thrown again, indicating that the `error` handler didn't return `false` as expected.

Once we have this method, we can add some wrappers around the DROP TABLE and CREATE TABLE SQL statements:

```
createTable({name, fields = [], constraints = [],
             ifNotExists = true, transaction} = {}) {
    let fieldSql = fields.map((field = []) =>
                             field.join(" ")).join(", "),
        constraintSQL = constraints.join(" ");
    let sql = `CREATE TABLE ${ifNotExists ? "IF NOT EXISTS" : ""}
               ${name} (${fieldSql}
               ${constraintSQL!=="" ? `, ${constraintSQL}` : ""})`;
    return this.exec({transaction, sql});
}


dropTable({name, ifExists = false, transaction} = {}) {
    let sql = `DROP TABLE ${ifExists ? "IF EXISTS" : ""} ${name}`;
    return this.exec({transaction, sql});
}
```

At this point, we could just create a simple table by calling `createTable` without a `transaction`, or we could create several tables in a row by first creating a `transaction`, as follows:

```
db.transaction((tx) => {
  db.dropTable({name: "definition", ifExists: true,
               transaction: tx});
```

```
db.dropTable({name: "lemmas", ifExists: true,
              transaction: tx});
db.createTable({name: "definition", ifNotExists: true,
                transaction: tx,
                fields: [["wordNetRef","INTEGER PRIMARY KEY"],
                         ["partOfSpeech", "TEXT"],
                         ["gloss", "TEXT"]]});
db.createTable({name: "lemmas", ifNotExists: true,
                transaction: tx,
                fields: [["wordNetRef", "INTEGER"],
                         ["lemma", "TEXT"]],
                constraints: ["PRIMARY KEY (wordNetRef, lemma)",
                              "FOREIGN KEY (wordNetRef)
                         REFERENCES definition (wordNetRef)"]});
}).then(() => console.log(
              "Promise Tables created successfully."))
  .catch((err) => console.log(`Promise Error: ${err}`));
```

Note that this isn't necessarily shorter; the point isn't to be *shorter*, but a bit clearer and easier to follow. It still does require some SQLite knowledge (especially with regards to primary and foreign keys), but you also don't having to deal with embedding lots of long SQL strings in your code.

Now that we've created some tables, let's actually start storing some data in them.

Inserting data and binding values

In SQL, we store data using two statements (usually): INSERT INTO and UPDATE. The first is used when you're adding data to a table, and the second is used to update data that already exists. There's also a variant that permits the merging of data: data that doesn't exist is added, and data that does exist is updated. Various SQL database servers do this differently, but SQLite uses INSERT OR REPLACE INTO.

The snippets in this section are located at snippets/08/ex4-insert-data/ in the code package of this book. When using the interactive snippet playground, select **8: Web SQL Database** and Example **4**.

The INSERT INTO statement looks as follows:

```
INSERT [OR REPLACE] INTO tableName (
    fieldName [, ...]
    ) VALUES (
    values [, ...]
    )
```

The UPDATE statement looks as follows:

```
UPDATE tableName
  SET fieldName = value
WHERE condition
```

In many ways, the UPDATE statement is a lot more readable than the INSERT INTO statement, mainly because with the latter, you're forced to mentally map the values to the field names. If you create a wrapper like we've been doing, it will not be as painful, so this is the path we suggest. Otherwise, long INSERT INTO statements become very hard to follow.

Furthermore, there's something you should be aware of. If you're ever inserting data that the user has given you into your database, you have to be aware of a security issue called SQL Injection.

SQL commands are built with strings, and you've seen quite a bit of this in our wrappers so far. If we allowed untrusted data into these commands, a malicious user could change our commands and change or destroy the database. While this isn't as critical when the database is local versus when the database is remote, it's still something your code should protect against whenever possible.

To do this, Web SQL Database has the concept of **bind values**. These allow you to specify placeholders within the SQL command (similar to ES2015 template strings), and then specify the values later. These values are never parsed as a part of the SQL command, so they can't change the command and change or delete data.

Let's take a quick look at what our statements look like when we use bind values:

```
INSERT INTO definition ( wordNetRef, partOfSpeech, gloss )
VALUES ( ?, ?, ? );

UPDATE definition
   SET partOfSpeech = ?
 WHERE wordNetRef = ?;
```

The question marks in the prior code indicate the placeholders. Then, when we actually ask the database to execute the command, we'll also pass the values along. This ensures that if `gloss` contained `; DROP TABLE definition`, inserting the data wouldn't actually drop our table.

So, you might be wondering why we've been building strings instead of using bind values in our wrappers so far. It's for a simple reason, actually: bind values aren't supported in statements that define the database structure (these are called **DDL** or data definition language statements), so there's no choice but to build strings instead of using bind values. To be extra safe, one should add additional escaping methods; but hopefully, you aren't ever building data structures based on untrusted data.

Statements that insert, change, or query data are collectively grouped as **DML** or data manipulation language statements. All DML statements accept bind values.

Now that we have our SQL statements, we can use the same `executeSql` method we used in the prior section to actually execute them. This is when we'll provide our bind values. For example:

```
let definitions = [
    {wordNetRef: "02124272", partOfSpeech: "noun",
     gloss: "feline mammal usually having thick soft fur and no
             ability to roar: domestic cats; wildcats"},
    {wordNetRef: "02130460", partOfSpeech: "noun",
     gloss: "any of several large cats typically able to roar and
             living in the wild"},
    {wordNetRef: "02085443", partOfSpeech: "noun",
     gloss: "nocturnal burrowing mammal of the grasslands of
             Africa that feeds on termites; sole extant
             representative of the order Tubulidentata"}
];

let lemmas = [
    {wordNetRef: "02124272", lemma: "cat"},
    {wordNetRef: "02124272", lemma: "true cat"},
    {wordNetRef: "02130460", lemma: "cat"},
    {wordNetRef: "02130460", lemma: "big cat"},
    {wordNetRef: "02085443", lemma: "aardvark"},
    {wordNetRef: "02085443", lemma: "ant bear"},
    {wordNetRef: "02085443", lemma: "anteater"},
```

```
        {wordNetRef: "02085443", lemma: "Orycteropus afer"}
    ];

    db.transaction((tx) => {
        let definitionSql = "INSERT INTO definition ( wordNetRef,
                        partOfSpeech, gloss ) VALUES ( ?, ?, ? )";
        let lemmaSql = "INSERT INTO lemmas ( wordNetRef, lemma )
                    VALUES ( ?, ? )";
        definitions.forEach(({wordNetRef, partOfSpeech, gloss}) =>
                        tx.executeSql(definitionSql,
                            [wordNetRef, partOfSpeech, gloss]) );
        lemmas.forEach(({wordNetRef, lemma}) =>
            tx.executeSql(lemmaSql, [wordNetRef, lemma]));
    }).then(() => console.log("Data inserted successfully."))
      .catch((err) => console.log(`Error: ${err.message}`));
```

Notice that, in the preceding code, the bind values are provided in an array. Unlike
ES2015 template strings, the bind values aren't specified by name, but by location.
This means that the first question mark is replaced by the first value in the array, and
so on.

Let's create a wrapper for this statement for our utility class:

```
insert({intoTable, data = {}, replace = false, transaction,
    template = false} = {}) {
    let fieldKeys = Object.keys(data);
    let fieldNames = fieldKeys.join(", ");
    let fieldBinds = fieldKeys.map(() => "?").join(", ");
    let binds = Object.values(data);
    let sql = `INSERT ${replace ? "OR REPLACE" : ""}
        INTO ${intoTable} (${fieldNames}) VALUES (${fieldBinds})`;
    return template ? sql : this.exec({transaction, sql, binds});
}
```

Essentially, the previous function will create the bulk of the statement based on the properties in `data`. For example, if we were to pass a `definition` object, the field names would be extracted as `wordNetRef`, `partOfSpeech`, and `gloss`. If `template` is `false`, the SQL statement and resulting bind values (extracted from the values of each property) would be executed. On the other hand, if `template` is `true`, it will just return to us a SQL statement that we can reuse.

That's another benefit of bind values: we can reuse SQL statements simply because we aren't encoding the values in each statement. This has tremendous performance benefits for both our code and the SQL parser. We don't have to construct the SQL statement each time, and the SQL parser doesn't have to decode it each time.

Now that we have this wrapper method, we can rewrite our code, as follows:

```
[ ["definition", definitions],
  ["lemmas", lemmas] ].forEach( ([ table, data]) => {
    let sql;
    data.forEach((item) => {
        if (!sql) {
            sql = db.insert({intoTable: table, data: item,
                            template: true});
        }
        db.exec({sql, binds: Object.values(item),
                transaction: tx});
    });
});
```

We'll leave writing a wrapper that handles UPDATE to you, but it wouldn't be terribly different from the INSERT INTO wrapper.

Querying data (single table, joins, and so on)

Now that we have data in the database, we need to have a way to get that data back out. In SQL, this is done by using the SELECT statement. It's a very versatile command, so there's no way that it can be covered completely in a single chapter. Instead, we'll go over some simple commands, and you can explore the commands more on your own.

The snippets in this section are located at `snippets/08/ex5-select-data/` in the code package of this book. When using the interactive snippet playground, select **8: Web SQL Database** and Example **5**.

At its simplest, a `SELECT` statement looks as follows:

```
SELECT fieldName[, ...]
  FROM tableName[, ...]
[WHERE condition[ ...]]
[ORDER BY field [direction], ...]
```

There's a whole lot more you can do with the `SELECT` statement than this, but this will suffice for now.

If we wanted to select all our definitions, we could write this command:

```
SELECT wordNetRef, partOfSpeech, gloss
  FROM definition
```

As you can see, `WHERE` and `ORDER BY` are completely optional. The `WHERE` clause lets us filter the data. For example:

```
SELECT wordNetRef, partOfSpeech, gloss
  FROM definition
WHERE partOfSpeech = ?
```

If we passed noun as the bind value, we'd only get the definitions of nouns. There are a number of operators you can use in your expressions. Here are a few:

- `<, <=, =, >=, >, <>`: These operators act like you would expect. If you prefer using `==` and `!=` for equality and inequality, respectively, you can do so. SQLite handles these in the same way. There's only one catch: `NULL` can't be compared using these operators.

- `IS`: To compare `NULL`, `IS` can be used. The full form looks like `IS NULL` or `IS NOT NULL`.

- `AND, OR`: These act to join expressions and clauses together.

- `NOT`: Acts as a unary `NOT`, negating the result of the following expression.

- `BETWEEN a AND b`: This is an easier way to state `value >= a AND value <= b`.

- `LIKE`: This operator acts as a wildcard match. `%` can be used to match any number of characters, and an underscore can be used to match a single character. These are akin to regular expressions, but are much simpler. By default, `LIKE` is case-insensitive, but only for the ASCII character set.

- `IN (a, b, c, …)`: This operator compares a value against a list of values.

There are many more operators that you can use. For a full description, see `http://www.sqlite.org/lang_expr.html`.

The `ORDER BY` clause, when specified, allows us to specify the order of the result set. You can specify which fields to sort first as well as the direction in which to sort them. For example, `ORDER BY wordNetRef ASC` would sort the results by the `wordNetRef` field in the ascending order. When a field is of numeric affinity, `ASC` will sort in the numeric ascending order, and `DESC` will sort in the numeric descending order. When a field is of text affinity, the same orders will apply, but the alphabetical order will be used instead. If the sort order isn't specified, ascending is assumed.

A `SELECT` statement doesn't have to operate on only a single table, and this is probably one of the biggest differentiators between IndexedDB and Web SQL Database. In IndexedDB, it is up to your JavaScript code to combine results from multiple schemas. In Web SQL Database, SQL itself can combine the values without any additional JavaScript code.

While joining multiple tables together, one has to be careful. If we just did `SELECT * FROM definition, lemmas`, we'd end up with a lot more results than we might expect, because SQL doesn't assume that we want to join them based on the primary key. Instead it returns a Cartesian product. Each row from one of the tables will be combined with each row from the other table. Even for the short list of definitions in our examples, it turns out to be quite a lot of rows.

`*` can be used in the `SELECT` statements to return all the fields. Generally, you should avoid using this, instead you should ask for the data you specifically require. This will result in faster performance.

Instead, one must always specify how the tables are linked. If we want to join both `definition` and `lemmas` together, we should write the following instead:

```
SELECT definition.wordNetRef, lemma, partOfSpeech, gloss
  FROM definition, lemmas
WHERE definition.wordNetRef = lemmas.wordNetRef
ORDER BY lemma
```

Where column names are duplicated, SQL needs us to specify which tables the columns come from. In the preceding case, `wordNetRef` is duplicated across `definition` and `lemmas`, so we can specify the table using `definition.wordNetRef` and `lemmas.wordNetRef`.

Now that we have a SQL statement, how do we actually execute it? Again, we can use `executeSql`. But this time, we will definitely need a success handler to retrieve the results. Let's take a look at what it would look like:

```
return db.transaction((tx) => {
  tx.executeSql("SELECT definition.wordNetRef, lemma," +
                "partOfSpeech, gloss FROM definition," +
                "lemmas WHERE definition.wordNetRef = " +
                "lemmas.wordNetRef ORDER BY lemma", null,
  (tx, results) => {
    let rows = [];
    for (let i = 0, l = results.rows.length; i < l; i++) {
      rows.push(results.rows.item(i));
    }
  })
});
```

Most of this looks pretty simple, but you might be wondering why we're taking the results and pushing them into an array. Oddly enough, the results from Web SQL Database are not returned in an array. Instead, each row has to be accessed by calling `rows.item()`. This is probably for performance reasons than anything else, but it does complicate things a bit. In order to prevent us from having to continually repeat it, we can add this ability to our exec method. Let's rewrite it as follows:

```
exec({transaction, sql, binds, readOnly = false} = {}) {
    if (!transaction) {
        return this.transaction((transaction) => {
            return this.exec({transaction, sql, binds, readOnly});
        }, {readOnly});
    } else {
        let returnResults = {};
        transaction.executeSql(sql, binds,
            (transaction, results) => {
                returnResults.rowsAffected = results.rowsAffected;
```

```
                returnResults.rows = [];
                if (results.rows && results.rows.length>0) {
                    for (let i = 0, l = results.rows.length;
                        i < l; i++) {
                        returnResults.rows.push(
                            results.rows.item(i));
                    }
                }
            });
        return returnResults;
    }
}
```

Once we do this, we can simplify our code to the following:

```
db.exec({sql:"SELECT definition.wordNetRef, lemma, partOfSpeech,"+
            "gloss FROM definition, lemmas " +
            "WHERE definition.wordNetRef = lemmas.wordNetRef "+
            "ORDER BY lemma"})
    .then((r) => { console.log(r); })
    .catch((err) => console.log(`Promise Error: ${err.message}`));
```

A row from the result set is actually a read-only JavaScript object. Each field from the query is present in the resulting object as a property. If we wanted to reference the `lemma` field value on the second row, we could use `results.rows.item(2).lemma` (assuming one doesn't push the results into an array), or `r.rows[2].lemma` (assuming one does push the results into an array). If a field name isn't a valid JavaScript property name, you can use bracket notation: `r.rows[2]["lemma"]`.

Before we go on to the next section, let's quickly show an example of how to filter our results using bind values:

```
tx.executeSql("SELECT definition.wordNetRef,lemma,partOfSpeech,"+
            "gloss FROM definition, lemmas " +
            "WHERE definition.wordNetRef = lemmas.wordNetRef "+
            "AND lemma = ? ORDER BY lemma", ["cat"],
            (tx, results) => { ... });
// or
db.exec({sql:"SELECT definition.wordNetRef,lemma,partOfSpeech,"+
            "gloss FROM definition, lemmas " +
```

```
        "WHERE definition.wordNetRef = lemmas.wordNetRef "+
        "ORDER BY lemma", binds: ["cat"]})
.then((r) => { console.log(r); })
.catch((err) => console.log(`Promise Error: ${err.message}`));
```

 We're not going to go into the code for our SELECT wrapper method. If you would like to see our version, you can do so by viewing the library using the snippets tool in the code package of this book.

Deleting data

Now that we've got data and can query it, what if we need to get rid of it?

Deleting is really pretty simple. The SQL statement looks as follows:

```
DELETE
   FROM tableName
[WHERE condition ...]
```

This will delete whatever rows match the conditions you supply and leave the rest. If no conditions are supplied, all the rows are removed.

We're not going to go over how to use this command in JavaScript; it uses the same executeSql method you're already familiar with. If you do want to see some code, you can look at the example snippets in the code package of this book.

The SQLite utilities

SQLite is used in a number of ecosystems. As such, there are lots of great utilities you can use to interact with SQLite databases. Some are as follows:

- Desktop browsers usually have embedded utilities:
    - Chrome and Safari provide both remote and local debugging support for Web SQL Databases. The functionality is exceedingly minimal, but you can perform queries and other commands against the database. If you're remotely debugging a device, do note that you won't be able to see the database created by the app. You'll either have to download it to your computer, or disable the plugin and use the platform's default Web SQL Database support. To access the database, open up the **Web Inspector** and navigate to the **Resources** panel. You should see a **Databases** section that expands to reveal the tables in your database. If you select the database instead of a table, you can also execute commands against the database.

- Cross-platform desktop clients are useful for inspecting databases copied from your device or for creating prepopulated databases.
    - DB Browser for SQLite (open source): `http://sqlitebrowser.org`
    - SQLite Studio (free): `http://sqlitestudio.pl/?act=about`
    - RazorSQL (commercial): `http://razorsql.com/features/sqlite_gui.html`
    - Navicat for SQLite (commercial): `http://www.navicat.com/products/navicat-for-sqlite`
    - Valentina Studio (free): `https://www.valentina-db.com/en/studio-for-sqlite`

Summary

We covered a lot of ground in this chapter. You've learned how to create and open databases, use transactions, create tables, insert and query data, and remove data.

In the next chapter, we're going to work with transferring files to and from a remote server.

9
Transferring Files

Many apps inevitably need to transfer files to or from a server. An app that stores photos in the cloud will need to upload files from the user's app. If the user needs to edit these files, then they will need to be downloaded again to the client. While XMLHttpRequest or Web Sockets can be used for this, Cordova supplies a core plugin that is made specifically for large file transfers: the "file transfer" plugin.

In this chapter, we'll cover the following:

- Configuring the whitelist
- Downloading files from a server
- Receiving files using PHP on a server
- Uploading files to a server
- Monitoring the progress
- Aborting transfers
- Security concerns

Getting started

Several of the snippets in this chapter are available using the interactive snippet playground that accompanies the code package of this book. Instructions to launch the playground are in the README.md file in the code package. Once it starts, select **9: Transferring Files** and then browse and experiment with the examples. Where applicable, each section and snippet will indicate which chapter and example you should select.

Configuring the whitelist

Because we'll be sending and receiving data over the network connection, we need to configure the network whitelist. Typically, Cordova's sample applications allow communication with any host. But generally, you should actively restrict the hosts your app can communicate with unless you have very good reasons for permitting unrestricted communication (for example, your app is a browser).

The first thing you need is the whitelist plugin. To add it using the Cordova CLI, you can do as follows:

```
cordova plugin add cordova-plugin-whitelist
```

On the other hand, since we're handling plugins in our app's `package.json`, we can add it to the `plugins` section, as follows:

```
...,
"plugins": {
    ...,
    "cordova-plugin-whitelist"
}, ...
```

Once this is done, we can run `gulp init` to rebuild the Cordova project with the necessary plugins.

 As of version 4.0 of the Cordova iOS and Cordova Android, all network access is denied unless the whitelist plugin is added. This is a breaking change from the earlier versions of each Cordova platform where network access was granted by default.

Now that the whitelist is added, we need to configure it. This is done in the `config.xml` file of our project (that, in our case, lives under `src/config.xml`). If you want to grant unfettered access to any or all the hosts, the following snippet will do just that:

```
<access origin="*" />
<allow-intent href="http://*/*" />
<allow-intent href="https://*/*" />
<allow-intent href="tel:*" />
<allow-intent href="sms:*" />
<allow-intent href="mailto:*" />
<allow-intent href="geo:*" />
<platform name="android">
  <allow-intent href="market:*" />
</platform>
<platform name="ios">
```

```
    <allow-intent href="itms:*" />
    <allow-intent href="itms-apps:*" />
</platform>
```

There's actually a lot going on here, especially if you're not familiar with the new whitelist plugin. Let's go over some of the interesting bits:

- `access` specifies the hosts with which our app is allowed to communicate. There can be any number of these tags, so you can get as specific as you like. Wildcards are also available; in this case, `*` allows communication with all hosts.

- `allow-intent` specifies what intents your application is allowed to trigger. An intent is a URL that will open a URL in another application that the user has installed on their app. For example, `http(s)://` would be opened in the user's web browser, while `tel://` would open the phone dialer, if available. The intents listed in this section are pretty generic and cover a wide number of use cases. If your app doesn't need a specific intent, you should remove it.

- `platform` allows us to indicate that certain settings are available only for certain platforms. For example, the `market://` URL scheme is valid only on Android devices, while the `itms://` and `itms-apps://` URL schemes are valid only on iOS devices (these open the app store).

In our case, let's imagine that the server we need to communicate with is `www.example.com`. We can use the access tag:

```
<access origin="http://www.example.com" />
```

 Our example assumes a data transfer over HTTP, which isn't secure. If you wanted to use a secure HTTP connection, you should specify `https://` instead.

If it's possible that you might need to access any of this host's subdomains, you can use a wildcard as follows:

```
<access origin="http://*.example.com" />
```

There are several other features that the whitelist controls, which you may be interested in (depending on your needs). For more information, see `https://github.com/apache/cordova-plugin-whitelist#network-request-whitelist`.

Downloading files from a server

It's always been possible to utilize XMLHttpRequest to send and receive content from external servers, which means that *technically* you could dispense with the File Transfer plugin entirely and use XHR, even for large files.

While it is possible, it's not ideal for several reasons. They are as follows:

- You're subject to any cross-origin restrictions, which may mean adding CORS support to the target server

- The data you receive isn't actually stored anywhere; you're still responsible for writing it out to a file

- You'll need to write a good deal of boilerplate code unless you are using an abstraction

The File Transfer plugin, on the other hand, has the following benefits:

- It reads and writes from the native file system without any additional code on your part

- It is not subjected to cross-origin restrictions; the request is made from the native code

- Operations can complete while the app is backgrounded (note that iOS does have a limit on how long the operations can continue in the background: roughly ten minutes)

So, when should you use the File Transfer plugin versus XHR? It really boils down to what you intend to do with the data. For example, if you're downloading a large JSON file that you immediately intend to parse, an XHR may make the most sense: you'd be provided the data immediately rather than having to write code to go read a file from the filesystem. However, if the file is, say, a SQLite file, it's a good idea to use the File Transfer plugin instead. Although you could use XHR to write the response to the filesystem in a binary format, it's far easier and less error-prone to use the File Transfer plugin. In short, if you want the file to exist on the user's device *as a file*, use the File Transfer plugin. If you just need to parse data from a response, use XHR.

The same applies with an upload: if the data you're uploading is something you've created dynamically in code, you can use an XHR to submit this data to a server. If the data you need to transfer resides in a file on the filesystem, use the File Transfer plugin instead. Again, you could use the File plugin to read the file's contents and then send it via XHR, but the File Transfer plugin is easier and less prone to error.

It is important to note that the File Transfer plugin only transfers data using HTTP(S). That is, the plugin won't attempt to do FTP or SFTP file transfers (or any other protocol). There are some plugins that support this functionality, but this is beyond the scope of this chapter.

Before we can use the File Transfer plugin, we need to install it.

We can use the Cordova CLI:

```
cordova plugin add cordova-plugin-file-transfer
```

Or, we can use `package.json`:

```
...,
"plugins": {
    ...,
    "cordova-plugin-file-transfer"
}, ...
```

Then, we need to execute `gulp init` to recreate the Cordova project with the new plugins.

> The snippets in this section are located at `snippets/09/ex1-downloading-files` in the code package of this book. When using the interactive snippet playground, select **9: Transferring Files** and Example 1.

The plugin provides a `FileTransfer` class that encapsulates both downloads and uploads. Before we can download or upload any files, we have to create a new instance of this class, as follows:

```
let fileTransfer = new FileTransfer();
```

> Remember, you can't actually use `FileTransfer` until the `deviceready` event is fired.

Once you have an instance, you can call the `download` method that it provides. It takes several parameters:

- `url`: The URL of the file that you want to download. You should use `encodeURI` to ensure the special characters are properly encoded or you may encounter errors.

- `downloadLocation`: This is the location where you want the file to be saved. This should be a `cdvfile://` location, but it can also be an absolute path. If the file is only going to be saved temporarily, save it to `cdvfile://localhost/temporary`. If the file is going to be saved permanently, save it to `cdvfile://localhost/persistent`. Note that the latter may be backed up by iCloud on iOS.

- `downloadSuccess`: This function is called when the file is downloaded successfully. It passes information on where the file was stored and the HTTP response that was generated.

- `downloadError`: This function is called if an error occurs during download. It will pass an error object indicating why the download failed (if available).

- `trustAllHosts`: This disables SSL certificate checking when `true`. It defaults to `false`, and you should avoid changing this unless you have a really good reason. You should definitely never use `true` in production code.

- `options`: This allows you to specify additional options, such as authorization headers.

Let's look at an example:

```
function downloadError(err) {
  console.log(`Encountered a download error:
    ${JSON.stringify(err, null, 2)}`);
}

function downloadSuccess(entry) {
  console.log(`Download completed successfully:
    ${JSON.stringify(entry, null, 2)}`);
}

function go() {
    let assetURL =
encodeURI("http://kerrishotts.github.io/Mastering-PhoneGap-Code-
Package/index.html");
    let downloadLocation =
        "cdvfile://localhost/persistent/index.html";

    let fileTransfer = new FileTransfer();
```

```
        fileTransfer.download(assetURL, downloadLocation,
            downloadSuccess, downloadError);
    }

    document.addEventListener("deviceready", go);
```

This example is pretty simple: it downloads a file from GitHub (the HTML page for this book's code package, actually), and saves it to the device's local filesystem as `index.html`. The name of the file could be anything you like; it doesn't have to match the original name (although you should endeavor to keep the same extension). Furthermore, it could be saved to a subdirectory; if the directory doesn't exist, it will be created automatically.

In the case of an error, the `downloadError` function is called. Our error handling is really pretty simple; it just logs out the `error` object. In production, you'd want to do quite a bit more to figure out what the problem was and whether there was anything you could do to work around it (or display a friendly error message to the user). The `err` object that is passed contains the following information that may be of use to you:

- `code` indicates the error code. This can be one of the following:
    - `FileTransferError.FILE_NOT_FOUND_ERR`: The file couldn't be saved at that download location.
    - `FileTransferError.INVALID_URL_ERR`: The source URL was invalid (did you forget to use `encodeURI`?).
    - `FileTransferError.CONNECTION_ERR`: A connection couldn't be established. Is there a network connection? Is the host reachable? If you're using SSL, make sure the certificates aren't expired and that they are signed by a trusted certificate authority.
    - `FileTransferError.ABORT_ERR`: The transfer was aborted by the app.
    - `FileTransferError.NOT_MODIFIED_ERR`: The source hasn't been modified since your last request. This occurs if an HTTP 304 code is returned for a request.
- `source` is the source URL that the plugin tried to download.
- `target` is the download destination.
- `http_status` indicates the response code from the server. This could be just about anything. But in general, the following are the typical codes:
    - **200 (OK)**: The request is completed successfully. At this point, the error occurred while saving the file, not at the server.

- ◦ **304 (Not Modified)**: The request has completed successfully, but the document hasn't been changed since the last time you requested it.
- ◦ **401 (Not Authorized)**: The request failed to complete, possibly because you aren't authenticated to the server.
- ◦ **403 (Forbidden)**: The request failed because you don't have access to the resource. You might want to ask the user for their credentials.
- ◦ **404 (Not Found)**: The request failed because the resource wasn't found.
- ◦ **500 (Internal Server Error)**: Something went very wrong on the server side. The error message may or may not have additional useful information.

- `body` is the response from the server. If you receive a status other than 200, you might want to check here for more information.

As you can see, there are a lot of opportunities for error handling here. At a minimum, you will want to display a notice to the user that you couldn't download the file; but you can use the information present in the passed `error` object to tailor the message to the user.

If the download completes successfully, the `downloadSuccess` function is called. Again, our handler is really simple here; it just logs the `file` entry (that represents where the file was stored on the filesystem). At this point in a production app, you would continue to work with the file; when this method is called, you're guaranteed to have the file on the file system. If you need to use the File API for additional processing, you can do so by using the passed `file` entry.

If you need to provide credentials for protected resources, you can do so as follows:

```
let fileTransfer = new FileTransfer();
let username = "testuser";
let password = "password";
let options = {
    headers: {
        "Authorization": `Basic ${btoa(`${username}:${password}`)}`
    }
}
fileTransfer.download(assetURL, downloadLocation,
    downloadSuccess, downloadError, false, options);
```

 If you're sending credentials, make sure you're using SSL to secure the communication.

Receiving files using PHP on a server

Before we can upload a file to a server, we need to have something on the server that can receive and process the file. At a minimum, this process writes the file to a specific location on the server, but there's usually a little bit more going on. Usually, the request is checked to make sure something fishy isn't going on (such as a file is too large or of the wrong type). Then, the file is almost always renamed to prevent naming collisions. After this, it's up to you: you could run a virus scan on the file, resize it (if it's an image), upload it to a backend database, send it to another server, and so on.

 The snippets in this section are located at `snippets/09/ex2-uploading-files` in the code package of this book. When using the interactive snippet playground, select **9: Transferring Files** and Example **2**.

The File Transfer plugin we've been using so far uses a multipart HTTP POST request to upload data, which is very useful. It means that we can use the same method we'd use to request files from users on a website, which typically involves an `<input type="file" />` widget on an HTML form and a PHP script that processes the results. In our case, we don't need the HTML form; our app is the one doing the uploading, not the user, so we can call the PHP script directly.

 If you've already got a system like this in place, you can skip this section. Also, note that, although we use PHP in this section, the concepts can be applied to any server-side language.

Let's start building our PHP script. We'll call it `upload.php`. At the top, we're going to place some configuration settings that we'll use later on:

```php
<?php
$maximumFileSize = 5 * 1024 * 1024;
$uploadLocation = "../upload/";
$validMimeTypes = array("text/plain", "text/html", "image/png",
"image/jpeg");
```

Although you may limit the maximum file size on the server in your `php.ini` settings, it's a good idea never to assume that these settings are what you want. As such, it's a good idea to check the file size in your upload script as well. One thing to remember, though, is that whatever size is specified here in `$maximumFileSize` won't override your `php.ini` settings, so you'll want to make sure the `post_max_size` and `upload_max_filesize` settings are large enough to accept a file of `$maximumFileSize` bytes.

The upload location is entirely up to you and your server configuration. The valid mime types are also up to you; these will let you filter out the files that aren't in the expected format. Of course, since our app is going to be the client that is uploading files, ideally, the app would never send a file of the wrong type, but it never hurts to check. Furthermore, your app may not be the only client for the upload script, so you will need to handle situations where the app may not be the one sending you data.

PHP automatically places information about the file being uploaded in a global variable called $_FILES. We can use this to extract information for our purposes:

```
$uploadedFile = $_FILES['file'];
$uploadedFileError = $uploadedFile['error'];
$uploadedFileSize = $uploadedFile['size'];
$uploadedFileType = $uploadedFile['type'];
$uploadedFilePath = $uploadedFile['tmp_name'];
```

One important thing to note is that the file index on $_FILES is the file key. If you had an HTML form, it would match the name of your file input element. We'll call this the "file key":

```
<form enctype="multipart/form-data" method="POST">
    <input type="file" name="file" />
</form>
```

Next, we're going to wrap everything we do in a try...catch statement. This will let us return an appropriate error if something goes wrong (otherwise we might return 200 even in an error condition):

```
try {
    // everything else we do in this section will be in this
    // try section
} catch (RuntimeException $err) {
    // generate a 500 server error
    http_response_code(500);
    // and give some error information
    echo $err->getMessage();
}
?>
```

All this does is it ensures that we return a 500 error code if we encounter an error. We also return the reason for the error so that the client can understand why the upload request failed.

With this in place, we need to start checking error conditions. There are several reasons to reject a file upload:

- The request is mangled or corrupt
- No files are provided or too many files are provided (this script will only work with one file at a time)
- The file is too large
- The file took too long to upload
- The file is of the wrong type
- The server encountered a problem saving the file (out of space, upload path is invalid, and so on)

> The code for error checking in this section is based on `http://php.net/manual/en/features.file-upload.php#114004`.

With this in mind, let's start checking these error conditions. We can check whether the request is mangled or if too many files were provided, as follows:

```
if(!isset($uploadedFileError) || is_array($uploadedFileError)) {
    throw new RuntimeException("Invalid arguments");
}
```

In PHP, all the file uploads will have an error condition set, *even if the file has been uploaded successfully*. We can check whether this is present to verify that someone isn't trying to send us a mangled or corrupt request. If an error condition isn't present, we can stop processing immediately. If there is more than one error condition (it's an array), then we will know that more than one file was sent our way; we can also complain.

Next, we check the error condition itself. It will tell us whether the file is uploaded correctly, if no file was sent, or if the file was larger than the server settings permit:

```
switch ($uploadedFileError) {
    case UPLOAD_ERR_OK:
        break;
    case UPLOAD_ERR_NO_FILE:
        throw new RuntimeException("No file sent");
        break;
    case UPLOAD_ERR_INI_SIZE:
    case UPLOAD_ERR_FORM_SIZE:
        throw new RuntimeException("File too large");
        break;
```

```
        default:
            throw new RuntimeException("Unknown error");
    }
```

Note that we throw `RuntimeException` in every `case`, except when the error is `UPLOAD_ERR_OK`. The latter case means that the server received the file correctly, and we can proceed with the processing. For any other case, we should immediately stop and complain.

Just because we've checked the file's size against the server settings, it doesn't mean that it isn't larger than the size we really want to accept. This snippet will check the size of the uploaded file against our `$maximumFileSize`:

```
    if ($uploadedFileSize > $maximumFileSize) {
        throw new RuntimeException("File too large");
    }
```

Unless you're running a server that can accept every kind of file type, chances are good you'll want to check the file type. We could just check `$uploadedFileType`, but the client sends us this information, which means that it could be inaccurate or incorrect. Instead, we should also check the file type based on what the filesystem tells us. This snippet does just that:

```
    $finfo = finfo_open(FILEINFO_MIME_TYPE);
    $actualFileType = finfo_file($finfo, $uploadedFilePath);

    if (!in_array($uploadedFileType, $validMimeTypes) ||
        !in_array($actualFileType, $validMimeTypes)) {
        throw new RuntimeException("File format isn't valid");
    }
```

The preceding snippet will check whether the file type specified by the client and the file type that the server believes the file to be are in the `$validMimeTypes` list. If it isn't, the script will complain and refuse to save the file.

This satisfies most of the error conditions mentioned earlier. Now, it's time to save the file to the desired upload location. But first, we should rename the file so that it is uniquely named, or we might overwrite a file someone else uploaded:

```
    $newFileName = "upload_" .uniqid();
```

uniqid is a function in PHP that returns a string based on the current time. This means that the name could actually be non-unique; but it's sufficient for our purposes here, assuming that the time on the server is never changed. You could use any renaming scheme you want, of course (for more information on the uniqueness of uniqid, see http://stackoverflow.com/questions/4070110/how-unique-is-uniqid).

Now that we have a unique filename, we can attempt to save the file:

```
if (move_uploaded_file($uploadedFilePath,
  $uploadLocation.$newFileName)) {
    echo "File uploaded successfully!";
} else {
    throw new RuntimeException("File failed to upload
      (".error_get_last().")");
}
```

Astute readers will notice that, technically, the server has already accepted the file if we've got to this point; it's just in a temporary location noted by $uploadedFilePath. move_uploaded_file is a PHP function that simply moves the file from the temporary location to a more permanent location.

If this move fails, we will throw another error along with the reason for the failure. At this point, it's probably something critical. Perhaps the server is out of space on the volume accepting uploads, or the location where we are trying to store the files doesn't exist.

If the move succeeds, however, we will return a success message. PHP will also return a 200 status code by default.

Just having the script doesn't do much good. You need a server that can run PHP scripts. That's a bit beyond the scope of this book, but if you want a very simple test environment to test PHP scripts, you can use Cloud9 (https://c9.io) that provides a complete development environment in the cloud that supports PHP. In fact, you can see this example at my public workspace (assuming you have a Cloud9 account) at https://ide.c9.io/kerrishotts/mastering-phonegap-ch8-server. Cloud9 isn't intended for an always-on server, but it's great for development purposes, especially when you can use it for free for public projects (up to one private project is also free).

Uploading files to a server

Now that we've got a script on a server that's waiting for us to upload content, we can use the File Transfer plugin to do just that. Instead of calling `download`, we'll be calling `upload`, as you might expect. This does require some options to be set, so it's not quite as simple as calling `download`.

`upload` accepts several parameters:

- `fileToUpload` indicates the file stored on the local device that you want to upload. Use the `cdvfile://` file path.
- `uploadURL` is the URL of your upload script. This should be passed through encodeURI.
- `uploadSuccess` will be called if the upload was successful.
- `uploadError` will be called if the upload didn't complete successfully.
- `options` specifies the file key, name, and mime type at a minimum. It can also supply parameters, headers, and other useful settings. This is an instance of `FileUploadOptions`.

 The snippets in this section are located at `snippets/09/ex2-uploading-files` in the code package of this book. When using the interactive snippet playground, select **9: Transferring Files** and example **2**.

Let's see an example:

```
function uploadError(err) {
    console.log(`Encountered an upload error:
        ${JSON.stringify(err, null, 2)}`);
}

function uploadSuccess(r) {
    console.log(`Upload completed successfully:
        ${JSON.stringify(r, null, 2)}`);
}

function doUpload() {
    let fileToUpload =
                    "cdvfile://localhost/persistent/index.html";
    let uploadURL = encodeURI(
                            "https://your.server.com/upload.php");

    let options = new FileUploadOptions();
    options.fileKey = "file";
```

```
options.fileName = "index.html";
options.mimeType = "text/html";

let fileTransfer = new FileTransfer();
fileTransfer.upload(fileToUpload, uploadURL, uploadSuccess,
                    uploadError, options);
}
```

The `options` we specify here are the minimum requirement. We have to specify the file key, the name of the file, and the file's type. The latter two are closer to suggestions: our script renames the file anyway (to ensure that there are no naming conflicts) and it doesn't assume that we are telling the truth with regard to the mime type either.

Notice that we specify the file for `options.fileKey`. This matches with the `name="file"` attribute on our imagined input element, and is what the PHP script uses to index `$_FILES`. If this is incorrect, the upload will fail.

If the upload encounters an error, `uploadError` will be called. It will have the same kind of structure as the error object passed to `downloadError`.

If the upload completes successfully, `uploadSuccess` is called with an object that includes data about the upload. You don't really have to do a lot with this; it just lets you inspect the response sent by the server. On Android, you can also inspect the number of bytes sent, but iOS doesn't support this feature, so you can't use it to determine whether the browser sent the number of bytes you were expecting.

You can specify other useful options:

- `httpMethod`: This changes the method used to upload the file. This is POST by default, but you can change it to PUT if you need to.

- `chunkedMode`: By default, the file is uploaded in chunks, which allows the native code to optimize how the files are transferred (especially large files). If you need to disable chunked uploading, set this to `false`.

- `headers`: You may need to send authentication information or other headers. You can do this by sending that information along in a `headers` object.

Here's a little more complicated example, using the earlier mentioned options:

```
let options = new FileUploadOptions();
options.fileKey = "file";
options.fileName = "index.html";
options.mimeType = "text/html";
options.chunckedMode = false;
options.httpMethod = "PUT";
```

```
options.headers = {
    "Authorization": `Basic ${btoa(`${username}:${password}`)}`
}

letfileTransfer = new FileTransfer();
fileTransfer.upload(fileToUpload, uploadURL, uploadSuccess,
                    uploadError, options);
```

> Technically, upload supports trustAllHosts as the sixth parameter. It operates the same way as trustAllHosts for downloading, but you should avoid setting it to true unless you really must accept self-signed certificates. You should never do such a thing in the production code.

Monitoring progress

As long as you're downloading or uploading small files, it's unlikely that the user will actually notice the length of time it takes to perform the operation. But once you transfer even moderately sized files, the time the operation takes will begin to be noticeable. As such, you're going to need a way to communicate the progress to the user.

How you do this is entirely up to you. You could just display a spinner or you could display a progress bar of some sort. But before any of these, we will have to listen for progress updates from our operation.

> The snippets in this section are located at snippets/09/ex3-progress in the code package of this book. When using the interactive snippet playground, select **9: Transferring Files** and example **3**.

Registering to receive progress updates is pretty simple. Once we've created an instance of FileTransfer, we can assign a handler to the onprogress property, as follows:

```
function reportProgress(progressEvent) {
  // we'll be adding to this function below.
}

let fileTransfer = new FileTransfer();
fileTransfer.onprogress = reportProgress;
```

The `progressEvent` that `reportProgress` will receive has a few useful properties:

- `lengthComputable`: If `true`, it's possible to compute the length of the operation. Not all servers return the size of a download, so this isn't always available.
- `total`: If the length can be computed, this is the total size of the operation.
- `loaded`: The amount of data that has been downloaded (or uploaded).

If `lengthComputable` is true, then it's possible to determine the percentage the operation is complete by dividing `loaded` by `total`:

```
let pctComplete;
if (progressEvent.lengthComputable) {
    pctComplete = progressEvent.loaded / progressEvent.total;
}
```

 At this point, `pctComplete` is a number between 0 and 1. If you want it in the typical range (0-100), you can multiply by 100.

Let's imagine that we have a `progress` element in the DOM that would render a progress bar on modern devices. We could update it as follows:

```
if (progressEvent.lengthComputable) {
    document.getElementById("progressBar").setAttribute("value",
        (progressEvent.loaded / progressEvent.total));
}
```

If the operation's percent complete can't be computed, it's up to you to decide what to do. You could display an indeterminate progress bar (although iOS 7 doesn't support indeterminacy on the `progress` elements). You could display additional information showing the user how much data has been downloaded; although this may or may not give them much information, since they are unlikely to know how much data should be transferred either. In short, the goal is to give them some certainty that the operation is proceeding, even if one doesn't know how long it will take. You could slowly increment a progress bar over time (this is often what web browsers will do while waiting for a server response) or display comforting messages, like "Hang on — we're still downloading data".

You are not guaranteed to ever receive a single progress update, however, so don't build any critical logic around it. If the file was already in the browser's cache or transferred very quickly, or if an error occurred, there may not be any time for progress events to be sent.

Aborting transfers

Users should always be able to terminate file transfers if at all possible, even if you don't expect that the transfer will take very long. You don't know their network conditions, and as such, it's possible that even a short file might take far longer than anyone would expect (especially if network conditions are very poor). That said, you don't have to offer an option immediately; you might want to wait a few seconds to give the transfer time to complete before offering the user a method for aborting the operation just to ensure they don't accidentally press whatever button they see appearing on their screen.

Aborting a transfer is easy: there's an `abort` method on any instance of `FileTransfer` that will stop the operation and call the error handler. The error code will always be `FileTransferError.ABORT_ERR`, so your error handler can properly notify the rest of your app about the termination.

 The snippets in this section are located at `snippets/09/ex4-abort` in the code package of this book. When using the interactive snippet playground, select **9: Transferring Files** and example **4**.

Here's an example. In this case, we have `<button id="cancelDownload">` in the DOM. When it is clicked, the transfer is aborted:

```
function go() {
    let assetURL = "https://github.com/kerrishotts/
Mastering-PhoneGap-Code-Package/zipball/master";
    let downloadLocation =
                    "cdvfile://localhost/temporary/index.zip";

    let fileTransfer = new FileTransfer();

    document.getElementById("cancelDownload")
            .addEventListener("click", () => {
                fileTransfer.abort();
            });
    fileTransfer.download(assetURL, downloadLocation,
                    downloadSuccess, downloadError);
}
```

Security concerns

Now that we've covered file transfers, it's important to go over some important security concerns, since your app is no longer a silo disconnected from the rest of the Internet.

- Your app shouldn't automatically trust the content that it receives from the server. The server could be compromised, or a man-in-the-middle attack might potentially modify the content.

- Your server definitely shouldn't automatically trust the content it receives from your app (or anywhere else). Your best bet is to scan every uploaded file using a virus scanner; but this is, of course, not an absolute guarantee.

- If at all possible, you should favor SSL connections (HTTPS) rather than unencrypted communication.

- While using SSL connections, self-signed certificates and certificates that are signed by a certificate authority that the device doesn't trust will be rejected. Rather than setting `trustAllHosts` to `true`, endeavor to provide trusted certificates on the servers you control.

- If you're sending authentication information, *always* use SSL.

- If you're going to display any data downloaded from a server, be sure to do so in a way that isn't vulnerable to injection attacks. Either escape the data so that dangerous HTML and JavaScript can't be supplied, or use `textContent` (instead of `innerHTML` or its variants). Note that `textContent` does *not* parse HTML, so if the content itself is HTML, you'll need to escape it instead, otherwise the user will just see the HTML source (not the desired output).

Summary

In this chapter, you learned how to download files from your server. You also saw how you can upload them using PHP scripts on the server. We discussed some security concerns with regard to trusting content downloaded from or uploaded to servers.

In the next chapter, we'll discuss the various performance issues your app might encounter, and how you can resolve these issues so that your users have a fantastic experience with your app.

10
Performance

While developing our application, it's often easy to overlook the performance of the application on a physical device for several reasons. One may be testing a lot of functionality in a desktop browser such as Google Chrome or Safari, especially while making quick iterations. For plugin testing, the developer may elect to use an emulator most of the time, especially if they need to quickly test across multiple platforms. As useful as this strategy is, it fails in one key area: it tells us nothing about the performance of our app on a real device.

In this chapter, we'll cover the following topics:

- Defining performance
- The performance difference between desktops, emulators, and physical devices
- Profiling your app
- Correcting input lag
- Correcting visual stutters
- Correcting memory problems
- Splitting up and delegating long computations

Getting started

This chapter assumes that you have a physical device on which you can test your app's performance. We also assume that you can connect this device to your development machine and debug the app remotely using Google Chrome (for Android) or Safari (for iOS).

If you haven't configured your device and development machine for remote debugging, the following articles should be of use:

- `https://blog.idrsolutions.com/2015/02/remote-debugging-ios-safari-on-os-x-windows-and-linux/`

- `https://developer.chrome.com/devtools/docs/remote-debugging`

Defining performance

Although it might seem obvious at first glance just *what* performance is, it's actually a pretty vague word that carries a lot of connotations. For example, does one mean speed when using the word? Do they mean frames per second? Or are they referring to memory use?

Because the word itself can be ambiguous, let's establish some terms and definitions:

- **Graphical performance**: The length of time taken to composite the elements in the DOM, send them to the GPU, and render them on the screen.

- **Computing performance**: The length of time a method takes to complete its task.

- **Frames per second**: This is related to both graphical and computing performance. This is the number of screen renders we can perform per second. Ideally, apps should target sixty frames per second.

- **Input performance**: The length of time from an input (such as a touch) to a visual confirmation that the action was understood. This does not imply that the action is complete, just that the device recognized the input.

- **Memory utilization**: The amount of memory consumed by the application. This is measured over a period of time to get a good feel of how much memory the app uses over a typical session.

- **Storage performance**: The length of time it takes to read and/or write data to the device's persistent storage.

- **Storage utilization**: The amount of data stored persistently by the application.

The performance difference between desktop browsers, emulators, and physical devices

Although we are building a mobile application, it is common to run our app in a desktop browser or an emulator, especially while rapidly iterating on the code. Unless there is functionality that directly requires a physical device (the accelerometer for example), a lot of development work can be done well before the app ever sees a physical device.

While developing in this manner saves enormous time up front, it does mean that performance problems could often be overlooked until it is too late. Thus, it's a good idea to periodically run your app on physical devices that represent your target market in order to ensure that the performance remains acceptable.

Let's go over the typical differences you'll encounter between desktop browsers and emulators and physical devices.

Desktop browser performance differences

Although mobile devices are increasing in computing and graphical performance, most development machines will easily outperform even a flagship mobile device in most tasks. There are several reasons for this, but they boil down to the power consumption of the components, the size of the components, heat dissipation, and cost. All of these tend to fight with each other; for example, one can find GPUs that are extremely fast, but they will cost more than their slower cousins and will tend to require more power and dissipate more heat.

Power availability and consumption

Desktops are much less constrained when it comes to power availability and consumption than mobile devices. Laptops fall somewhere in between, since they operate using a battery (like a mobile device), but these batteries can also deliver more power than a mobile device (more like a desktop, but not to quite the same degree). As such, desktop class CPUs and GPUs can draw significant amounts of power when under heavy load, whereas mobile devices don't have the same luxury: they are limited by both the size and output of their small batteries. Heat dissipation also becomes problematic. In desktops and laptops, there are typically one or more fans that kick in when the internal temperature becomes too high, and there is usually more room between the various internal components for air to move more efficiently. If the internal cooling can't fully compensate, the CPU or GPU will throttle their performance to avoid burning themselves up. This latter fact is true for mobile devices as well, but mobile devices don't have fans that can dissipate internal heat. They rely on heatsinks and the ability of the outer casing to radiate heat outside, but this is obviously far less efficient than using fans. Furthermore, if a device is too hot to touch, it severely restricts the user's ability to interact with it.

All of this means that desktop class devices can operate at faster speeds and higher power consumption for a considerably longer duration than a mobile device. This has tremendous impact upon computationally heavy and graphically heavy applications, because the desktop may be able to perform as expected, but the mobile device may simply be too taxed to deliver. It's a good idea to remember that your development machine is likely to be at least an order of magnitude *faster* than even a recent mobile device, if not more.

Battery life

Along with power consumption comes battery life as well. A desktop, of course, doesn't have to worry about battery consumption very much, because it's connected to your mains (of course, a power outage will take your desktop with it). Thus, it may not be immediately obvious that we may need to enable our app to change its behavior on the basis of the available battery life remaining. If you use a laptop for development, of course, this will tend to be a bit more obvious, because you already have to manage the battery during development. But most laptops have considerably larger batteries and different discharge patterns than a mobile device. Thus, it's still worth thinking about how your app both drains the battery and behaves in low power situations.

Browser impacts

Because of all the earlier mentioned factors, desktop *browsers* are also orders of magnitude faster than their mobile counterparts. And, because Cordova apps are hybrid apps that utilize the system's web view, the same applies to our apps. Thus, what might take 5 ms to compute on a desktop might take 50 ms on a mobile device. What might take a few milliseconds to draw on screen using a powerful desktop GPU might take longer using a mobile device.

Memory

Along with the earlier mentioned factors, desktops usually have much more available memory. It isn't unusual for a development machine to have between 8 and 32 gigabytes of RAM (or more!), while a mobile device might have between 1 and 4 gigabytes of RAM (and older devices have even less). This means that mobile devices must be much stricter with regard to allowing tasks to consume memory (especially in the background), and are more apt to jettison apps in the background whenever the memory is low. This becomes a potential issue for hybrid apps, because the web view itself requires a large amount of memory just to generate the contents of the DOM on the screen. On a desktop with lots of memory, this often goes unnoticed; but on a mobile device, rendering a complicated layout may get your app terminated by the mobile operating system.

Storage

Storage is also often very different. A desktop or laptop is likely to have anywhere from 256 gigabytes to several terabytes of available storage, while mobile devices usually top out at 128 gigabytes of persistent storage. Of course, most devices that your app finds itself running on will actually contain even less storage and may have very little (or no) storage available for the app. In short, our hybrid apps need to properly handle low or no available storage without just crashing outright.

Storage read/write speeds can also vary widely. Your development machine might have a very speedy solid state drive that operates very quickly, or it might have a spinning drive that is relatively slow. A mobile device has solid state storage, but the speeds at which it can operate are much slower than a solid state drive you'd install in your desktop machine. This isn't a big deal while working with small files, but it can definitely present a problem while reading or writing very large files.

Lag

There's another area that we need to cover, and it's related to the delay between input (say, from your mouse) and the output on the screen. This depends on the potential performance the device can offer and what it is doing; but there is always some minimal amount of processing that must go on. This is called *lag*, and it needs to be kept to an absolute minimum to remain unnoticed by users.

When we interact with the physical world, there's very little lag. Even so, although it feels to our brains as if an action and the recognition of that action occur simultaneously, there is actually a small amount of lag from the time you generate an action impulse to the moment the your brain recognizes the consequences of that impulse visually. The fact that our actions and the physical responses feel immediate is because our brain uses a buffer of sorts. If the events arrive within a short time frame, they are considered to be simultaneous. If they arrive outside of that time frame, the events are no longer simultaneous.

You can see this effect while watching a video of a person who is talking. Usually, a video is edited such that the audio appears to be synchronized. But occasionally, one will encounter a video where the audio is *not* properly synchronized, and the effect is, at best, disturbing, and at worst, so annoying that the viewer will stop watching. However, if you look at the actual video frames and audio, you'd likely notice that it can be very difficult to perfectly synchronize audio and video (especially when the audio and video are coming from different sources). Because of the buffer in our brains, we can tolerate a small degree of misalignment, say, +/-20 ms; although this can vary widely. For some, a delay of 100 ms and more won't cause any issues.

This has tremendous implications while interacting with our devices. Imagine yourself moving a mouse pointer on your computer's screen. There are several processes that are occurring that all take finite time to complete. Your brain has to decide where the mouse pointer should go, compute the appropriate muscle commands, and send these commands to the muscles. At this point, the computer receives a notification that the mouse has been moved, computes where the pointer should end up (based upon position difference and acceleration), composites the screen with the new location of the mouse pointer, and sends that off to the GPU for rendering. Your brain then processes the screen, and makes additional movements and adjustments based on what just occurred. It's one big feedback loop; as long as it all occurs within a few milliseconds, it will feel simultaneous. But if the process takes too long (say more than 50 ms), people are bound to notice.

If you've ever mirrored your display to a television or other remote device, you've likely experienced the preceding phenomenon. Alternatively, if you've logged into a remote machine over a poor network connection, you've probably also experienced this. The delay between your input and the final output is increased from the norm due to the additional latency involved in transmitting the information across the air or a poor network connection. Thus, one starts to feel disconnected from the output, and it becomes difficult to anticipate the results of our actions. It's most obvious when you introduce a delay in mouse movement. Our brains will tend to overcompensate and miss the mark, and this is extremely frustrating. We can adapt to the delay eventually, of course, but it's far from ideal.

I say all this for the following reason: the delay between input and output on a desktop is *different* than the delay on a mobile device; if the response time is *too* high, users are going to get frustrated. Users will put up with a long-running computation as long as they have a progress indicator, but users don't appreciate a user interface that lags dramatically behind their touches. Just as a lagging mouse pointer is a problem, scrolling that doesn't match the user's finger is similarly problematic. Clicking a mouse button gives us pretty immediate feedback that yes, we actually *clicked* the button (even if the computer is slow in recognizing it), but a mobile device responds to touch without that intermediate physical click. If the device is slow to respond, users will often repeat their actions, thinking that they didn't press hard enough or that the device didn't register their touch. If one isn't aware of this, individuals can inadvertently trigger unwanted actions that could even result in data loss.

It is important to recognize that you can't eliminate all the lag between input and output, but you can attempt to minimize it. Even with your minimization, you'll find it difficult to generate responses any faster than 33 ms (two screen frames at 60 fps). If you find that your app is lagging more than 50 to 100 ms, your app is definitely going to cause frustration for your users.

This lag doesn't have to mean that the operation the user is initiating must also be complete within a short time frame. All that's important is that the device lets the user know that "yes, I heard you" as quickly as possible. A user isn't going to expect a video to encode in a few milliseconds, but they do expect that the user interface will do *something* in that time frame so that they know their touch was understood.

Because the lag on a desktop or laptop is *different* than the lag on a mobile device, one shouldn't trust that just because things occur immediately on a desktop, the same is true on a mobile device. A mouse click often feels pretty immediate on a desktop, but if we used the same JavaScript event in our code, our app would feel very slow, because it often has to wait about 300 ms to be sure there isn't a double-click coming. Desktops have to wait for a double-click as well, but the delay is *much* shorter, so it will feel much more immediate.

There's one last thing I need to mention: obviously, desktop browsers, although related to their mobile cousins, are *not* the same. They are optimized for desktop class CPUs, support different operating systems, and support different feature sets. Generally, they are updated with much more frequency than their mobile counterpart (although this is changing on Android). Thus, just because your app works on a desktop browser, it does *not* mean it will work on a mobile browser. The absolute best way to test your app is always on the physical device, but if you want to verify that your HTML, JavaScript, and CSS code works on the mobile device, you can also fire up the emulator.

Emulator performance differences

As a developer, you'll typically use emulators fairly often during your app's development and testing. Although these emulators are technically at the desktop level, they have their own share of quirks that make judging performance difficult.

First, a reminder: there is no iOS *emulator*, only an iOS *simulator*. This is key, because there is a pretty big difference between a simulator and an emulator. In practice, this means that the iOS simulator tends to be much faster than a physical device, whereas an Android emulator may be slower or faster depending on the architecture being used for emulation.

iOS devices use the ARM architecture, so when the apps are compiled, the native portion of the code will be converted into instructions that the ARM CPUs can recognize. Development machines, on the other hand, are mostly x86-based machines (Intel/AMD), and can't natively understand these instructions. There are two ways to deal with this: either recompile the app into x86 code or emulate the ARM CPU.

Of course, there are a lot of support frameworks and libraries that need to be present for an app to run. That's largely where the difference between an iOS simulator and an Android emulator lies. Android has, for a while now, been able to target both ARM and x86 architectures (in fact, there are a few Android devices with x86 CPUs). Thus, there's no real fundamental difference between what the simulator and the emulator is doing at this level.

The real difference between the iOS simulator and the Android emulators is that the iOS simulator runs your app as a native Mac OS X application, whereas an Android emulator will run your app within a completely virtualized environment. This doesn't usually make *too* much of a difference, but it can change how you access resources such as the network or storage. For example, while using the iOS Simulator, `localhost` refers to your development machine just like it would in any other process. While using the Android emulator, `localhost` refers instead to the virtualized device. You can ignore the difference by simply referring to your machine's actual IP address on the network (or the hostname). But it illustrates the difference: the iOS app being simulated runs alongside all your other processes, while the Android app runs inside a virtualized container.

So what does this mean in terms of our app's performance? Well, it boils down to this: don't trust your emulator. Not because it's trying to deceive you, but because it can't accurately replicate the performance profile of a physical device. Here's a few of the things that are different:

- Graphical performance is usually reduced, often greatly. This has been improved in more modern Android emulators that can access the host GPU. But neither the iOS simulator, nor the Android emulator, accurately reflects the physical device's GPU performance. From my experience, you might achieve approximately 80% performance, but you're not bound to see perfectly fluid interfaces running at 60 fps all the time.

- Computation performance can vary widely. If running on the x86 architecture like the iOS simulator does and some Android emulators can do, then performance will most likely exceed that of the physical device, because it is running at the same speed (or slightly slower) as that of your desktop's CPU. If your CPU is emulating the ARM architecture, on the other hand, expect the performance to be dismal and much slower than the physical device.

- Available memory can vary widely, as follows:
  - While simulating an iOS app, the app actually has access to all the available memory on your development machine, which almost certainly guarantees it will never be low on memory. Furthermore, your development machine has an operating system that supports swap files; thus, it can devote all the remaining space on persistent storage to your app's memory needs as well. There's a utility in the iOS simulator to *simulate* a low memory condition, but that's it.

- When you create an Android Virtual Device or use a GenyMotion device, a certain amount of memory is provided to the virtual device. This more closely matches the physical devices, since the Android operating system, the web view, and your web code must coexist within a more limited confine. Unfortunately, these emulators don't reflect real-world device usages (usually, other apps are in memory alongside your own), so it's not a perfect substitute.

- Available storage can vary widely, but the same caveats apply with respect to the read/write speed of the storage as in the prior section:
    - Again, while simulating an iOS app, the app has the same access to your persistent storage as any other app on the device. This means that the iOS app could fill up your hard drive, although it shouldn't be able to escape the sandbox provided by Mac OS X, so it can't hurt any of your other files. This means that given most development machine specifications, your app isn't likely to encounter a low or no space situation.

    - Android devices are also provided virtualized persistent storage with a maximum size. This more accurately reflects what happens on a physical device; but again, it's not entirely representative of the real world. Most users stuff their devices with apps, reducing the available storage for your own, whereas the emulator is apt to be quite Spartan.

- Lag can also be a big issue, mainly as a side effect of the computational and graphics performance of the emulator, but also because one is often using a mouse in place of touch gestures This already destroys any resemblance to the actual feel of the app on a real device; but it also means that you're subject not only to the lag that's built in to the development machine's OS, but also to that of the simulator or emulator. Add slower graphical performance, and the lag will not be so great. In short, if the lag is bad on an emulator, don't panic. Test it on a physical device before you panic!

- Although it is not directly associated with performance, it is also important to note that emulators do not always provide the same functionality as a physical device. GPS support may be emulated, but it's not the same as a physical device's GPS reporting capabilities. If you were developing a game that uses an accelerometer, you're almost certainly out of luck on anything other than a physical device, not just because the accelerometer isn't supported on the emulator, but because of the other performance and lag differences.

So, what's the point of the emulator? Well, it lets us verify that our hybrid app works with the system web view that we're targeting. It lets us test a lot of plugins as well, which isn't possible on a desktop browser. But don't forget, the emulator is never a replacement for the real thing.

Profiling your app

Now that we've hopefully convinced you to verify performance on physical devices, how does one identify that performance is becoming a problem? There are a couple ways:

- Physical testing involves an actual interaction with your app on the device. As you test your app, you may encounter visual stutters, delays, lags, or worse. It's also important to test on as many different classes of devices as possible, since each kind and model often have very different performances. This can quickly become expensive, but this can be mediated to some degree with a large beta test with lots of human testers.

- Profiling looks at several different metrics to identify where potential problems may be. Memory is the most obvious metric; you can record your app's memory utilization during your interactions in order to identify any potential memory issues. You can determine long-running processes in your app that may be causing visual stutters as well. Profiling inevitably introduces its own performance impact (always slower), so don't rely on profiling as the sole measure of performance. Unplug your device from your development machine and use your app without any debuggers attached in order to get a true feeling for the actual feel of your app.

The first method is pretty self-explanatory: pick up your device and play with your app. Make sure the app is disconnected from your debugger, since the debugger can negatively impact your app's performance. If you notice any stuttering, lag, or delays, you know you have a problem. At these points, you can diagnose the problems using the second method: profiling.

Profiling depends upon platform-specific tools. For Android, you'll be able to profile your app using Google Chrome's remote web inspector tool. For iOS, you'll need to use a recent version of the Safari browser for mobile debugging, and you'll also need to use Instruments to check the memory usage.

Profiling on Android

Assuming your device or emulator has Android 4.4 or higher, profiling your app is pretty simple. Assuming you have configured your device for remote debugging, your app is installed and running, and your device is connected to your development machine, you should be able to navigate to `chrome://inspect` in Chrome and see your device and app listed.

Once you click on the device and app you want to debug, you should see the familiar Web Inspector tool that Google Chrome allows you to use to debug and inspect regular web pages. In the inspector, there should be a **Timeline** tab that you can click on. Initially, this will be blank; but you can tap the **Record** icon in the upper-left corner and Google Chrome will begin recording your application's memory use, CPU utilization, frames per second, and more. Once you're done interacting with your app, click on the **Stop** icon to finish recording.

A sample profiling looks similar to that shown in the following screenshot:

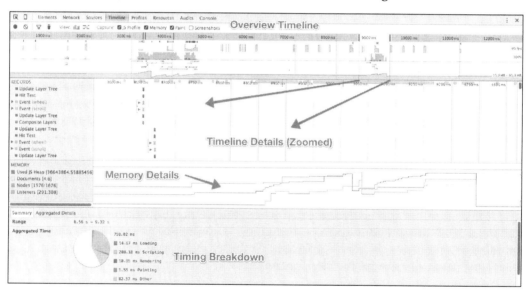

There are many different sections, and you can resize most of them depending upon what you are interested in. The following toolbar the tabs allows you to change the data visualization. The preceding screenshot is a highly compressed timeline of your app's performance, both graphically and computationally, and your app's memory usage. You can select a portion of this timeline to view more details, which are displayed in the **Timeline Details** section. Below this is the same selected period's memory utilization broken down into a few different categories. At the bottom of this screenshot is a pie chart that represents the portion of the selected time that was spent rendering, painting, executing scripts, and so on.

This particular view is especially useful to track memory utilization. Notice the blue graph on the timeline? That's a compressed representation of the app's memory allocations. The **Memory Details** section gives a close-up of the selected area in the timeline. The key indicates which line colors represent which categories; of great importance is **Used JS Heap**, which represents the total memory allocated. Also useful are **Nodes** and **Listeners** that represent the number of nodes in the document and the number of event listeners, respectively.

If you switch views (by clicking on the icon directly to the right of **View** in the toolbar), you should see something that looks like this:

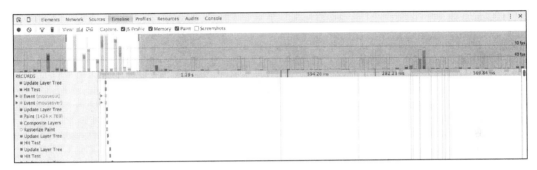

In this screenshot, the graph at the top is still a timeline of your app, but it represents the time it took your device to draw each frame. This is useful because it indicates where our app took time to cause visual stutters as it couldn't generate a frame fast enough. In the bottom section of the screenshot, you can see details expanded to show which portions of your code are taking a long time to execute.

Profiling on iOS

Unfortunately, Safari's Inspector tools aren't quite as advanced as Chrome's; thus, it is necessary to use two tools. We can profile frames per second using version 9 or higher of Safari. To profile your app's memory, you'll need to use Xcode's Instruments tool.

First, if you've configured your device for remote debugging and have your app installed and running on your device, you should be able to plug your device into your development machine. Then, you need to start Safari and navigate to **Develop | Your Device | Your App** to open Safari's inspector.

You should see a **Web Inspector** window. At the top, below the toolbar, there should be a list of tabs. Click on **Timelines** and then click on **Rendering Frames**. You should see something similar to the following image, although devoid of data:

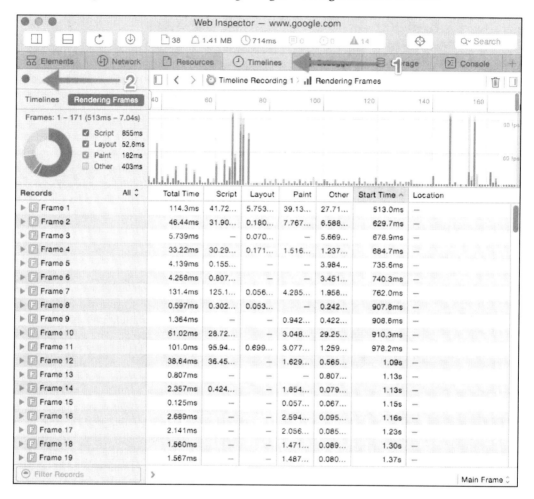

To start recording your device's performance, click on the **Record** icon as indicated by **2**, and then interact with your device. When you're done interacting with your app, click on the icon again; the inspector will populate with a lot of useful information.

At the top is a timeline that represents the graphical performance of your app; for example, how long it took to draw each frame. This is useful when we want to avoid visual stuttering. You can select a range of frames, or even a single frame, and then drill down into each to see the time that was taken.

To profile your app's memory, however, Safari has to be abandoned in favor of Xcode's Instruments tool. Furthermore, the two cannot be profiling the same app; thus, you'll need to close Safari's Inspector before launching Instruments.

Although you can profile a running app's memory usage, it's wise to get memory consumption trends from the very start of the app. To do this, you'll need to restart your app; but you don't need to do this manually—Instruments can launch it for you.

To launch Instruments, you can perform either of the following steps:

1. Open Xcode and then navigate to **Xcode | Open Developer Tool... | Instruments**
2. Search `Instruments` using Spotlight

Either method works fine. You should be presented with a dialog like the one shown in the following screenshot:

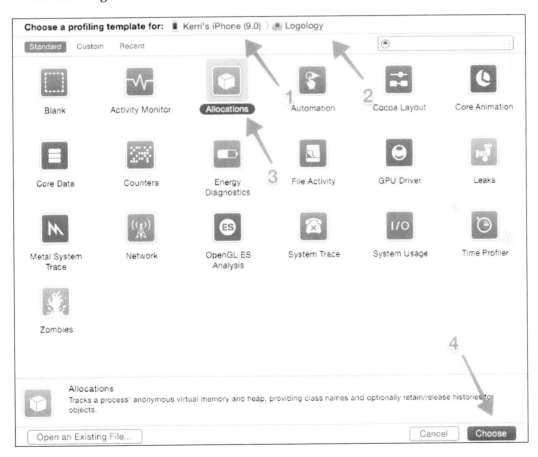

The first thing you'll want to do is select your device. If you're lucky, it will be already selected. If not, click on **1** to reveal the available devices. Then, you need to select the app to be profiled; click on **2** to reveal the installed and running apps. You'll want to pick an installed app so that we can capture the memory utilization as the app initializes.

Next, select what you want to profile. You'll probably want to use **Allocations (3)**, but the other options are also very useful. Once you've chosen, click on **Choose** and you should be presented with something similar to what is shown in the following screenshot:

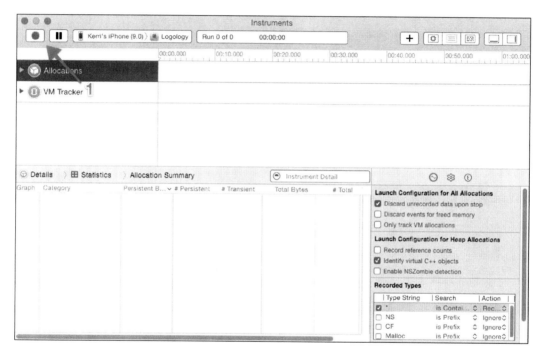

At the moment, the view doesn't look very populated, but that's just because Instruments is waiting for you to start profiling. Click on the **Record** icon and interact with your app. Click on the **Stop** icon when you are done interacting with the app. You should see something similar to what is shown in the following screenshot:

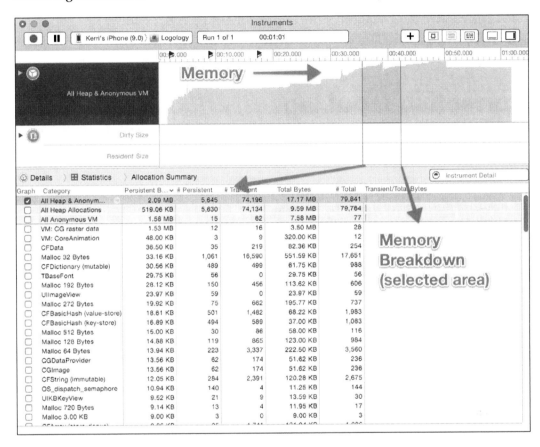

As you can see, this profile run is focused solely on memory utilization. You can select a range within the timeline. The details are presented in the area below the timeline.

Caveats

There's one important detail you need to be aware of: Click profiling reduces your app's performance, which means it is something of a catch-22. In short, if you don't see any stuttering during normal usage of your app, but you *do* during profiling, don't fret: the profiler is getting in the way. If you're checking for memory problems, don't assume that the graphical performance you see is representative. The only *true* representation of how your app runs graphically is when your device is untethered from your development machine.

Correcting input lag

As should be obvious, we can't eliminate *all* of the input lag. There's always going to be some present. What we *can* eliminate are those frustrating times when it doesn't immediately appear as if the device has understood our intent.

Because mobile devices rely on touch and generally have pretty small screens, gestures are the primary input mechanism. Also, because we like to do a lot of things with the data on the screen, apps tend to recognize several gestures. Tapping is the obvious gesture, but while browsing a web page, the double-tap-to-zoom gesture is also often used. Because our hybrid app lives within a web view, it inherits the same double-tap-to-zoom gesture, which is often problematic. How many apps have you seen that let you zoom in on their user interface elements? Not many, if any at all.

This double-tap-to-zoom gesture comes with a problem: at first, it appears no different than a single tap on the screen. This means that the web view has to wait some additional amount of time before determining whether or not a second tap occurred quickly enough to count it as a double tap. For most web views, this is 300 ms, or almost a third of a second. Until this time is up, the single tap event can't be sent. This leads to enormous input lag.

More recent versions of Android have recognized this problem and have provided various attributes that you can use so that this delay isn't required. iOS, on the other hand, does not provide any way to disable the gesture completely, as of this writing. Instead, we have to work around it.

Android and iOS web views generate both *mouse* and *touch* events. The mouse events are present for compatibility with the existing web pages that may not be touch-aware. These include the `click` event that has a delay of 300 ms. Touch events, however, avoid the problem entirely, because they are more akin to `mouseup`/`mousedown` than they are to `click`, so they can fire immediately. One way to avoid the `click` 300 ms delay is to simply use `touchend` events instead, except that `touchend` really isn't `click`. All sorts of quirks can arise, which make it far simpler to involve a support library that abstracts all the pain away. That's the tact we'll take in this section.

If your app relies on a lot of `click` events, then the easiest way to fix the problem is to include the `FastClick` library (`https://github.com/ftlabs/fastclick`). It's been deployed in quite a number of hybrid apps and works on a large number of platforms. It listens to the touch events and generates a synthetic `click` event when your finger leaves the screen. It then suppresses the `click` event that the browser would normally generate. While it sounds pretty simple, the commented code comes in at 841 lines of code. Needless to say, things are rarely as simple as they may appear.

Personally, I take the route of avoiding `click` and building the app to respond to gestures. So, instead of `click` (that is a mouse event), my code listens for gestures like `tap` and `swipe`. There are many different libraries that provide this gesture support, but my personal favorite is Hammer.js (`https://github.com/hammerjs/hammer.js`). It's not as easy to set up as the `FastClick` library is, but it provides support for more gestures than just a tap. For flexibility, one trades off simplicity.

If your app doesn't need gesture support beyond a single tap, then `FastClick` is probably your best and simplest bet. But if you need to respond to swipes, pinches, and more, you'll want to look at a gesture library.

The following is a list of useful gesture libraries:

- **Event.js** (`https://github.com/mudcube/Event.js`): This supports many different events, including taps, long presses, swipes, and more.

- **Hammerjs** (`https://github.com/hammerjs/hammer.js`): This supports different events, such as tap, long presses, and swipes.

- **Interact** (`https://github.com/taye/interact.js`): This supports drag and drop, resizing, and more, with inertia.

- **Zepto** (`http://zeptojs.com/#Touch%20events`): This is a lightweight jQuery replacement, but it has support for simple gestures, such as swipe and tap.

- **tap.js** (`https://github.com/alexgibson/tap.js`): This is similar to `FastClick`, but it uses a tap event instead of overriding `click`.

While all of this goes a long way in reducing the perceived lag, there's still more we can do. Typically, the earlier listed libraries are useful in responding to an event once it has finished, but what if an event is in progress? For example, apps don't usually wait to register that an onscreen button has been pressed until one lifts their finger; instead they usually display a depressed button (or some other state) while the finger is on the screen. This reduces the feeling of lag and increases the perception of performance, because now we can see the app responding directly to our touch, not just to the completion of a gesture.

The easiest way to do this is simply to use the various states that CSS already provides us, namely, the `:active` and `:focus` states. While `:hover` is supported by mobile web views, it has quirky behavior and is best avoided.

`:hover`, of course, has no real analog in a touch environment, because the device isn't capable of recognizing when your finger is actually hovering over the screen. So, the browser takes a different tact: one tap on an element will transition it to the `:hover` state, and then another tap will invoke a `click` event. Although I understand the reasoning, it's terribly frustrating when I encounter it on web pages, because it means that I have to start tapping everything twice. So please, don't use it in your apps!

The `:focus` state occurs when an element receives input focus. This is valid only for `input`, `textarea`, `select`, and other similar elements. By changing the visual state of the element, even subtly, the user can be assured that the app is focused on the appropriate element. This also has benefits if the user has paired a hardware keyboard, since they can then *Tab* through the elements like on a desktop browser.

The `:active` state occurs when the element receives a touch. This is probably the most critical state to implement, because it gives nearly immediate feedback to the user, *without any JavaScript code whatsoever*. This means that it also generates the least lag. You shouldn't try do to anything *too* fancy while changing to the `:active` state, because you don't want to force the browser to recalculate the positions of every element; but changing the text color (even subtly) is usually sufficient and extremely fast.

Correcting visual stutters

This particular issue is most obvious when you see visual stutters while scrolling or animations are playing. The stutters occur because the device can't perform all the necessary computations to render the screen fast enough to meet the target 60 fps. To reach this target, the device must execute *your* code, layout the DOM, composite various elements together, and send the result to the GPU within roughly 16 ms. If it sounds like a really short time, that's because it is. For a computer, of course, this is a reasonable amount of time. But while dealing with computing the locations and sizes of DOM elements that are relative to each other, compositing transparent and translucent elements on top of one another, and then pushing all the data across to the GPU, these milliseconds quickly disappear.

If you are seeing this particular issue, the profiling tools we've already mentioned should help point out where the potential issues are lurking. This is because the profilers record how long it takes to generate each frame. Consider the following example:

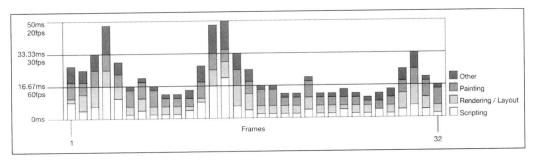

This graph is a representative of what you can see on both Google Chrome and Safari. The height of each bar indicates how long the frame took to render, and the various segments indicate where the time was spent.

As you can see in the preceding graph, our app only achieves 60 fps when the height of the bar is below the **60fps** line. Both Google Chrome and Safari will indicate the 60fps line. They will also show a **30fps** line if necessary.

Once our frames start taking longer than 16.67 ms, we can't sustain 60 fps. If we're slower than 33.33 ms, we can't sustain 30 fps. If this occurs infrequently, it's not such a big deal, because you're never in *total* control of the device (the operating system might be performing an install, the browser might be collecting garbage, and so on). But if it's consistent, it will be obvious in the form of visual stuttering.

Reaching 60 fps

So, how do you tame the frames-per-second beast? Here are some suggestions:

- Keep the DOM simple. If an element doesn't need to belong in the DOM, don't add it.

- Avoid deeply nested elements in the DOM. Changes made to the child elements will invariably force the parent elements to recalculate their position and size, which can be a costly computation.

- Avoid long lists of DOM elements. Scrolling through long lists can quickly become laggy and slow, so it's better to limit the number of elements that can be presented. You can use paging to accomplish this pretty simply or you can use a variation of infinite scrolling, which is closer to what native SDKs use. However, the latter is much more complicated. Some infinite scrolling libraries are, as follows:
    - **Infinity** (`http://airbnb.io/infinity/`)
    - **iScroll** (`http://iscrolljs.com`)

- Cache references to DOM elements. Typically, you will need to use some sort of CSS selector rule to locate the DOM elements you need. This can be expensive, especially if the DOM is nested to any degree. Looking up elements by ID is the fastest option, but you may not always have this option. So, instead of searching the DOM repeatedly when you don't need to, cache the results.

- Avoid unnecessary DOM reflow. This occurs whenever the browser needs to calculate the position, size, and styling of elements, usually in response to either a query for a specific property (such as `window.getComputedStyle(element).width`), or when various styles change (like `element.style.width="100%"`). Adding elements to nodes can also cause the DOM to reflow, which means that you should avoid using `parentElement.appendChild(element)` in a loop where `parentElement` is in the DOM (Use document fragments for this purpose.) A reflow also occurs while removing elements, so it is often faster to hide an element (`visibility: hidden`) in comparison to removing it, especially if you know you'll need the element in the future (as in the case of a sidebar menu).

- Keep your CSS pruned. The more complicated your CSS is, the more complicated it is to compute the various properties on your DOM elements. Remove unneeded rules and avoid complex selectors.

- Keep your CSS layouts simple. It's important to remember that the browser is actually solving some very complex equations in order to satisfy your layout requirements, and these can add up quickly. For example, Flexbox, while easy to use, is also difficult to compute. You can avoid some of the computations by positioning elements absolutely or using CSS transforms, but this can also remove the benefits of HTML and CSS: apps that are responsive to the viewport's size. If you position everything absolutely, it will be incumbent upon your own code to recalculate every element's position. Depending on the structure of your app, it might actually turn out to be more time-consuming than letting the browser handle this responsibility.

- Avoid *fancy* CSS styles. This includes all sorts of things, but it boils down to this: minimize the use of transparency, translucency, shadows, and gradients. This means that you should minimize the use of `box-shadow` and `opacity`, for example, but it also means that you should try to avoid overdoing `border-radius` (which requires translucency) as well. Images of gradients and shadows are more performant than the equivalent CSS styles. None of this is to say that you must *eliminate* these graphical flourishes completely, but that you should try to avoid overdoing it. If you find that some slower devices can't handle the flourishes, you might also want to add a setting that lets the user lower the graphical quality (or detect it automatically).

- Use CSS 3D transforms, but don't overdo it. These 3D transforms force the GPU to render the DOM elements affected, which can improve the performance. You have to be a bit careful here, because overusing it can have the reverse effect. It also uses a lot of memory. Furthermore, you should avoid nesting these transforms too deeply each time you use it. The GPU has to get involved, and those memory transfers are not free.

- Use CSS animations or `requestAnimationFrame` with the CSS transforms. Always avoid animating the typical positional styles (`top`, `left`, and so on) and animate using the CSS 3D transforms. You can use CSS animations when no user interaction is required during the animation, or you can use `requestAnimationFrame` to smoothly animate user interactions using CSS transforms.

- Reduce the number of event listeners attached to the DOM elements. Ideally, use event delegation (that our demo app has used from the start). When a user touches the screen, the DOM is required to determine all the elements that can respond to that particular touch. The more event handlers you have, the longer the list gets. Event delegation speeds up the process by reducing the number of event handlers, because only one handler needs to be added at the view's root level. These may still be nested (views within views, for example), but you will end up with far fewer than adding event handlers to every list item in a long list.

The following websites provide very useful performance information:

- Top 10 performance techniques for PhoneGap applications: (`http://coenraets.org/keypoint/phonegap-performance/`)

- Minimizing browser reflow: (`https://developers.google.com/speed/articles/reflow`)

- Performance and UX considerations for successful PhoneGap apps: (`http://www.tricedesigns.com/2013/03/11/performance-ux-considerations-for-successful-phonegap-apps/`)

Correcting memory problems

This one can be immediately obvious or an exceedingly insidious bug to track down. If your app is allocating lots of memory quickly and not releasing it back to the operating system, your app will find itself terminated in a hurry. On the other hand, a slow memory leak may not rear its head until your app's session is several hours or days old.

Profiling can help if you suspect a memory leak, but it's a good idea to profile your app anyway in order to determine whether it is just using too much memory in general. Not all memory problems are leaks, after all.

This said, what would a memory leak look like? Well, it would look like an ever-rising line in the profiler graph, as follows:

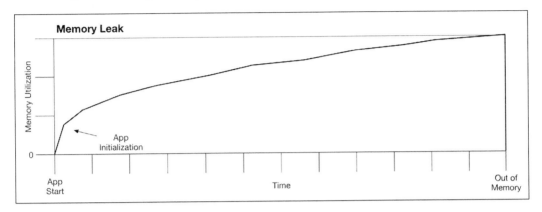

The time frame here is important; this is over a significant period of time, not just a couple of seconds. Due to the way the browser manages memory, there will always be some small period of time where you will see the graph continually rising. The catch is that, in this example, the memory is never released. So, the graph rises for minutes and perhaps longer, until the operating system terminates the app due to memory pressure.

So, what should the graph look like? It should look like a ragged saw tooth, as seen in the following image:

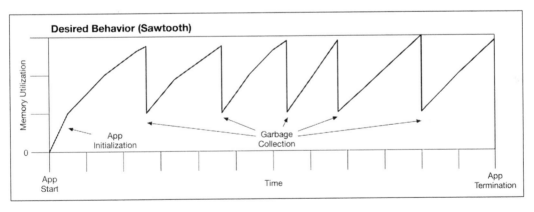

As you probably already know, the web view is a garbage-collected environment. Garbage collection occurs periodically during the app's lifetime and occurs simply to release memory back to the operating system when the memory is no longer needed. The catch here is that there's no mechanism to explicitly tell the garbage collector that an object is no longer needed; it just figures it out on its own. If the object has nothing else referencing it, the garbage collector feels free to release it back to the operating system. But if an object has even one reference, the collector will hold on to it.

Because of this fact, the best thing you can do to avoid holding on to objects unnecessarily is to null them out when you're done with them.

Closures also contribute to memory pressure. This occurs whenever a function inherits the lexical environment around it. For example, let's say we have the following code:

```
function a() {
  var anArray = [1,2,3];
  function b() {
    console.log(anArray);
  }
  b();
}
```

When b is called, you'd expect to see [1, 2, 3] logged to the console. While this makes sense, it also implies that b has a reference to the data stored by a. In JavaScript, especially with regards to event handling and asynchronous methods, it's easy to capture a large amount of data because we're often creating functions within functions. Each function gets access to its parent's lexical environment; this can add up in a hurry.

Normally, this isn't a *huge* deal, because the functions will just be deleted when the parent is no longer being referenced. However, this is more problematic when we start attaching event listeners to the DOM elements, because then the parent function and all its data can't be released until the DOM element is also removed and no longer referenced by anything else.

While dealing with event listeners, the one thing you should always do is remove handlers from elements when you're done with them. In short, for every addEventListener (or similar), there should be a corresponding removeEventListener. For every on, there should be an off. This not only reduces the chances of unexpected behavior in your app, but it allows the browser to release all the memory being retained by the listeners.

Sometimes, the problem isn't so much that you're holding on to memory for too long, but that you're holding on to too much. Browsers are getting better at optimizing this case and are retaining variables in the lexical scope that the method only actually references; but this is far from perfect. Thus, if you have a large object *that your method doesn't need* in the lexical scope, you should set it to `null` to release that memory.

There are a lot of articles available that you should definitely absorb:

- JavaScript memory profiling: (`https://developer.chrome.com/devtools/docs/javascript-memory-profiling`)

- Memory management: (`https://developer.mozilla.org/en-US/docs/Web/JavaScript/Memory_Management`)

- Fixing memory leaks in AngularJS and other JavaScript applications: `http://www.codeproject.com/Articles/882966/Fixing-Memory-Leaks-in-AngularJS-and-other-JavaScr`

- High-performance, garbage-collector-friendly code: (`http://buildnewgames.com/garbage-collector-friendly-code/`)

Splitting up and delegating long computations

A lot of data entry and productivity applications are usually waiting around for the user to do something rather than the reverse. However, if your app performs long computations (whatever they may be), you're likely to find yourself with an unwelcome occurrence of the dreaded frozen app.

JavaScript itself is single-threaded. This means that your code has control until it relinquishes control back to the browser, at which point the browser can begin to render the DOM and detect events. These events will often trigger more of your code, and the cycle will repeat.

Normally, your code will execute quickly enough that the user won't notice. That is, they'll be scrolling around in your app, or they will be switching views or tapping buttons. They hopefully won't notice when your code is running. But if you need to compute a complex calculation that takes more than 16.67 ms, they'll start noticing, because you'll see visual stuttering again.

The problem lies within the run loop used by JavaScript. While your code has control, the browser can't respond to any user input, and it can't render any DOM elements. If your app is running a short calculation that doesn't take too long, this will just look like a little visual glitch. But if it's a long calculation, the user will think your app has frozen up. While your app *hasn't*, the user can't tell, because all the input and output have stopped.

Profiling is useful once again, and it'll show up in much the same way as slow rendering. But you will be in a better position to know which is which, because you'll have just performed an action that results in a long calculation. For example, if you tap a button named "Calculate Big Prime Number", you will know that if the device pauses for a few seconds afterwards, it was probably because it was doing what you asked, not because your DOM is overly complex or because the CSS styles you've used are taxing the GPU. However, you can use the profiler during this time to determine the duration for the various methods, which presents you with targets for optimization.

Optimization is highly dependent on your code, so there's no concrete direction we can steer you. However, there are a couple of other things you can do to help with the problem:

- Chop the task up into discrete tasks that can be executed in short bursts (with `setInterval` or `requestAnimationFrame`).
- Use Web Workers. This is unfortunately beyond the scope of this chapter, but the following websites have lots of great information:
  - Using Web Workers: (`https://developer.mozilla.org/en-US/docs/Web/API/Web_Workers_API/Using_web_workers`)
  - The basics of Web Workers: (`http://www.html5rocks.com/en/tutorials/workers/basics/`)

Web Workers are supported on most modern devices, so it's advisable to place long running computations in a worker. This simulates multithreading, because the worker gains its own run loop. The browser's loop can then remain responsive to user input.

Chopping up your task can achieve similar results, although it requires that the task can be split into discrete parts. Consider a simple example:

```
function countToX(x) {
  var i = 0;
  while (i<x) {
    i++;
  }
  console.log ("done!");
}
```

This example doesn't do anything *useful*, but it illustrates the problem well. If we call this method with a small value, the user won't notice anything, because the computer can count upward very quickly. However, if we call it with a sufficiently large value (and it would need to be pretty large), the user will notice that the device freezes while the task is going on.

We could, however, split it up into small tasks:

```
function countToX(x) {
  var i = 0;
  var intervalId;
  function countALittleBit() {
    var j = 0;
    while (j<10) {
      if (i<x) {
        i++;
        j++;
      } else {
        console.log ("done");
        clearInterval(intervalId);
        j = 10;
      }
    }
  }
  intervalId = setInterval(countALittleBit, 0);
}
```

Now, regardless of how large of a number we pass to countToX, the browser will always remain responsive to the user. The task itself will take longer, perhaps, quite a lot longer, but the user can still interact with the app.

Essentially, the important thing is this: keep the runtime of your methods low. Don't perform *too* lengthy a computation in your code without either splitting it up into separate pieces or using Web Workers.

Summary

We covered a great deal in this chapter, from clarifying what we mean when we use the word performance to the various differences between desktops, emulators and simulators, and physical devices. We also touched on how to profile your app and went over some common problems and ways to approach them.

In the next chapter, we'll start preparing our app for submission to the Apple and Google Play stores by creating app icons and splash screen assets.

11
Graphical Assets

No doubt you've seen the default launch screen and icon that Cordova/PhoneGap projects use. These are sufficient during development; but when you're getting ready to publish your app to the masses, you need appropriate graphical assets. These come in three categories: app icons, launch screens, and in-app graphics. We've talked to some degree already about how to make your in-app graphics responsive to the user's device in *Chapter 4*, *More Responsive Design*. Some of what we talked about does apply to your app's icon and launch screens. However, these particular assets require special configuration to ensure that Cordova/PhoneGap uses them correctly.

In this chapter, we'll cover the following topics:

- App icon requirements
- Creating an app icon
- Launch screen requirements
- Creating a launch screen
- Configuring your app
- Useful resources

Getting started

This chapter assumes that you have some experience with graphic design applications such as Adobe Photoshop, Adobe Illustrator, GIMP, Sketch, and so on. If you aren't already familiar with such an application, you should consider finding an application that supports *vector* illustrations. There are many applications that are *raster* based, that is, you control each pixel in the resulting image. Because the mobile landscape is changing quickly with respect to the device's screen size and resolution, it's safer to develop your images in a resolution-independent manner so that you can generate new images at specific resolutions without the loss of detail.

If you've heard of *bitmap* images, it is important to know that these are raster images.

Adobe Photoshop is frequently used for this task even though it isn't a pure vector graphics editor. Most of Photoshop's functionality is specific to raster images, but there is enough vector support built in Photoshop that is capable of creating resolution-independent images. A lot of useful resources are also available for Photoshop when it comes to creating app icons and launch screens, which further simplifies their development.

Technically, *any* graphics editor can create icons and launch screens, of course. So, you aren't required to use Adobe Photoshop in this chapter. Though our examples will use Photoshop, most graphic editors have analogues of the tools we will be using. If you need to find a vector editor, check out the *Useful resources* section at the end of this chapter.

App icon requirements

Your app icon is a very important graphical asset. It's typically how users will start your app on their mobile devices. As such, it has to be easily distinguished from the other icons on the user's screen. For a game or a highly graphical app, the icon might be a more literal representation of the app itself. But for many other apps, the icon is an abstract representation. If your app has a recognizable brand, the icon can be a play off the brand, such as the app icons for Facebook, Twitter, and the like.

Each platform your app supports will have different *physical* requirements for your icon. But in most cases, the aesthetic is largely the same across platforms and the only difference is the size and whether or not there are rounded corners (and to what degree). In many ways, this makes designing a cross-platform icon fairly easy. It isn't difficult to target all the various sizes as long as you avoid the corners. This isn't to say that your icon must be identical across platforms. In some cases, you may need to tune your icons for each platform (an icon that looks fine with somewhat square corners may not look fine with rounded corners).

Before we cover how you can create an icon, we first need to address the various requirements regarding physical size. Each platform requires that we generate icons in different sizes for various system purposes. Let's go over them, starting with iOS:

Category	Size (dpi)
Icon used in Settings app	29 × 29 (@1x), 58 × 58 (@2x), 87 × 87 (@3x)
Shown in the Spotlight search	40 × 40 (@1x), 80 × 80 (@2x), 120 × 120 (@3x)

Category	Size (dpi)
Shown on the home screen	76 × 76 (@1x iPads), 152 × 152 (@2x iPads), 120 × 120 (@2x iPhones), 180 × 180 (@3x iPhones)
Backwards compatibility (<= iOS 6.1)	57 × 57 (@1x iPhones), 114 × 114 (@2x iPhones), 72 × 72 (@1x iPads), 144 × 144 (@2x iPads), 100 × 100 (@2x iPads, Settings app)
App store	1024 × 1024

Not every icon is required. Technically, you can get away with supplying only the 1024 × 1024 dpi icon to the app store and the 120 × 120 dpi icon to the app if you are targeting iOS 6.2 or later and the 57 × 57 dpi icon if you are targeting iOS 6.1 or lower. But the others are all marked as recommended, even though they are optional, and the Cordova/PhoneGap app templates have several defined for you already. You would either need to remove any icons you didn't use in order to ensure that the default icon didn't show in an unexpected place, or you should overwrite them all. I prefer the latter option, even if it is a bit more work to generate multiple versions of the icon.

For Android, a similar situation exists, but there aren't nearly as many variants. Technically, you only need one icon for Android as well. But for best results, you should provide icons in the following sizes:

DPI	Resolution
mdpi	48 × 48
hdpi	72 × 72
xxdpi	96 × 96
xxxhdpi	144 × 144
xxxxhdpi	192 × 192
Google Play Store	512 × 512

Like Apple, you'll also want to create a version of the app for the Google Play Store. This icon should be sized at 512 × 512.

You may be asking yourself why we have to worry about so many different sizes. In most cases, shrinking an icon from a large source resolution down to a small size will generate an icon that is usable, but there's an inevitable loss of detail. Of course, we typically plan for this and design our large icons with the expectation that they will be reduced in size later. This works up to a point where one encounters problems with these very small icons. If you had a lot of detail being rendered in an icon at 72 × 72, that detail would blur together in a 48 × 48 or a 29 × 29 pixel icon. As such, both platforms give you the opportunity to make tweaks to those smaller icons as desired. Technically, the same could be applied in reverse. You could add more detail to the icons with higher resolutions, although there is a visual limit here. Larger icon sizes are usually being displayed in roughly the same amount of physical space, and there is a limit to how much the eye can perceive.

Thankfully, in most cases, we can automate the process of creating icons of each size and then tweak them as necessary. There are some useful Photoshop actions (macros essentially) and other useful utilities in the *Useful resources* section at the end of the chapter.

Creating an app icon

It isn't necessarily easy to create an app icon that stands out from the crowd, and we can't really cover *how* to do that in this chapter. This requires creativity, and there really isn't a set of steps that guarantee a creative result. But there are some general ideas that you can use to create an icon that will work for your app.

Here are some things that you typically find in great app icons:

- The icon plays off the brand or the logo. Note that this isn't the same as saying that the icon *is* your brand or logo (your brand or logo may not fit within the icon's size without modification, for example). Furthermore, this only works if the brand or logo is well-known (such as Facebook, Twitter, and more)

- The icon is distinguishable. That is, the icon shouldn't look too much like the other apps the user might have installed on their device. This typically means that you shouldn't go around making an icon that looks a bit too much like the Facebook icon with similar colors and fonts. Not because you *can't*, but because your user may easily become confused as to which app they are launching.

- The icon fits the platform's aesthetic. The current design trend is mostly flat (though shadows and layer effects are still present). Highly skeuomorphic designs are out, and they will look out of place on a platform where the other icons are typically flat. Although this might allow your app's icon to stand out by using a photorealistic icon, it may also lead to a negative impression on the part of your users that the app is dated and following old design trends.

- The icon is legible. Your icon will be displayed in many different sizes on the device, and it must remain legible and recognizable in all those sizes. On the iPhone, for example, your icon may be rendered in the space the size of your pinky fingernail in the Settings app, while it may be rendered in the space the size of your thumbnail on the home screen. In other places such as the App Store, it may be rendered at even larger sizes. As such, your icon needs be easily recognizable at a variety of scales.

- The icon is engaging. Unless your app has something to do with black and white photo processing or is a mostly monochrome game, your app icon should probably have some color in it. Drawing from the colors your app itself uses for a good start.

- The icon is a representative of your app. Your icon should connect with your app in a tangible, meaningful way. Don't always go with the most obvious; for example, a camera app doesn't *always* need to use a camera for the app's icon, but the user must be able to see the icon and then make the connection to your app. This is why using your brand or logo only works well when they are well-known; the user already has an established connection. Most apps don't have this luxury.

- The icon is professional. This is a bit subjective, of course, and it's incredibly difficult to actually write about, because there's no set of steps that will guarantee the result. In short, however, the icon needs to look as if there was some care taken in the design. Elements should line up appropriately, text should be kerned, images and shapes should be rendered at their correct aspect ratio, and so on. Not all of us are amazing artists, but lining things up on a grid and ensuring proper text rendering alone goes a long way to improving user perception.

Let's take a look at some icons that excel at meeting the earlier mentioned criteria and some others that could do better:

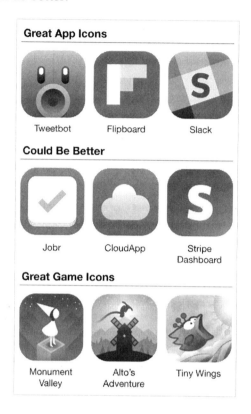

None of these icons are unprofessional. They all look fine, but some do the job of connecting with the app they represent better than others. Those in the top row are great examples of icons that do a very good job of representing their app. They are memorable, not overly skeuomorphic, easily legible in various sizes, engaging, and a representative of the app and the associated brand. The **Tweetbot** icon is easily anthropomorphized, which makes the connection even easier. **Flipboard**, on the other hand, plays off their brand. Note that it's not a simple *F*, but a stylized version that also plays on the notion of how articles are presented in the app itself. Finally, while **Slack** does use an *S* in their icon, the colors match their branding and app experience.

In the second row, however, are icons that, while professional, could be better. I bet you can't guess what the first icon is supposed to represent. My initial guess was that of a to-do or task list application. I was wrong, though. The app is actually about job searches. It's a little more obvious from the app title, but still; checkmarks do not automatically make a good icon. The middle icon is for a cloud-based service, which is fine, but there are lots of cloud services. Furthermore, there are a lot of other apps that use the cloud as a symbol, which means that this particular icon has very little connection with the app. Finally, we look at the icon on the right-hand side. Although it matches the app's color scheme, it tells the user nothing about the app other than that the title starts with an *S*. The letterform isn't highly stylized to make it iconic. As such, the user is going to have a hard time remembering that this icon launches the **Stripe Dashboard** application.

Finally, in the third row are some excellent icons for gaming apps. It's not impossible to make a bad game icon, but games usually lend themselves to good icons very easily. In each of these examples, the icon accurately represents the game world itself, they are all memorable, and make it easy to connect with each game.

Now that we've talked a little about what makes a good app icon, let's go through a little design process I used for the demo application in the code package of this book, Logology. My initial designs won't be perfect—they are proofs of concept. Once I find a design I like, I can always flesh the icon out even further.

Your proofs of concept don't need to be done in the same editor you'll use to create the final version of your icon. Many designers like to sketch out ideas on a piece of paper first, or use some other application that lets the user play with shapes and colors quickly. Personally, I use both Omnigraffle (akin to Microsoft Visio) and Adobe Photoshop at this stage, as well as the occasional paper sketch. Let's take a look at some first attempts:

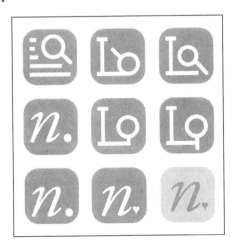

There are some promising ideas here, and then there are some that are not. One thing you should never be afraid of is to put your ideas down on paper, even the ones you don't like. Sometimes, what works while envisioning it in your mind doesn't work on paper and *vice versa*. Allow yourself to play with ideas, even if you don't think they'll go anywhere initially. You might surprise yourself.

Even once you settle on what you think is the best idea, you should probably develop at least two icons simultaneously. This lets you do A–B testing later to see what your beta testers think of your icon. They may prefer something different than you. Although too many options can be paralyzing, a few options (say, two or three) won't hurt.

Now that we've got some ideas, it's time to start designing our icons in an editor that supports vector editing. Regardless of the platforms your app is targeting, you will want to start out with a *square* canvas. You might find it useful to overlay various grids on top of this square in order to assist you with layout. We'll mention a few of these in the *Useful resources* section of this chapter.

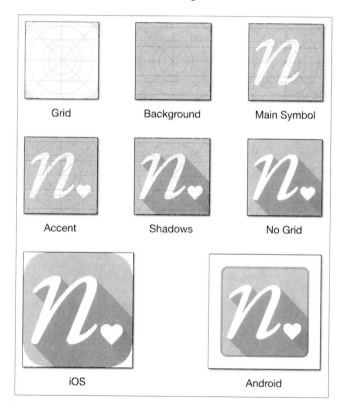

Grid   Background   Main Symbol

Accent   Shadows   No Grid

iOS   Android

The previous image shows the approximate steps we took in the creation of this particular icon. Let's quickly go over these steps:

1. The first image (top left) shows the blank grid on a square canvas. In our case, the square is 1024 × 1024 pixels. Technically, nearly everything will be done using vectors, so it really doesn't matter what resolution you use, as long as it is square.

2. The next step (top middle) shows a color wash applied to the background. In our case, we used a solid color that's a little brighter than our app's navigation bar. Many icons will use a gradient for the background, but solid worked best in our case.

3. Next, we start applying our symbols. In this case, we added the *n* that represents noun. This is a little abstract, but *l* wouldn't really mean anything with respect to a dictionary definition.

4. At the start of the middle row, you can see that we've applied our accent symbol. We're using a heart in place of the typical period you would have after abbreviating a noun in a dictionary.

5. The results are still a bit flat, so to help things out a bit, we have added some long shadows, as you can see in the middle image.

6. As we complete the process, we removed the grid lines, so we have an unobstructed view.

You can see the iOS icon on the lower left-hand side and the Android icon on the lower right-hand side. There are some differences between the two, notably:

- The iOS icon fills the entire canvas and has very round corners. The rounded corner effect is actually generated by the operating system, so we actually package the *square* icon with our app, not one with rounded corners.

- The Android icon does not fill the entire canvas and has relatively sharper corners when compared with iOS. Android expects that we'll supply the icon as we want it to be seen on the device, so we have to supply the rounded corners and spacing.

 iOS enforces the separation between grid elements on the home screen and doesn't permit transparency in your app's icon. As such, you are responsible for filling the entire icon canvas. Android, however, expects that you'll apply some spacing within the canvas so that your icon has some separation from other icons. Since Android supports transparencies as a part of the app icon, this lets you get very creative with the shape of your icon.

Now that we have our icon, we need to package it with our app. Unfortunately, both iOS and Android require many different versions of the icon to be generated. This is painful to do by hand, so we can take advantage of various Photoshop actions (your tool may use the term "macro") to generate all the icon sizes for us. You can see the various actions we use in the *Useful resources* section at the end of this chapter.

Launch screen requirements

Unlike your app's icon, the launch screen only appears briefly, while your app is actually loading into the device's memory. This means that it isn't visible for very long. If it is seen for too long, you've already got problems. As such, your launch screen is probably *not* the best place to be displaying something overly intricate or fancy. The whole point of a launch screen is meant to cover up the time it takes to launch your app, and on iOS, to give the impression that your app loads much faster than it really does. On Android, many apps dispense with launch screens entirely. But due to the way the Cordova/PhoneGap apps initialize the underlying web view, a launch screen is something you'll still want to use.

 On Android, the system web view for your app tends to take a moment to initialize. During this time, your app may present an undesirable display (akin to the flash-of-unstyled-content that is sometimes present while using some websites). Because of this, a launch screen is highly suggested so that the end user doesn't see any flashes or misrendered content.

Technically, your launch screen could be a simple black background and this would work. If your app's background color is black, you could indeed get away with this. If your app has a white background, a black launch screen is a little distracting, so you should endeavor to match your launch screen with your app's interface.

Apple has the idea that your launch screen should appear as if your app has been loaded into memory, but has yet to be populated with data. This gives the impression that your app loads quickly, but this is really a trick; your app is still unresponsive at this point. Personally, I find this a little frustrating from the end user perspective, because it seems to make the app's load time feel slower than it would otherwise. I have the tendency to start interacting with the apps that do this earlier than the app expects, so I have to repeat my actions when the app finally initializes.

 Most devices have a **watchdog** that ensures your app starts up within a certain amount of time. For example, on iOS, if your app doesn't complete the startup within ten seconds, your app is automatically terminated. The operating system decides that your app has crashed if it remains unresponsive for this time period, and to prevent the user from having to manually terminate the app, the operating system does it for them.

Most app developers will instead create something a little more abstract that still represents their app. The colors that the app uses will be present on the launch screen, but the rest of the launch screen may not accurately reflect the app's actual appearance. Although Apple frowns on this kind of launch screen, most apps fall into this category, so clearly Apple isn't terribly concerned that you follow their guidelines on this issue.

Other apps will use the launch screen as an opportunity to get really artsy. This is most common with games, but the launch screen really isn't about *delaying* the user's interaction with the app, it's solely about covering up the loading time. So, if your app loads quickly, your user may never get to notice the intricate details of your art. In short: keep it simple, not complex. Furthermore, games usually render *several* splash screens in quick succession. For example, the publisher might have a screen all to themselves, while the development company might get another. Some actual game art might be displayed just prior to launching the menu. This particular use of splash screens should be handled by your app, *not* the operating system. As such, you would be better off using a very simple launch screen (perhaps, simply with the *Your Publisher presents* message, as seen in many Nintendo games).

This translates into several different styles of launch screens. Let's look at a few:

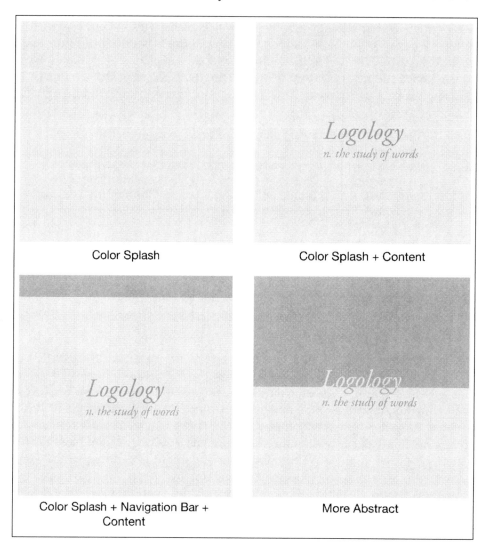

As you can see, the first launch screen (upper left) is very bland. It's a solid color, and that's it. In this case, it would match the background color of our demonstration app if it didn't have any data. This isn't so much to present the unpopulated user interface we've been talking about; it's just trying to prevent the jarring transition from one color to another. If I had used a black color, the transition from the launch screen to the app would be extremely obvious.

The second launch screen (upper right) takes things a step farther. In this case, I added the name of the app and a tag line. These never appear in the app in this particular form, but it tells the user that *yes, the app is loading and, by the way, you did start the right app.*

The third launch screen (lower left) starts to work off the unpopulated user interface metaphor. There's an orange bar at the top exactly where the navigation bar would be in the app. The transition to the app would be virtually seamless, except for the disappearance of the app title and tag line.

The final launch screen (lower right) starts to be a bit more abstract. The colors are still the same, but I've given up on the navigation bar concept. Instead there are two different kinds of color here dividing the screen (in a way, like a book), and the app title is imposed over the separation between these two colors creating an inverse effect. This is definitely *not* what our app looks like with no data, but the launch screen still works.

Like your app's icon, your launch screen needs to be rendered in various resolutions. For each platform, this means creating a launch screen that matches the various screen sizes and orientations that your app targets. On iOS, this adds up to quite a few versions. You would follow the same example on Android, but you can also use nine-patch images instead.

Nine-patch images are *resizable* raster images. You can recognize them by their extension: .9.png. They are PNG files, so you can technically create them in any editor. Around the border is a series of black and white pixels. These pixels tell Android what portions of the image can be scaled and what portions should always remain the same size. This allows you to create a launch screen that completely fills the screen of any device while not stretching the important content (such as a logo or other user interface elements). We'll cover creating these images later on in this chapter.

It should be pretty obvious at this point that creating lots of versions of the launch screen for each different resolution can be quite time-consuming. If you keep your important content near the center of the canvas, you may be able to use some utilities to create these images for you (and I listed a few at the end of the chapter). But if you have content that's near the edges (like a navigation bar), you will have to do the hard work yourself. In the preceding example, this makes the third launch screen the hardest to export.

Let's quickly go over the required resolutions for iOS:

Device	Portrait	Landscape
iPhone (@1x)	320 × 480	N/A
iPhone 4, 4s (@2x)	640 × 960	N/A
iPhone 5, 5s (@2x)	640 × 1136	N/A
iPhone 6, 6s (@2x)	750 × 1334	1334 × 750
iPhone 6+, 6s+ (@3x)	1242 × 2208	2208 × 1242
iPad (@1x)	768 × 1024	1024 × 768
iPad (@2x)	1536 × 2048	2048 × 1536
iPad Pro (@2x)	2048 × 2732	2732 × 2048

Android also has several different suggested resolutions for the launch screen, as follows:

DPI	Portrait	Landscape
ldpi	200 × 320	320 × 200
mdpi	320 × 480	480 × 320
hdpi	480 × 800	800 × 480
xhdpi	720 × 1280	1280 × 720

These sizes aren't a hard and fast rule. Android devices have many different screen sizes and pixel densities. This is why we'll use nine-patch images: they can scale to fit any device size without distorting the content.

Creating a Launch Screen

As we've mentioned, both iOS and Android have differing opinions as to what a launch screen should be, and whether or not it is even required. What's really important to know is that neither Apple, nor Google, particularly *requires* you to adhere to their guidelines when it comes to launch screens. For Apple especially, it's just important that the launch screen exists. They *won't* check whether it matches what your user interface would look like with no data.

For our app, we'll take the slightly abstract launch screen approach (the fourth launch screen in the prior section). This lets us simplify the export of the launch screens in all the various resolutions by using automation utilities rather than doing it all by hand.

We can't cover *all* the steps involved in creating the initial launch screen, since they would vary based upon your use cases, your app's user interface, and your graphic editor, but we can cover what you'll have to do at a high level. You should be able to look at my source and output images in order to see how it worked out for me.

1. The first thing I do is create a blank canvas that is 3072 x 3072 pixels square. This lets me target the @3x devices that are currently in the market. As with the icon, it really doesn't matter how large your canvas is as long as it's square, because you should design the splash screen with as many vector-based shapes as you possibly can.

2. Next, I added a new layer that filled the entire canvas with a solid background color. I used the same background color used by the app so that the transition from the launch screen to the live app isn't jarring.

3. Next, I added a vector shape that filled the top half of the canvas and filled it with the app's navigation bar color.

4. I then added the app's title to the center of the canvas. I masked it with a duplicate of the shape I just created (as well as the inverse) so that I could create the inverse effect on the text. Depending on your colors, you could also just use the blend modes to get the same (or similar) effect.

5. Below the app title, I added a tag line.

At this point, we'd be ready to export the launch screen. I used Ape Tools—Image Gorilla (the link is at the end of the chapter) to create all the various sizes of the launch screen. I could do this simply because the content is in the middle of the launch screen.

This works well for iOS, where you know for certain what screen resolutions your app might encounter. On Android, you don't really have any idea what screen resolutions you will see. You could aim for the typical sizes (which is what the automation tools do), but if your launch screen is displayed on a device that doesn't fit one of these sizes, you may see black bars or have a portion of your launch screen cropped. That's where nine-patch images come in.

In order to create a nine-patch image, you add a single-pixel transparent border to your PNG files. On the right and bottom, you can then draw a line of black pixels, leaving the corner pixels transparent. This is the **fill area** and is the portion of the image that Android will use while filling the screen. At the top and left, you draw two lines of black pixels each with each one covering the nonresizable content of the image. This is called the **scale area**. Android will freely scale the contents of the areas where these lines intersect to fill the entire screen. The remaining transparent area will not be scaled, so the content won't be distorted.

When it comes to nine-patch images, it always helps to have a visual. Here's what the single-pixel border looks like for the demonstration app's launch screen (the border is magnified here to help you see it better):

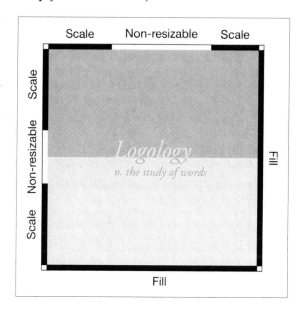

 The white portions of the border should be *transparent* in your output image, not white.

When you save a nine-patch image, you should use the .9.png extension, so Android knows that it can resize the image. Furthermore, your border *must* be one pixel wide or it will start to leak through into the image on the screen.

Although you can create your nine-patch images in any raster editor (such as Adobe Photoshop, GIMP, and so on), there are also specialized tools to help with the creation of these images. I've listed a few at the end of this chapter.

Configuring your app

Now that we've created our app's icon and launch images, we need to configure our app to use them. In both the cases, you'll need to rename your exported files to specific names and move them into a specific directory. Then, we'll edit the configuration files to point at those files.

If you've downloaded the code package for this book, or if you've created an app using the typical Cordova/PhoneGap templates, chances are you already have the directory structure needed to configure your app. In case you don't, here's how it should look:

```
<project root>
`-- src
    |-- config.xml
    |-- res
    |   |-- icon
    |   |   |-- android
    |   |   `-- ios
    |   `-- splash
    |       |-- android
    |       `-- ios
    `-- www
```

> If you are going to use PhoneGap Build, you should also symlink in your www directory and point it at `src/res`. This will let PhoneGap Build access the image files.

If you're using our app's code, you might remember that we do a lot of configuration using the `package.json` file. This is a little simpler than having to fight with XML. In order to use the images we have created, we have a snippet as follows (the full version is in the code package of this book):

```json
{
    "cordova": {
        "icon": {
            "ios": [
                { "src": "res/icon/ios/icon-60.png",
                    "w": 60, "h": 60 },
                { "src": "res/icon/ios/icon-60@2x.png",
                    "w": 120, "h": 120 },
                { "src": "res/icon/ios/icon-60@3x.png",
                    "w": 180, "h": 180 },
                ...
            ],
            "android": [
                { "src": "res/icon/android/ldpi.png", "d": "ldpi" },
                { "src": "res/icon/android/mdpi.png", "d": "mdpi" },
                ...
            ]
        },
```

```
          "splash": {
            "ios": [
              { "src": "res/splash/ios/Default~iphone.png",
                  "w": 320, "h": 480 },
              { "src": "res/splash/ios/Default@2x~iphone.png",
                  "w": 640, "h": 960 },
              { "src": "res/splash/ios/Default-Portrait~ipad.png",
                  "w": 768, "h": 1024 },
              ...
            ],
            "android": [
              { "src": "res/splash/android/splash-land-ldpi.9.png",
                "d": "land-ldpi" },
              { "src": "res/splash/android/splash-land-mdpi.9.png",
                "d": "land-mdpi" },
              { "src": "res/splash/android/splash-land-hdpi.9.png",
                "d": "land-hdpi" },
              ...
            ]
          }, ...
      }
  }
```

On the other hand, if you're using `config.xml`, you can do the same with the following:

```
<icon src="res/icon/ios/icon-60.png" platform="ios"
 width="60" height="60" />
<icon src="res/icon/ios/icon-60@2x.png" platform="ios"
 width="120" height="120" />
<icon src="res/icon/ios/icon-60@3x.png" platform="ios"
 width="180" height="180" />
...
<icon src="res/icon/android/ldpi.png" platform="android"
 density="ldpi" />
<icon src="res/icon/android/mdpi.png" platform="android"
 density="mdpi" />
...
<splash src="res/splash/ios/Default~iphone.png" platform="ios"
 width="320" height="480" />
<splash src="res/splash/ios/Default@2x~iphone.png" platform="ios"
 width="640" height="960" />
<splash src="res/splash/ios/Default-Portrait~ipad.png"
```

```
platform="ios" width="768" height="1024" />
...
<splash src="res/splash/android/splash-land-ldpi.9.png"
 platform="android" density="land-ldpi" />
<splash src="res/splash/android/splash-land-mdpi.9.png"
 platform="android" density="land-mdpi" />
<splash src="res/splash/android/splash-land-hdpi.9.png"
 platform="android" density="land-hdpi" />
...
```

 If you use PhoneGap Build, the XML source code is slightly different. See the code package of this book for an example or see `http://docs.build.phonegap.com/en_US/ configuring_icons_and_splash.md.html`.

For Android, the names of the files themselves don't matter. It is wise to use the pixel density so that you can keep track of which files are which.

iOS is a different story. The names of each image are also very important. It's best to rename your files to the names that follow:

Type	Resolution	Filename
Icon	60 × 60	`icon-60.png`
	120 × 120	`icon-60@2x.png`
	180 × 180	`icon-60@3x.png`
	76 × 76	`icon-76.png`
	152 × 152	`icon-76@2x.png`
	40 × 40	`icon-40.png`
	80 × 80	`icon-40@2x.png`
	57 × 57	`icon.png`
	114 × 114	`icon@2x.png`
	72 × 72	`icon-72.png`
	144 × 144	`icon-72@2x.png`
	50 × 50	`icon-50.png`
	100 × 100	`icon-50@2x.png`
Launch	320 × 480	`Default~iphone.png`
	640 × 960	`Default~iphone@2x.png`
	768 × 1024	`Default-Portrait~ipad.png`
	1536 × 2048	`Default-Portrait~ipad@2x.png`

Type	Resolution	Filename
	1024 × 768	`Default-Landscape~ipad.png`
	2048 × 1536	`Default-Landscape~ipad@2x.png`
	640 × 1136	`Default-568h@2x~iphone.png`
	750 × 1334	`Default-667h.png`
	1334 × 750	`Default-Landscape-667h.png`
	1242 × 2208	`Default-736h.png`
	2208 × 1242	`Default-Landscape-736h.png`

Recent versions of iOS are a lot more forgiving when it comes to the naming of icon and launching image files, but earlier versions weren't. As such, it's good practice to adhere to the naming convention that Apple suggests.

> iPad Pro does not support the use of raster launch screens. Instead, you have to use a storyboard launch screen. The same is also true if you want to use iOS 9's multitasking features. Unfortunately, at the time of this writing, Cordova does not yet support a storyboard launch screen.

Useful resources

There are almost too many vector and graphic editors with vector support to count. Here are some of the most popular:

- Pure vector editors:
    - Adobe Illustrator (`http://www.adobe.com/products/illustrator.html`, subscription, Windows and Mac OS X)
    - Affinity (`https://affinity.serif.com/en-us/`, commercial, Mac OS X)
    - CorelDRAW (`http://www.coreldraw.com/us/product/graphic-design-software/`, commercial, Windows)
    - DrawPlus (`http://www.serif.com/drawplus/`, free starter edition and commercial version, Windows)
    - Inkscape (`https://inkscape.org/en/`, free, cross-platform)
    - Sketch (`http://bohemiancoding.com/sketch/`, commercial, Mac OS X)

- Raster editors with vector support:
  - Adobe Photoshop (`http://www.adobe.com/products/photoshop.html`, subscription, Windows and Mac OS X)
  - GIMP (`http://www.gimp.org`, free, cross-platform)
  - Photoline (`http://www.pl32.com`, commercial, Windows and Mac OS X)

- Photoshop actions and templates:
  - iOS grid icon: `https://www.brownbagmarketing.com/ios-7-and-the-golden-ratio/`
  - Long shadow action: `https://dribbble.com/shots/1205511-Free-Long-Shadow-Photoshop-Action`
  - iOS app icon template (with actions): `http://appicontemplate.com/ios8`
  - Android app icon template (with actions): `http://appicontemplate.com/android`

- Nine-patch editors:
  - Draw 9-patch (supplied with Android SDK): `http://developer.android.com/tools/help/draw9patch.html`
  - Simple nine-patch generator (website): `https://romannurik.github.io/AndroidAssetStudio/nine-patches.html`
  - Nine-patch editor (Java): `https://github.com/mgarin/weblaf/releases` (download and launch the `ninepatch-editor-1.28.jar` file)

- Automation:
  - MakeAppIcon: `http://makeappicon.com/` (app icons only)
  - Icon Generator: `http://icon.angrymarmot.org` (app icons only)
  - Ape Tools: `http://apetools.webprofusion.com/tools/imagegorilla` (app icons and splash screens)

- Inspiration:
  - `http://www.iconsfeed.com`
  - `http://iosicongallery.com`
  - `http://www.iospirations.com`

Summary

In this chapter, we've discussed about how you should create your app icons and launch screens. We've covered the various resolutions you need to export your images into. Finally, we covered configuring your app to use your images.

In the next chapter, we'll deal with the actual submission of your app to the Apple App Store and the Google Play Store using step-by-step instructions. When done, you'll have an app ready for download on the app store!

12
Deployment

Once your app is fundamentally complete, it's unlikely that you'll want to be the only user of your app; thus, you can now start considering the various avenues for deployment. Deployment comes in several different flavors, and we'll cover most of these in this chapter. You'll be guided through the process of signing up for developer accounts as well.

In this chapter, we will be covering the following topics:

- Building modes
- Distribution methods
- Signing up for developer accounts
- Generating signed release builds
- Deploying ad hoc releases
- Deploying app store releases

One kind of build that we won't be discussing in this chapter is the *enterprise* build: these are deployments intended for internal use by a company (usually, for their own employees). This typically requires specialized configuration within the environment and, as such, is outside the scope of this book.

Build modes

Before we go much further, we need to define some terms when it comes to building your app for deployment. There are several variations, and it is important to understand them well.

There are typically two build modes: **debug** and **release**. Depending on your needs, you may actually have more. For this chapter, we'll focus only on these two. Let's go over what they are used for and the differences between them.

A **debug** build is the *default* build generated by Cordova. It's loaded with debugging information (hence the name), which is extremely useful during the development and debugging phases. Your app might have additional debugging aids as well. For example, there might be a simple tool to query a local database. The output might be ugly, but it doesn't matter much while debugging.

A debug build is never *ever* meant for typical end users. This means that you should never have debug code in an app deployed to an app store (your app may be rejected because of it). As obvious as this sounds, it's a little scary how often debugging code ends up in the production code. Although generating lots of logging data may not necessarily be the worst thing in the world, at minimum, your app will experience a performance hit. At the opposite end of that spectrum, debugging code is rarely the most secure stuff in the world.

A **release** build is simply a build suitable for release to end users. Cordova will generate native code that is stripped of debugging information, and will also prevent remote debugging connections. Release builds are often tighter about verifying security. For example, Android debug builds don't necessarily check whether a SSL certificate is signed by a trusted certificate authority, but release builds definitely do.

You can take advantage of the release build process as well, by minifying and compressing your assets. Not all users have a lot of free space on their device and you can make their lives a little easier by reducing the amount of space your app takes up. Eliminating source maps goes a long way in this regard too, since they can consume a significant amount of storage. Any other debugging aids your app might have in place should be either eliminated or polished up into something you can use to support your end users should the need arise.

Once you have a build, you obviously need to distribute it. But here lays a problem: how does the device (and the end user, by proxy) *trust* that the code they are downloading is the same code you published? The answer is simple: code signing.

A signed build is just a build *signed* using a specific signing identity. This signing identity is essentially a public/private key pair that links the signed build to you as a developer. Any unauthorized modifications to the build itself will fail to match your signature, so the user can be reasonably assured that the code is, indeed, from you. For typical Android users, the app they install will indeed be signed by you. For iOS users, the app they install will be signed by you initially, but Apple resigns it using their identity.

Of course, you should realize that if Apple can resign your app using their own signing identity, then so can just about anyone else. For iOS, this isn't a huge issue, since the device typically only trusts Apple-signed code. For Android, however, this does mean that someone else can resign your app and the device won't complain. They can't, however, release a version update to your app; resigned apps would always install as a new app, not an upgrade.

On Android, builds can be signed or unsigned. Unsigned builds require additional steps on the part of the end user in order to permit installation. So, one shouldn't rely on this for a reliable distribution model. On iOS, *all* the builds are signed and the user cannot permit the installation of apps signed by untrusted sources. This effectively means that while one can sideload apps on Android, iOS blocks this feature completely (unless one is a developer).

Signed builds are one way to ensure that users have the bits that you, the developer, think they should have. It's also a great way, for better or worse, to control distribution channels. Notice that we've said that iOS doesn't permit sideloading or the installation of unsigned apps. Apple makes a big deal about the security model here, but it also wants to control the distribution channel. As such, if you want to deploy an app on Android, you have a lot of distribution channels available; but on iOS, these channels are very limited.

Distribution methods

When it comes to actually deploying your builds, there are several different distribution methods:

- **ad-hoc**: It requires no real infrastructure for deployment. You might send the build via e-mail or by a website. These builds typically target specific users (especially on iOS). They aren't typically intended to be the method by which end users install the app.

- **beta-tester**: This is similar to an ad-hoc deployment with the following key difference: your app is beyond the initial development stage and you are asking a small group of users to try and break your app in any way they can think of. This is useful because a single developer won't be able to catch all the bugs in their own code (for many different reasons). These kinds of deployment can have no infrastructure behind them or they can use tools that assist the testing process (such as TestFlight and HockeyApp). Usually, additional support libraries are added so that you can be notified when the app crashes and see what the user was doing to make the app crash.

- **enterprise**: If you've ever worked for an enterprise, you probably are already familiar with the fact that these businesses typically have pretty tight controls over what technologies can be used and where and how they can be installed. As such, enterprises will tend to control app deployment through various automated solutions, all of which are technically beyond the scope of this chapter.

- **app store**: For most individuals and companies, this is the goal: your app on the Apple App Store or Google Play. This lets your target audience search, purchase, download, and install your app just as they would in case of any other app. This consistency lowers the bar to your user's wallet, but it also lowers the user's bar to your app. The stores typically have a lot of their own infrastructure in place to host your content, which is why they all take a portion of the cost of the app as their cut. On the flip side, however, you don't have to worry about hosting a copy of the app on your own infrastructure. An app store release will *always* be a release build.

> In all the earlier cases, iOS requires that you have an active developer account, even for ad-hoc deployment. Android is a bit more lax here: you only need a Google Play market developer account to submit to the Google Play market.

Signing up for developer accounts

Before you can deploy any app to physical iOS devices other than your own, you need to be a registered Apple developer. In the past, Apple required you to pay $99 USD per year to test apps on even your own physical devices, but this requirement has been lifted since the release of iOS 9. While this assists with your own testing, you'll still need to pay the subscription fee to deploy your apps on the devices you don't own, which is usually the point.

Google only requires an account when you intend on submitting your Android app to the Google Play market. Until then, you don't need an account. As of this writing, this costs a one-time fee of $25 USD. However, for consistency, we'll go over registering yourself on both the platforms in this first section.

> Although we'll only be focusing on iOS and Android, instructions for other platforms are largely similar.

Becoming an Apple iOS developer

To deploy applications to devices other than your own, you need to enroll in Apple's developer program. To start the process, you should navigate to `https://developer.apple.com/programs/enroll/`. Immediately, you are presented with a choice: you can choose to register as an individual or as a company. Which one you should use really depends upon your situation and this book can't cover all the various scenarios.

However, if you are a single developer, not working for another company, you should be safe registering for an individual account. If, for some reason, you need to transition the account into a company developer account, you can do so later. You can also usually transfer your app to another account as well.

If you are a developer working *within* a company, you should probably create a company account. This is more complicated, because Apple needs to verify that you have the ability to enter into contractual agreements on behalf of the company. Your company also needs to have a D-U-N-S number, which uniquely identifies your company. Unless your company is very small or recently formed, chances are pretty good that you'll already have one. If not, the process, though free, can take up to a few days in order to obtain one; although in some areas, the process takes much less time.

Before you begin the enrollment process, you *will* also need an Apple ID. If you don't have one already, you'll need to set one of those up first. In fact, even if you *already* have one, you should probably create a separate one to manage your deployments. If Apple were ever to disable your account for some reason, you would lose access to both your personal apps and the apps you have deployed to the store: better to be safe than sorry.

We'll assume that, at this point, you don't have an ID. So, let's go through the process to create one:

1. Navigate to `https://appleid.apple.com`.

2. You should see a screen similar to the following:

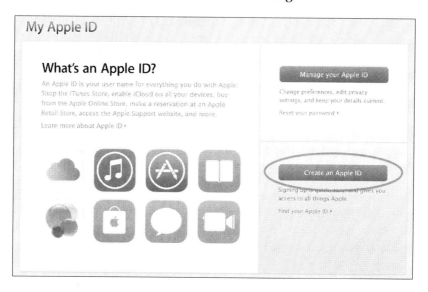

3. Click on **Create an Apple ID**.

4. You'll be presented with a blank registration form. Fill in your *legal* name, e-mail address, and choose your password. The results should look similar to the form shown in the following screenshot:

5. Scroll down and answer the security questions and enter your birth date. The form should look similar to the form shown in the following screenshot:

6. Next, you need to scroll down a little further and enter your mailing address (at a minimum). It's a good idea to set up a rescue e-mail address if you have one. Your form should look similar to this (we've left off the rescue address):

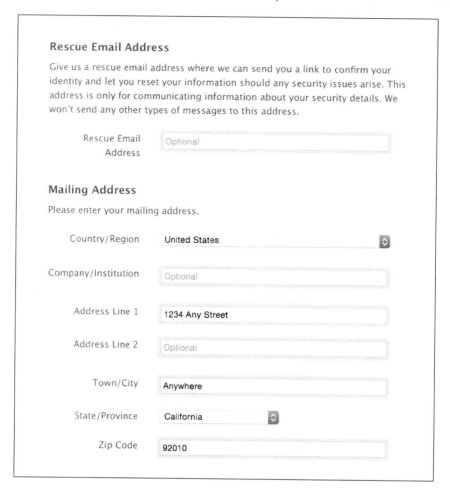

7. Scroll down a little further and select your preferred language and e-mail preferences. If you've already got an Apple ID, you can probably uncheck both the checkboxes under **Email Preferences**. If you want to keep up on Apple news and announcements, you might only want to leave the first checkmark checked. Either way, your form should look something like the following:

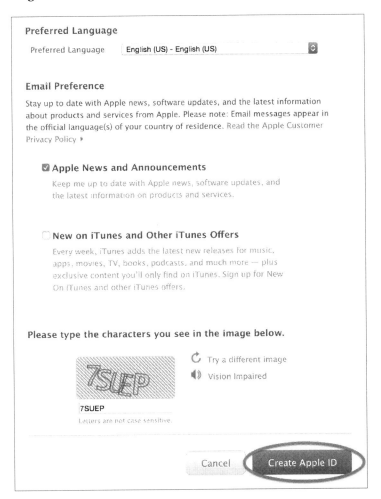

8. Finally, click on **Create Apple ID**, and you'll be prompted to verify your e-mail address. Apple will send an e-mail to the address you provided, and that e-mail will contain a verification link. Click on the link and you'll let Apple know that you can be reached at the provided address. You'll be prompted to log in again with the username and password that you just set up. The screen looks as follows:

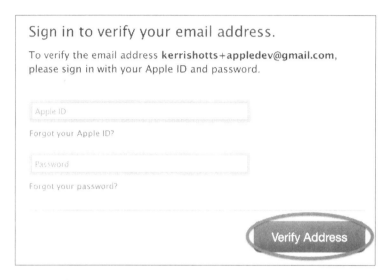

9. Once you click on **Verify Address**, you should see the following screenshot, indicating that the e-mail address was verified:

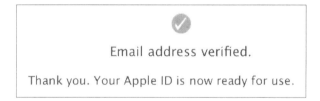

 You'll almost certainly want to enable two-factor authentication for your account in order to increase security, but that's beyond the scope of this chapter.

If you set up a rescue e-mail address, you'll also need to verify that address. The verification e-mail for rescue e-mail addresses is sent separately.

Now that you have an Apple ID, we can start the developer enrollment process. Go back to `https://developer.apple.com/programs/enroll/` and click on the **Start Your Enrollment** button, as follows:

Enrolling as an Individual

If you are an individual or sole proprietor/single person business, sign in with your Apple ID to get started. You'll need to provide basic personal information, including your legal name and address.

Enrolling as an Organization

If you're enrolling your organization, you'll need an Apple ID as well as the following to get started:

A D-U-N-S® Number

Your organization must have a D-U-N-S Number so that we can verify your organization's identity and legal entity status. These unique nine-digit numbers are assigned by Dun & Bradstreet and are widely used as standard business identifiers. You can check to see if your organization already has a D-U-N-S Number and request one if necessary. They are free in most jurisdictions. Learn more ›

Legal Entity Status

Your organization must be a legal entity to so that it can enter into contracts with Apple. We do not accept DBAs, Fictitious Businesses, Trade names, or branches.

Legal Binding Authority

As the person enrolling your organization in the Apple Developer Program, you must have the legal authority to bind your organization to legal agreements. You must be the organization's owner/founder, executive team member, senior project lead, or have legal authority granted to you by a senior employee.

Start Your Enrollment

Next, follow these steps to enroll in the developer program:

1. You'll be prompted to log in using the Apple ID you just created. Once this is done, you'll be prompted to review and agree to the **Apple Developer Agreement**, as you can see in the following screenshot:

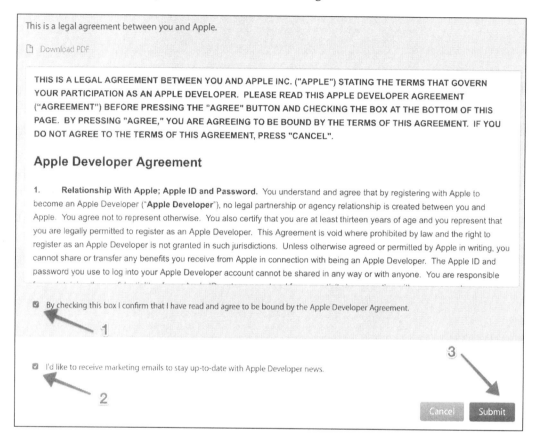

2. Check that you have read and that you agree to the terms (1). You should ideally check that you want to stay up to date with Apple Developer news as well (2), unless you have another developer account somewhere that already receives this information. Then, click on **Submit** and you'll be prompted to verify that the Apple ID you are using is the one you really want to use. You'll then be asked to choose whether you want to continue as an individual developer or a company, as follows:

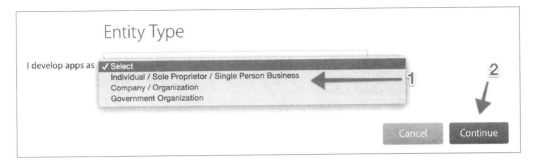

I proceeded as an individual, so if you register as a company, your steps will be different. Apple also verifies that you have the authority to participate in legal agreements, and so they will verify the information that you provide. This can take several days.

3. Once you click on **Continue**, you'll be asked for your contact information as well as your address. Note that your name is not editable, so your Apple ID must also use your legal name. The form should look as follows:

4. Scroll down a little, and then read and accept the presented agreement, as shown in the following screenshot. Then, click on **Continue**.

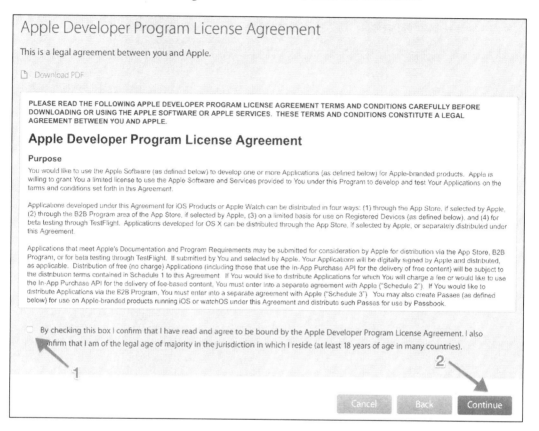

5. At this point, you'll be presented with a verification screen. Make sure the information you have provided is correct and then click on **Continue**.

6. You'll now be asked to complete the purchase, as shown in the next screenshot. If you want, you can have Apple automatically renew your agreement by checking the box indicated by (**1**). Either way, click on **Purchase** to continue.

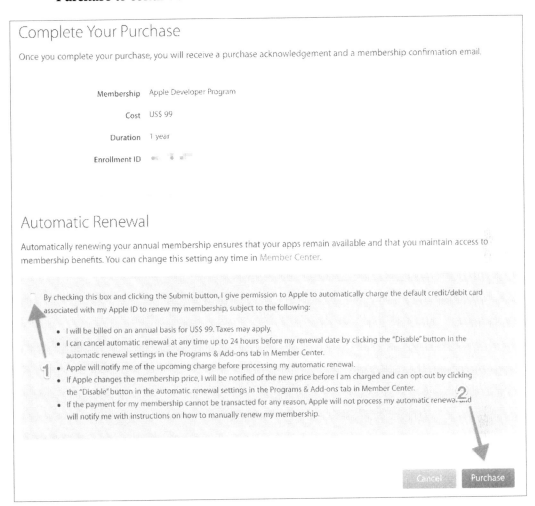

7. You'll be redirected to the Apple store, where you'll again be prompted for your username and password. Enter them and click on **Sign In**.

8. You should see an order screen similar to the following one. Enter your address, contact information, and credit card information, and then click on **Continue**.

9. At this point, you'll need to verify your information again, and then click on **Place Your Order**. You'll receive a confirmation message and e-mail as well.

Congratulations, you are now officially an Apple developer! Note that it may take up to twenty-four hours to process an individual's developer account, while a company account can take substantially longer depending upon how speedily the verification process is completed.

Becoming a Google Play Store developer

Google doesn't require that you be a Google Play market developer in order
to deploy your apps to your local devices, nor do they require it prior to you
distributing your app ad-hoc. However, if you want to be listed in the Google Play
market, you *do* need an account. You'll need a few things, all of which we'll set up in
this section:

- A Google account
- A Google Wallet account
- A Google merchant agreement

As with the Apple developer account, we suggest that you create a completely
separate identity for your app distribution purposes, such that if something ever
happens with the account, it doesn't affect your personal account.

1. Navigate to `https://play.google.com/apps/publish/`. You'll be
   prompted to sign in if you want to use an existing account. You can also
   create a new account by clicking on **Create Account**, as indicated by the
   following screenshot:

2. You'll be taken to a typical registration screen, where you'll be asked for your name, password, and other information. By default, Google assumes you'll also want a separate e-mail address. But if you click on **I prefer to use my current email address**, you can use your current e-mail address instead. The following screenshot shows an example of this:

3. Either way you proceed, you'll need to fill in your name, password, and the like, as shown in the following screenshot:

If you create a new e-mail account, Google will ask for an existing e-mail account as well. It's akin to Apple's rescue e-mail address.

4. Assuming you enter all the requested information and properly respond to the captcha, Google will respond with the following:

 You'll also receive an e-mail with the same information.

5. At this point, you can click on **Back to Google Play Developer Console** and you should see the following screen. Make sure you read the distribution agreement (**1**) and check **I agree…** (**2**) before clicking on **Continue to payment**.

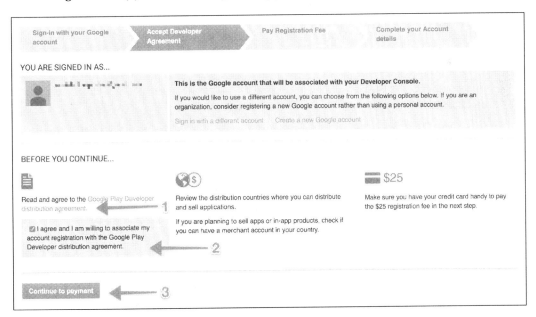

6. Google will now prompt you to set up your Google Wallet, as shown in the next screenshot. Enter your payment information, uncheck the second checkbox (**8**) (otherwise, you'll get special offers sent to your e-mail), and click on **Accept and continue**.

7. Google will display the cost, which is $25 USD at the time of this writing. Click on **Buy** to complete the transaction.

8. Google may ask you to update your billing information. Enter the same address and phone number used for your payment method. Then, click on **Buy**.

9. You should receive the following notice when your payment is processed; click on **Continue registration**:

10. You're almost there: the next step asks for your developer name, e-mail, website, and other contact information. This is the information your users will see, and it doesn't need to match the information already provided in your Google account setup. For example, you may wish to enter a company name instead of your personal name in the developer name field. (If you do, ensure you have the authority to do so.) Once entered, click on **Complete registration** as shown in the following screenshot:

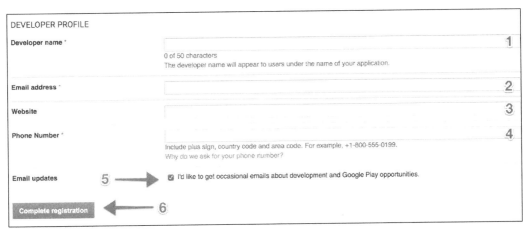

11. If your intent is only to offer apps for free, you're done at this point. But if you want to sell your apps or add in-app purchases, you need to set up a merchant account. Click on **set up a merchant account** as follows:

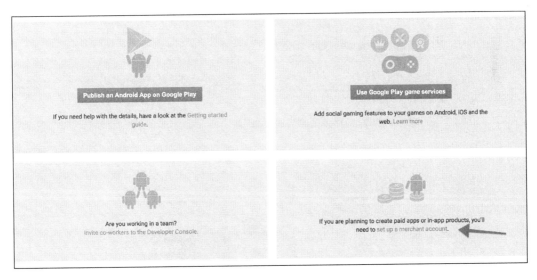

12. You'll be presented with yet another registration form. The top part is familiar by now. It asks for your name, address, and so on. Note that Google is now asking for your *legal business information*. Enter it and scroll down a little further.

13. When you scroll down, you should see something like the following screenshot. Here, you will provide customer-facing information, such as your website, what products you are selling (you should select **Computer Software** if you are selling apps), as well as what should appear on the end user's credit card statement (note that the credit card statement field is short; you may have to abbreviate). After reading the terms of service, click on **Submit**.

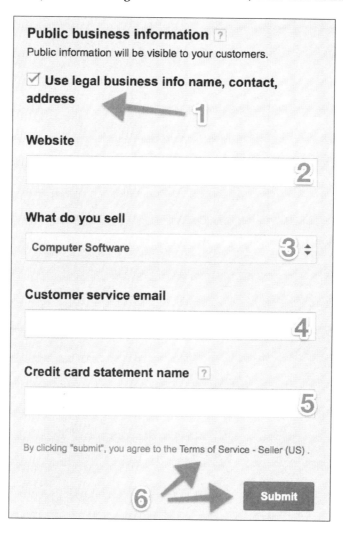

14. Assuming all goes well, Google should return the following, indicating that your merchant account has been approved:

> YOUR GOOGLE PAYMENTS MERCHANT ACCOUNT IS
> APPROVED.
>
> You can now sell applications in Google Play.
>
> Go to Developer Console.

Congratulations! At this point, you are a Google Play market developer and you can submit your apps to the store!

Generating signed release builds

If you've executed the app on an emulator or even on your device, chances are pretty good you've already generated a debug build; this is the default setting for the Cordova apps. To generate a release build, you have to explicitly request it. To generate a release build that is suitable for deployment, you also need to sign it. By signing the app, you will allow other devices to ensure that the app really did come from you and reduce the potential of others tampering with your app.

In this section, we'll cover how to create builds and sign them. Since the signing steps are different on each platform, we'll cover them in separate subsections.

Managing the iOS signing identities

In order to sign your code (for debug or release), you need a signing identity. On iOS (where all the builds are signed regardless of their debug status), you have at least two identities: a *development* identity and a *distribution* identity. These identities uniquely identify you as the developer. The development identity is only used for debug builds, while the distribution identity is used to deploy release builds.

On iOS, Xcode is typically used to manage your signing identities. If Xcode notices that something isn't correctly set up, it will usually correct it on its own. You do, however, need to let Xcode know your Apple ID account information so that it can properly manage your identities for you.

To do so, follow these instructions:

1. Launch Xcode.

2. Open the **Xcode** application menu, then click on **Preferences…**.

3. Click on the **Accounts** tab, as seen in the next screenshot:

4. Click on the **+** button in the lower left corner of the sheet. You should see a drop-down menu similar to the following:

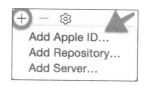

5. Click on **Apple ID…**. You should be presented with a dialog prompting you for your Apple ID login credentials:

6. Enter your account information and click on **Add**. Wait a moment while Xcode retrieves your information. You should then see the account added to the list on the left-hand side of the **Accounts** sheet.

7. Click on the newly added account. The account information should then be displayed on the right-hand side of the sheet. Click on **View Details…** located in the lower right corner of the sheet.

8. At this point, Xcode will display your installed signing identities, which may be empty. If this is the case, you can click on the refresh icon in the lower left corner of the dialog, which should prompt Xcode to ask you if it can create several certificates for you (these are your signing identities). Allow it to do so, and you should end up with a list that looks partially like this:

Signing Identities	Platform	Status
iOS Development	iOS	Valid
iOS Distribution	iOS	Valid

9. Click on the **Done** button to close the dialog. You can shut Xcode down at this point if you so choose, but you'll need it again in a few minutes, so you may want to leave it running for the time being.

It's possible Xcode won't pick up your signing identities automatically. If this is the case, click on the **+** button in the middle of the dialog and then click on **iOS Development** to add your development identity. Repeat these steps, but then select **iOS Distribution** to add your distribution identity. The following screenshot should help:

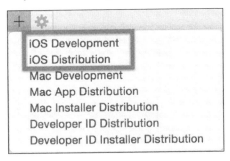

Managing iOS App IDs

Apple provides a wildcard application ID, but it is suggested that you create a specific ID for each app you intend to distribute. This is especially important if your app can receive push notifications or handle in-app purchases, since these are very granular settings and have to be targeted at a single app, not at a range of apps.

In order to create an iOS App ID, follow these steps:

1. Log in to the Developer member center (`https://developer.apple.com/membercenter`). You should see a link titled **Certificates, Identifiers & Profiles**. When you click on the link, you should see something similar to the following image:

2. Click on the **Identifiers** link as shown in the earlier screenshot, and you will probably see only one defined App ID: **Xcode: iOS Wildcard Apple ID**.

3. Above the list, there is a **+** button; click on it. You'll be taken to a form that looks like the following:

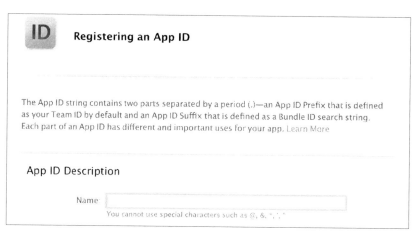

4. In the **App ID Description** field, enter the name of your app. This is only for your information, so it only needs to make sense to you.

5. If you scroll down, you should see an **App ID Suffix** section, as follows:

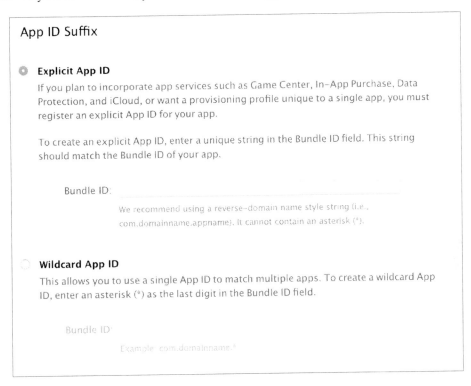

6. Enter the same value you used to create the Cordova app. This is in the `config.xml` file. If you're using the same build system we are using, it's present in the `package.json` file. For our demonstration app, I used `com.packtpub.logology`.

7. If you scroll down a little further, you should see a section titled **App Services**, as follows:

App Services

Select the services you would like to enable in your app. You can edit your choices after this App ID has been registered.

Enable Services:

- [ ] App Groups
- [ ] Associated Domains
- [ ] Data Protection
    - Complete Protection
    - Protected Unless Open
    - Protected Until First User Authentication
- [x] Game Center
- [ ] HealthKit
- [ ] HomeKit
- [ ] Wireless Accessory Configuration
- [ ] Apple Pay
- [ ] iCloud
    - Compatible with Xcode 5
    - Include CloudKit support (requires Xcode 6)
- [x] In-App Purchase
- [ ] Inter-App Audio
- [ ] Passbook
- [ ] Push Notifications
- [ ] VPN Configuration & Control

---

8. Make any selections you think you need. If your app uses push notifications, you'll want to enable this feature. If you aren't sure, you can always make changes later on, so don't get too hung up on this question. Note that **Game Center** and **In-App Purchase** are already checked. All the nonwildcard app IDs will have these features enabled. Should you want to use these features, you'll still need to add the appropriate code to your app.

9. Click on **Continue**. You'll be shown a confirmation screen. Click on **Submit**. Then, click on **Done** on the confirmation screen to return to the list of App IDs.

If you ever need to edit an existing App ID, click on the App ID in the list and then click on **Edit**. You may have to scroll down a little, since the feature information that appears after clicking a row may fill your screen. You can also delete existing App IDs using this same method. There's a **Delete** button on the form that will appear after you click on **Edit**.

An App ID by itself doesn't do a lot, but it's the key for the really important bit: your app's provisioning profile.

Managing iOS devices

In order to deploy your app on an ad-hoc or development basis, you need to let Apple know what devices the app should run on. Doing this is pretty simple, thankfully. But there *is* a limit on how many devices you can target in a year. This is to ensure that you don't try to avoid Apple's distribution channel. Unless you have a lot of devices or run a larger company, you'll probably not run over the limit.

Xcode is usually pretty good at automatically registering your attached devices when you first deploy an app to them. But you may want to register a device that you don't physically have access to, such as a remote team member's device.

To add a device, you first need to know the device's **UDID** (Universal Device Identifier). You can determine this by following these steps:

1. Attach your device to your computer.
2. Launch Xcode.
3. Open the **Window** menu and click on **Devices**.
4. You should see a screen that looks as follows:

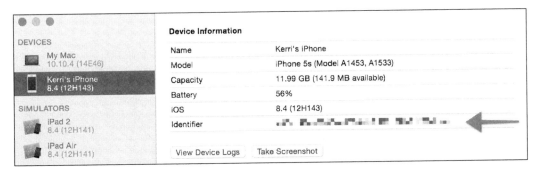

Now that you know the UDID, you can follow these steps to add the device to your developer account:

1. Log in to the Developer member center (`https://developer.apple.com/membercenter`). You should see a link titled **Certificates, Identifiers & Profiles**. Click on the link. If you're already logged in, skip to step 2.

2. Click on **Devices**.

3. In the upper right corner of the page, there is a + button. Click on it to add a new device.

4. Enter a name by which you can recognize the device in the **Name** field, and enter the UDID in the **UDID** field. Click on **Continue**.

5. You'll be prompted to review your information. If it is all correct, click on **Register**.

Managing the iOS provisioning profiles

Provisioning profiles are iOS's way of verifying that a device has permission to run your app. There are three kinds: development, ad-hoc, and app store distribution. Development is obvious: it's for debug or test builds. The latter two are for release builds—either for ad-hoc distribution or for eventual distribution by the app store. Your app can have any number of these profiles.

To create a provisioning profile, follow these steps:

1. Log in to the Developer member center (`https://developer.apple.com/membercenter`). You should see a link titled **Certificates, Identifiers & Profiles**. Click the on link. If you're already logged in, skip to step 2.

2. Click **Provisioning Profiles**.

3. You should see a rather short list of profiles; possibly none at all.

4. In the upper-right corner, there is a + button. Click on it to add a new profile.

5. You should see a form like the following:

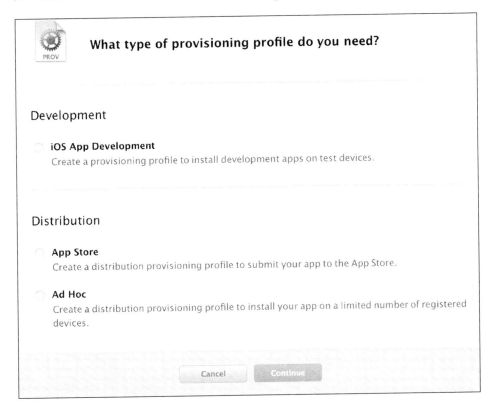

6. Select the choice you need. This will, of course, depend on what kind of build you're creating and how you intend on deploying it. If the build is for your own devices, select **iOS App Development**. If the build is going to be distributed outside of the app store on an ad-hoc basis (to a limited number of devices), select **Ad Hoc**. If the build is going to be submitted to the app store, select **App Store**. If you make a mistake in the choice, you can always remove the profile and create another one.

7. Click on **Continue**.

8. You'll now be asked which App ID you want to associate with this profile. Select the one you created in the prior section from the drop-down list and click on **Continue**.

9. Next, you'll be asked which certificates to include in the profile. These are the same thing as your signing identity you created earlier. Which ones are visible will depend on if you're creating a development or a distribution profile. Select the one you want to use, and click on **Continue**.

10. If you selected an ad-hoc or development profile, you'll be asked which devices you want to include. Select the devices that should be able to run the app, and then click on **Continue**. If you selected an App Store profile, skip to the next step.

11. Enter a name that you can use to identify this profile in the **Profile Name** field, as shown next. Then, click on **Generate**:

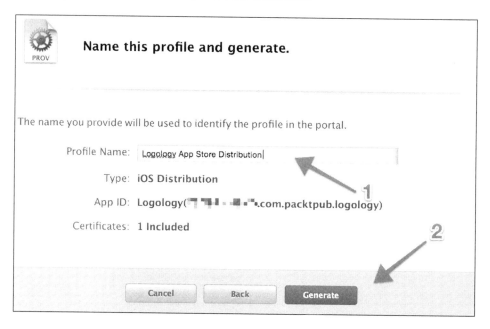

12. Once the profile has been generated, you'll see a message indicating that the profile is ready to be downloaded and installed. You can do this if you want, but we'll allow Xcode to manage them for us in the next step.

13. Return to Xcode (or open it if you've closed it). Navigate to **Xcode | Preferences**, and then select the **Accounts** tab sheet. Select your Apple ID on the left sidebar and then click on **View Details** in the lower right corner.

14. Click the refresh icon in the lower left corner of the resulting dialog and wait a moment. After a couple seconds, Xcode should add the new provisioning profile to the list in the bottom half of the dialog.

At this point, you can use this provisioning profile to sign your builds. There's one more thing that we'll need for future reference, however, and that's the provisioning profile's UUID. To get it, follow these steps:

1. In the bottom list where the provisioning profiles are listed, find the newly added profile.

2. Right-click on the profile. A menu should appear with **Show in Finder** as an option.

3. Click on **Show in Finder**. Finder should now open a folder with the provisioning profile identified.

4. Note the filename; the UUID of the provisioning profile is the name of the file minus any extension.

5. Repeat steps 1 to 4 for all the added provisioning profiles you need to build with.

6. Once you're finished, click on **Done** and exit the preferences pane.

Creating an Android keystore

While iOS manages signing identities for you, Android requires you to handle this aspect yourself. Android stores your signing identity (really, a private key) in what's called a **keystore** that is typically specific to your application.

> In this section, we assume that you're using the command line to build your app. If you use Android Studio, Eclipse, or any other IDE tasked with creating Android apps, they could handle this aspect for you (see the *Resources* section at the end of this chapter).

In order to create a private key, you can execute the following command at a command prompt, replacing `app_name` with the name of your app:

```
keytool -genkey -v -keystore .release.keystore -alias app_name -keyalg
RSA -keysize 2048 -validity 10000
```

> You must have Java installed on your development machine in order to use the `keytool` utility.
>
> The number after `validity` is expressed in days, and you should make sure this is for quite a number of them! In this case, the key is valid for just over 27 years.

The utility will now ask a series of questions, as follows:

```
Enter keystore password: (1)
Re-enter new password:
What is your first and last name? (2)
[Unknown]:  Johnny Appleseed
What is the name of your organizational unit? (3)
[Unknown]:  Department
What is the name of your organization? (4)
[Unknown]:  Company
What is the name of your City or Locality? (5)
[Unknown]:  Anytown
What is the name of your State or Province? (6)
[Unknown]:  CA
What is the two-letter country code for this unit? (7)
[Unknown]:  US
Is CN=Johnny Appleseed, OU=Department, O=Company, L=Anytown, ST=CA, C=US
correct? (8)
[no]:  yes


Generating 2,048 bit RSA key pair and self-signed certificate
(SHA256withRSA) with a validity of 10,000 days
for: CN=Johnny Appleseed, OU=Department, O=Company, L=Anytown, ST=CA,
C=US
Enter key password for <app_name> (9)
(RETURN if same as keystore password):
Re-enter new password:
[Storing .release.keystore]
```

Let's go over what you need to provide in each step:

1. **Keystore password**: This password protects your keystore itself. Technically, keystores can have many different private keys stored, although this probably won't be your case. Be sure to use a strong password; if an attacker has possession of your keystore and can guess the password, they are one step closer to compromising your users.

2. **First and last name**: Your first and last name. There's not really any checking done on this, so use whatever makes sense for your particular situation.

3. **Organization unit**: `keytool` assumes you're operating within an organizational hierarchy. If you're creating an app for a company, your organizational unit might be Information Technology or Application Development. You can leave it blank, but the utility will assume Unknown. So, you may as well come up with something that makes sense. If you're an individual developer, you could just specify Developer.

4. **Name of your organization**: If you're working for a company, this one is obvious. If you are an individual developer that has a registered company name, you could use the company's name. If not, just use your name again.

5. **Name of your City or Locality**: Your or your company's location.

6. **Name of your State or Province**: Your or your company's state or province.

7. **Two-letter country code**: Your or your company's country's two-letter identifier. See `https://en.wikipedia.org/wiki/ISO_3166-1_alpha-2` if you aren't sure what code you should use for your country.

8. **Is ... correct?**: Answer `yes` if the information displayed is correct. If you specify `no`, the utility will ask the questions again, allowing you to edit your answers.

9. **Key password for...**: Because a keystore could contain multiple private keys, you need to specify a password for this particular private key (or alias). You could use the same password that you used for the keystore with the understanding that if an attacker guesses the keystore password, they would then have access to your private key and could generate updates to your app for your end users. Better to use two separate strong passwords.

At this point, you should have a new file in your current directory named `.release.keystore`. Guard this file with your life; it contains the data necessary for signing your app (and delivering any future updates). If it were to be lost, you could lose the ability to generate updates to your app. If someone else were to gain access to it, they could issue updates to your app as if they were you; which is not a good thing.

Don't let this file go into any source code repository! Immediately tell Git (or whatever source code repository you use) to ignore the file.

For Git, we need to add the following to our `.gitignore` file:

```
.release.keystore
```

 Back up your keystore someplace secure. If you lose it, you won't be able to issue app updates!

Signing the release build

In *Chapter 1, Task Automation*, we covered how one can build a release build that includes minified code stripped of source maps. We also covered how to create such a build using our Gulp configuration:

```
gulp build --mode release [--for platform-list]
```

Doing this will create a release build, but it won't be ready for deployment. We need to make some more changes to our project structure and our Gulp configuration before we get a result that we can deploy.

First, regardless of whether or not you're using `gulp` or another build tool, you need to create a `build.json` file. This file includes information on signing your apps. It exists in the root directory of your project. The format looks as follows:

```json
{
    "android": {
      "release": {
        "keystore": "../.release.keystore",
        "alias": "app_name"
      }
    },
    "ios": {
      "debug": {
        "codeSignIdentity": "iPhone Developer",
        "provisioningProfile": "<UUID>"
      },
      "release": {
        "codeSignIdentity": "iPhone Distribution",
        "provisioningProfile": "<UUID>"
      }
    }
}
```

 Android doesn't require you to sign your debug builds. If you want to, you can add a `debug` section that duplicates your `release` section, except you'd want to create a debug keystore and use that instead.

Note that there is a section for iOS's provisioning profile UUIDs. If you recall from *Managing iOS Provisioning Profiles*, Xcode can show you what these UUIDs are. Follow the steps at the end of this section and you should be able to determine which UUIDs you want to use.

If you're using the Cordova CLI to build your apps, you can then build it using the following configuration:

```
cordova build [platforms] --release --device --buildConfig=build.json
```

If you're using `gulp` and our Gulp configuration, the following changes need to be made:

1. The `build.json` file needs to be copied to the `build` directory prior to actually executing the build steps. This can be done by adding the following to the `config.assets.copy` object in `gulp/config.js`:

```
var config = {
    ...
    assets: {
        copy: [
                {src: "../build.json", dest: "."},
                ...
        ], ...
    }, ...
}
```

2. The `buildCordova` function in `cordova-build.js` task needs to be modified so that it passes the `--device` and `--buildConfig` flags to Cordova:

```
function buildCordova() {
    var target = settings.TARGET_DEVICE;
    if (!target || target === "" ||
        target === "--target=device") {
        target = "--device";
    }
    return cordovaTasks.build({
        buildMode: settings.BUILD_MODE,
        platforms: settings.BUILD_PLATFORMS,
        options: [target, "--buildConfig=build.json"]});
}
```

Now you can build the project using the following command:

```
gulp build --mode release [--for platform-list]
```

Regardless of whether or not you use Cordova to build a release version or `gulp`, the release build should proceed in a similar fashion to your previous debug builds. There is one difference when you build an Android release: you'll be prompted twice for a password. The first time, you'll enter your keystore's password. The second time, you'll enter your alias password. Although you can specify the passwords in the `build.json` file, this is highly discouraged as it creates a security risk.

Now that you've built a release version, you can access the corresponding files at the following locations:

- **Android**: [build/]platforms/android/build/outputs/apk/android-release.apk.

- **iOS**: Cordova doesn't generate a format that can be readily distributed. You can use Xcode or you can use the following command-line steps (from your project root), replacing app_name with your app name:
    - ○ If you are using our project format: xcrun -sdkiphoneosPackageApplication "$(PWD)/build/platforms/ios/build/device/app_name.app" -o "$(PWD)/app_name.ipa".
    - ○ If you are using the Cordova CLI directly: xcrun -sdkiphoneosPackageApplication "$(PWD)/platforms/ios/build/device/app_name.app" -o "$(PWD)/app_name.ipa".
    - ○ Move the resulting .ipa file to the desired location.

 You'll probably want to automate the moving of .apk and .ipa files to a different location, such as a dist folder within your project. We leave this as an exercise to the reader, but it's not difficult to automate.

Deploying ad hoc releases

Deploying ad hoc releases is pretty simple, once you've generated a signed build. The resulting .apk and .ipa files are transmittable via e-mail or downloadable via a website, so it's not difficult to transfer them around. There are various tools that make deploying this way easy.

Deploying via e-mail

To deploy it using e-mail, follow these steps:

1. Create a new message in your e-mail application.

2. Attach the .apk or .ipa file to your e-mail. Be careful of sending/receiving limits. If your app is large, you might want to deploy it a different way.

3. Send it to the recipients.

Once a recipient receives the build, they can install it using the following steps:

- For Android, use the following steps:

    1. The user should remove any prior versions of the app, especially if they were downloaded from the Google Play market or any other store.

    2. Download the attachment.

    3. Tap it to open the attachment.

    4. Android will ask whether the user wishes to install the app, along with any permissions the app requires.

    5. The user should tap on **Install**.

    6. The app will install on their device.

    7. If an error occurs, the user should remove the app from their device before trying again.

- For iOS, use the following steps (iOS requires that the user have access to iTunes and can connect their device to their computer):

    1. A copy of these instructions is available at `https://developer.apple.com/library/ios/documentation/IDEs/Conceptual/AppDistributionGuide/TestingYouriOSApp/TestingYouriOSApp.html#//apple_ref/doc/uid/TP40012582-CH8-SW6`.

    2. The user should remove any prior versions of the app, especially if they were downloaded from the app store.

    3. Download `.ipa` on their computer.

    4. Connect their device to the computer.

    5. Double-click on the `.ipa` file.

    6. In iTunes, navigate to the **Device** tab (either in the sidebar or in the upper-left corner).

    7. Click on **Apps** in the sidebar. The new app should appear in the application list. If it isn't immediately visible, use the search field to locate it.

    8. Click on **Install** next to the new app. The text changes to **Will Install**.

    9. Click on **Sync** or **Apply**. The app will now be deployed to the device.

    10. If the app fails to deploy, delete the app from the device (if it is visible) before you try again.

Deploying via URL

If you have your app stored on a Dropbox account (or similar service), or have uploaded your build to a web server, you can share a link with your users instead. Android users can install the app directly, just as in the last section. iOS users will still need access to a machine with iTunes on it to plug in their device in order to install the build.

Deploying via Diawi

If you would rather avoid the messy installation steps for iOS, you can have users install your app from a special website: `http://www.diawi.com`. This website takes your `.ipa` file and returns a shortened link that you can send to all your users. They can install it by tapping on the link.

You can do this online without Diawi if you'd rather. Just follow the instructions at any of these sites:

- `http://3qilabs.com/how-to-ad-hoc-distribute-your-ios-app-via-a-website-and-ota/`
- `http://gknops.github.io/adHocGenerate/`
- `http://aaronparecki.com/articles/2011/01/21/1/how-to-distribute-your-ios-apps-over-the-air`

Deploying app store releases

Once your app has been tested, you're ready to deploy your app to the respective stores. Each store uses a different process, so we'll detail the steps separately per platform.

Deploying to the Apple App Store

Follow these steps to deploy your app to the Apple App Store:

1. Navigate to `https://itunesconnect.apple.com`.

2. Log in with your Apple ID.

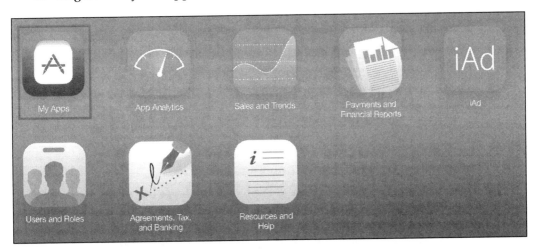

3. You should be greeted with a grid of various icons, as follows:

4. Click on **Apps**.

5. Click on the **+** button in the upper-left corner of the page. A drop-down menu will appear. Click on **New iOS App**.

6. A new form like the following appears:

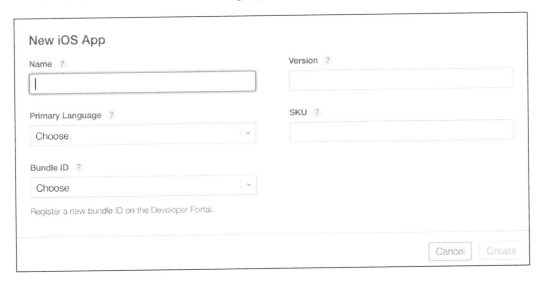

7. Supply the name of your app in the **Name** field. This is visible to your end users.

8. Select **Primary Language** for the app from the select list.

9. Select **Bundle ID** for your app from the select list. This will match the App ID you created in the *Managing App IDs* section.

10. Enter your app's version into the **Version** field. This should match the version in your app's `config.xml` and `package.json` files.

11. Select a unique ID for your app's **SKU**. This isn't visible to the end user and is only for your use.

12. Click on **Create**.

13. You'll be taken to a screen with several sections, including **Version Information**, **General App Information**, and so on.

14. There will be a large blank area at the top of the form below the field name **App Video Preview and Screenshots** followed by a selector that lists several screen sizes. This is where you supply your app's screenshots so that the end user can get a good feel for your app. At least one is required for all the devices your app supports, but you can have up to five screenshots per device form factor. We can't go over the creation of these screenshots here, but there are several links available in the *Resources* section.

15. Scroll down below the screenshots section. You should see a form requesting the name, description, and other information about your app. Your app's name should already be filled in.

16. Enter your app's description in the **Description** field. Whitespace is respected, so you can (and should) use paragraphs and spacing to make your description clear.

17. Enter some keywords into the **Keywords** field separated by commas. You can use up to 100 characters. Use the terms that you think your potential users will use while searching for your app.

18. Enter a valid URL into the **Support URL** field. This link is visible to your end user, and should provide them a means of getting support for the app.

19. If your app has a marketing web page, you can enter that URL into **Marketing URL**. This will visible be to the end users.

20. If your app or company has a privacy policy (and it should!) available on a website, enter that URL into the **Privacy Policy URL** field.

21. Scroll down to **General App Information**.

22. Click on **Choose File** below the **App Icon** field heading. Select the `iTunesArtwork@2x.png` file that you created in the last chapter. This icon is visible to the users browsing the app store.

23. Select a primary and secondary category for your app using the **Category** section. If your app only fits one category, you don't need to supply a secondary category. Make sure the categories apply to your app in some form or fashion, since this also assists users in finding your app.

24. Next to the **Rating** field, click on the **Edit** link. A form will appear that looks like the following:

Edit Rating

For each content description, select the level of frequency that best describes your app. To learn more about the content description, see the App Rating Detail page.

Apps must not contain any obscene, pornographic, offensive, or defamatory or materials of any kind (text, graphics, images, photographs, and so on), or other content or materials that in Apple's reasonable judgement may be found objectionable

Apple Content Description	None	Infrequent/Mild	Frequent/Intense
Cartoon or Fantasy Violence	○	○	○
Realistic Violence	○	○	○
Prolonged Graphic or Sadistic Realistic Violence	○	○	○
Profanity or Crude Humor	○	○	○
Mature/Suggestive Themes	○	○	○
Horror/Fear Themes	○	○	○
Medical/Treatment Information	○	○	○
Alcohol, Tobacco, or Drug Use or References	○	○	○
Simulated Gambling	○	○	○
Sexual Content or Nudity	○	○	○
Graphic Sexual Content and Nudity	○	○	○

	No	Yes
Unrestricted Web Access	○	○
Gambling and Contests	○	○

Cancel Done

---

25. Select the appropriate items for each category. Once you've made a selection for each row, Apple will display the final rating. If the app is eligible for the Made for Kids category, Apple will display it as an option, which you can check if the app is made for kids. When done, click on **Done**.

26. Enter your app's copyright information in the **Copyright** field.

27. Scroll down to the **App Review Information** section.

28. Enter your contact information in the provided fields. If the review team at Apple has any questions regarding your app, they will contact you with the information you provide. If you want Apple to contact another individual, enter their information instead.

29. If your app requires credentials in order to work, Apple will require a demo account. Enter the username and password in the **Username** and **Password** fields, respectively.

30. Enter any notes into the **Notes** area that you might think the app review team will need.

31. Scroll down to the **Version Release** section.

32. You can choose **Automatically release this version** when the app team accepts your submission, or you can choose **Manually release this version**. The latter allows you to have more fine-grained control over the app when it is released into the app store. If you're releasing an iOS and an Android app together, this can be useful. Or, if your marketing department has a specific date when the app should be available on their marketing material, you can wait until that date before you release the app into the wild.

33. Click on **Save** in the upper-right corner to save your changes.

34. Click on the **Pricing** link at the top of the web page.

35. Select your app's anticipated availability date. You don't have to be exact with this.

36. Select a price tier. If your app is free, select **Free**.

37. Choose whether or not an educational institution should get a discount by checking or unchecking the **Discount for Educational Institutions** field. This is checked by default.

38. Leave **Custom B2B app** unchecked, unless you are participating in that developer program and are delivering a B2B app.

39. Click on **Save**.

40. The page will reload and now give you the option to select the effective date the price takes effect, and (optionally) when it ends. This can be useful for temporary price reductions.

41. Click on **Save**.

42. To return to your app's listing, click on **Cancel**.

This takes care of the metadata for our app, but we will need to upload our app. You can do this using one of two methods: via Xcode or Application Loader. Application Loader works well when you already have an `.ipa` file, which is what we have. In order to submit it, use the following steps:

1. Open Application Loader on your Mac.

2. If prompted to agree to a license agreement, read it and agree to it.

3. Sign in with your Apple ID.

4. Click on the **Deliver Your App** button. Click on **Choose**.

5. You'll be prompted for the location of your `.ipa` file. Navigate to the location and click on **Open**.

6. Review the information on the screen at this point. It should list the title of the app, SKU, and version number, among other things.

7. Click on **Next**.

8. Application Loader will go to work. It will upload your app to Apple, validate that it isn't using any private APIs, and more.

9. When the process is complete, you'll see a nice big green checkmark. Click on **Next**.

10. Click on **Done** on the final screen that appears.

11. Wait a few moments and then refresh your app details in the browser. Scroll to the **Build** section. You should see the following image. If you don't, wait a few more moments and then refresh again.

> Click + to add a build before you submit your app.
>
> Submit your builds using Xcode 5.1.1 or later, or Application Loader 3.0 or later.

12. Click on the **+** button.

13. Select the newly uploaded build from the pop-up dialog and click on **Done**.

14. The build now appears below the **Build** heading.

15. Click on **Save**.

16. Review the app information. When it looks correct, click on **Submit for Review**.

17. Assuming there are no errors in your description, you will be taken to another screen, where you'll be asked a series of questions regarding the export compliance and legality of the app. Answer truthfully, or your app will be rejected (or pulled at a later date). Click on **Submit**.

18. Wait. App reviews typically take a week or more (a useful website to see typical review times is `http://appreviewtimes.com/`). Don't be discouraged if you get rejected the first time (or even the second). Address the issues indicated by the reviewer and then resubmit the app.

19. If you elected to release your app manually, your app will not be released into the app store automatically. Return to the app page in iTunes Connect, and then click on the **Release** button in the upper-right corner.

20. You're done! The hardest part, honestly, is creating the screenshots and the description text. If you aren't quite sure how to create the screenshots, take a look at it in the *Resources* section. We've got some links for you.

Deploying to the Google Play Store

To deploy an app to the Google Play market, follow these steps:

1. Navigate to `https://play.google.com/apps/publish/` in your browser.

2. Log in with your Google account.

3. Click on **Publish an Android App on Google Play**. You'll see a form that looks like the following:

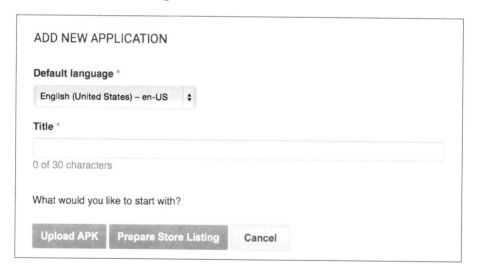

4. Choose your app's default language if necessary.

5. Enter your app's name into the **Title** field.

6. Click on **Prepare Store Listing**.

7. You'll be taken to a long form, where you can enter your app's information, upload screenshots, and so on. Your app's title should already be filled in.

8. Enter a short description into the **Short Description** text area. You only have eighty characters, so make it succinct and intriguing.

9. Enter your app's description into the **Full Description** text area. Whitespace and line breaks are respected, so use paragraphs and spacing to your advantage in order to make the description easy to read.

10. Scroll down to **Graphic Assets**.

11. Upload your app's screenshots. You need at least two, but you can supply up to eight for each category. Only supply screenshots for the form factors that your app supports. Unlike Apple, you do *not* need to submit screenshots for *every* form factor that your app supports.

12. Once you've uploaded your screenshots, scroll down and upload your app's icon. You created this in the prior chapter.

13. **Feature Graphic** is also required; these images are displayed on your app's listing page. **Promo Graphic** and **TV Banner** are optional, however.

14. Scroll down to **Categorization**.

15. Indicate whether your app is a game or an application by using the **Application type** select list.

16. Select the category your app belongs to from the **Category** select list.

17. Indicate a content rating using the **Content Rating** select list. You'll need to fill in a rating questionnaire before submission, but we'll come back to it shortly.

18. Scroll down to **Contact Details**.

19. Enter your website URL in the **Website** field if you have one.

20. Enter a publicly available e-mail address into the **Email** field. This will be visible to the users who use your app.

21. Scroll down to **Privacy Policy**.

22. If you have one, enter the URL into the **Privacy Policy** field.

23. If you don't have a privacy policy, check **Not submitting a privacy policy URL at this time**.

24. Scroll all the way to the top of the page and click on **Save Draft**.

25. Navigate to **Pricing & Distribution** in the left-hand sidebar.

26. Click on **Free** if your app is free. Click on **Paid** if your app is paid. Note that you cannot later change your app to paid once you release the app for free.

27. If your app is paid, enter the price in the **Default Price** field.

28. Click on **Auto-convert prices now** to make sure that your price is updated for all the regions in which your app will be available.

29. Scroll down to **Distribute in these countries**.

30. If you want to distribute everywhere, check **SELECT ALL COUNTRIES**.

You're now ready to upload a build to the app store. Use the following steps to upload your build to app store:

1. Click on **APK** on the left-hand side.

2. Click on **Upload your first APK to Production**.

3. Click on **Browse files** in the resulting dialog.

4. Select the .apk file that you have generated. It will need to be a signed release build. Once you choose the file, it will begin to upload to Google Play.

5. Once the upload is complete, the dialog will disappear and the APK information will appear. Note the **Draft in Prod** designation; the app isn't yet available.

Now that we have .apk uploaded, we can set the content rating using the following steps:

1. Click on **Content Rating** in the left-hand sidebar.

2. Click on **Continue**.

3. Enter your e-mail address in the **Email address** field.

4. Scroll down and select your app category.

5. Google will now ask questions related to the category. They are presented one section at a time; answer the questions in each section and the next section will appear.

6. When done, click on **Save Questionnaire**.

7. Click on **Calculate Rating**.

8. Your rating will appear. Scroll down and click on **Apply Rating**.

You're now ready to publish your app. Click on the **Publish App** button. You'll be asked to review the information and eligible devices. If everything looks right, publish the app. It will be available on the app store within a few hours.

If it is disabled, click on the **Why can't I publish** link to see what fields need to be entered.

Resources

The following links can be useful while dealing with creating signed builds:

- Android-specific signing:
  - Signing with Android Studio: `http://developer.android.com/tools/publishing/app-signing.html`
  - Signing with Eclipse: `https://developer.android.com/tools/publishing/app-signing-eclipse.html`

- Beta-testing websites:
  - TestFlight (Apple, iOS only): `https://developer.apple.com/testflight/index.html`
  - Google beta testing (Google, Android only): `https://support.google.com/googleplay/android-developer/answer/3131213?hl=en`
  - Hockey App (Microsoft Windows, iOS/Android): `http://hockeyapp.net/features/`

- Creating the App Store screenshots:
  - `http://www.raywenderlich.com/71175/make-great-app-store-screenshots`
  - `https://launchkit.io/screenshots`
  - `http://sketchtoappstore.com`
  - `http://www.smashingmagazine.com/2015/03/create-effective-app-screenshots-for-app-page/`
  - `https://support.google.com/googleplay/android-developer/answer/1078870?hl=en`
  - `http://blog.placeit.net/make-google-play-screenshots/`

Summary

Congratulations! In this chapter, we covered a lot of information, from creating your developer accounts to signing your app for release and submitting it to the various app stores. Hopefully, your app will now be enjoyed by your users, and you'll get great reviews.

You've also completed the final chapter in this book, but this doesn't that mean your work as a developer is over. Your users might find a few bugs in your app that demand fixes or you might want to add new features. Either way, you'll likely be releasing new versions of your app to the store. Along the way, you'll be growing as a hybrid app developer.

There's always the chance you'll need some assistance. I suggest the following resources if you ever get stuck. There are a lot of great volunteers who are happy to help if they can:

- Stack Overflow: `http://stackoverflow.com/tags/cordova`
- The PhoneGap/Cordova CLI Google group: `http://groups.google.com/group/phonegap`
- The PhoneGap Build community: `http://community.phonegap.com/nitobi`
- Cordova's Slack community: `http://slack.cordova.io/`

Index

Symbols

:active state 278
:focus state 278
:hover state 278

A

accessibility
  about 119
  for free 124-126
  reference link 120
Accessibility DevTools for Chrome
  reference link 142
accessibility examples
  about 131
  accessible alerts 136, 137
  accessible dialog 136, 137
  accessible icon buttons 132, 133
  accessible lists 135, 136
  accessible navigation 133, 134
  separation of presentation and content 131
accessibility features
  about 120
  auditory disabilities 123
  blindness 122
  color vision deficient 120, 121
  Dyslexia 123
  low vision 121, 122
  motor disabilities 123
  seizures 124
Accessible Rich Internet Applications 126
addPlatforms 28
ad-hoc distribution method 313
ad hoc releases
  deploying 348

deploying, via Diawi 350
deploying, via e-mail 348, 349
deploying, via URL 350
Adobe Photoshop 290
Affinity
  URL 308
Android
  app, profiling 270, 271
Android app icon template
  URL 309
Android keystore
  creating 343-345
Android-specific signing
  references 359
Ape Tools
  URL 309
app
  configuring 304-308
  exploring, with Appium 163-177
  profiling 269
  profiling, caveats 276
  profiling, on Android 270, 271
  profiling, on iOS 271-275
app directory structure
  root directory 5
  setting up 5-9
  src/, root directory 5
app icon
  creating 292-297
  requisites 290-292
Appium
  app, exploring with 163-177
  installing 161, 162
  reference link, for desktop application 162
  used, for running UI Automation
    tests 182, 183

Apple Developer member center
  reference link 336, 340
Apple iOS developer 315-321
Apple iOS developer program
  enrolling in 322-326
app store distribution method 314
app store releases
  deploying 350
  deploying, to Apple App Store 350-356
  deploying, to Google Play Store 356-358
App Store screenshots
  references, for creating 359
arrow functions 44-46
aspect-ratio filters 102
assertions 144, 145
automated testing 144
Autoprefixer
  reference link 112
await, ES2015
  reference link 59

B

Babel
  URL 32
babel-eslint utility 12
beta-tester distribution method 313
beta-testing websites
  references 359
block scope 43, 44
Broccoli
  URL 5
Browserify
  URL 65
  using 65
buggyfill
  reference link 100
build 28
build artifacts 7
build modes
  about 311
  debug 311
  release 311
builds, distribution methods
  ad-hoc 313
  app store 314
  beta-tester 313

enterprise 314

C

Cake
  URL 5
cdProject / cdUp 28
Chai
  reference link 150
  used, for writing tests 146-150
chai-as-promised plugin
  reference link 147
Chrome
  URL 270
classes 60-63
Cloud9
  reference link 251
code
  linting 35-37
  uglifying 37
collections
  testing 153, 154
Cordova-IndexedDB
  about 189
  URL 189
Cordova-Plugin-IndexedDB
  about 189
  URL 189
Cordova SQLite plugin
  about 215
  reference link 215
Cordova tasks
  executing 24-31
CorelDRAW
  URL 308
CSS 71
CSS3 units 97-100
cursors
  using 208-211

D

data
  deleting 236
  inserting 227-231
  querying 231-235
database
  closing 211

creating 193-218
   object store, creating within 197-200
   opening 215-218
database upgrades
   handling 200-202
DB Browser for SQLite
   reference link 237
debug build 311, 312
default arguments 49
desktop browser, performance differences
   about 261
   battery life 262
   browser impacts 263
   consumption 262
   lag 264-266
   memory 263
   power availability 262
   storage 263
destructuring 51-53
developer accounts
   Apple iOS developer 315-321
   Google Play Store developer 327-333
   signing up 314
device-pixel-ratio filters 103
Diawi
   ad hoc releases, deploying via 350
   references 350
Draw 9-patch
   URL 309
DrawPlus
   URL 308
Dyslexia 123

E

Electron
   URL 7
e-mail
   ad hoc releases, deploying via 348, 349
emulator
   performance differences 266-268
enterprise distribution method 314
equality
   testing 152, 153
ES2015
   about 32
   references 64

using 32-35
ES2015, benefits
   about 42
   block scope 43, 44
   classes 60-63
   default arguments 49
   destructuring 51-53
   fat arrow functions 44-46
   modules 63, 64
   named parameters 51-53
   promises 56-59
   simpler object definitions 47, 48
   string interpolation 54, 55
   variable arguments 49, 50
ESLint
   URL 35
Event.js
   URL 277

F

FastClick library
   URL 277
files
   downloading, from server 242-246
   receiving, PHP on server used 247-251
   uploading, to server 252, 253
fill area 303
flex-box layout
   about 111-118
   reference link 111

G

Google beta testing
   reference link 359
Google Play Store
   app store releases, deploying to 356-358
Google Play Store developer 327-333
graphic design applications 289
Grunt
   URL 5
Gulp
   about 4
   for task automation 4
   installing 10, 11
   tests, integrating with 184-186
   URL 4

gulp-babel utility 11
gulp-bump utility 11
gulp-concat utility 11
Gulp configuration
  modifying, for using Browserify 66-68
Gulp configuration file
  creating 12, 13
gulp-eslint utility 12
gulp-jscs utility 12
gulp-notify utility 12
gulp-rename utility 12
gulp-replace-task utility 12
gulp-sourcemaps utility 12
gulp-uglify utility 12
gulp-util utility 12

H

Hammer.js
  URL 277
height filters 102
Hockey App
  reference link 359
HTML 93
HTML 2.0 124
HTML 4.0 124

I

Icon Generator
  URL 309
image sizing 104-111
IndexedDB
  about 188
  mobile browser support 188
  references 211
IndexedDBShim
  about 189
  URL 189
indexes
  using 208-211
Infinity
  URL 280
init 28
Inkscape
  URL 308
input lag
  correcting 276-278

installation, Appium 161, 162
install base, Android version
  reference link 100
Interact
  URL 277
iOS
  app, profiling 271-275
  reference link 100
iOS app icon template
  URL 309
iOS App IDs
  managing 335-339
iOS devices
  managing 339, 340
iOS grid icon
  URL 309
iOS provisioning profiles
  managing 340-342
iOS signing identities
  managing 333-335
iScroll
  URL 280

J

JavaScript Code Style checker
  reference 35
JavaScript memory profiling
  URL 285
jsdom
  reference link 160

K

key-object storage
  versus relational storage 189-193
keystore 343

L

lag 264
language chains 151
launch screen
  creating 302-304
  requisites 298-302
lint tasks 35
logical words 151

Logology
about 3
features 3, 4
long computations
delegating 285-287
splitting up 285-287
Long Shadow Action
URL 309

M

MakeAppIcon
URL 309
media queries
about 101-103
reference link 103
memory management
URL 285
memory problems
correcting 282-284
reference links 285
merge-stream utility 12
Mobile Accessibility Plugin
installing 139
URL 139
Mocha
URL 154
used, for running test suites 154-160
used, for running UI Automation
tests 182, 183
modules 63, 64

N

named parameters 51-53
native accessibility features
about 138, 139
custom text, speaking 141
screen reader, detecting 140, 141
user's preferred text size, detecting 140
Navicat for SQLite (commercial)
reference link 237
Nine-patch editor
URL 309
Node.js
including, for using Browserify 68, 69

O

objects
deleting 207, 208
retrieving 206, 207
storing 204, 206
object store
creating, within database 197-200
OpenDyslexic
reference link 123
orientation filters 102

P

performance
about 259
computing performance 260
defining 260
frames per second 260
graphical performance 260
input performance 260
memory utilization 260
reference links 282
storage performance 260
storage utilization 260
testing 259
performance differences
between desktop browsers and
emulators 261
between desktop browsers and physical
devices 261
PHP on server
used, for receiving files 247-251
pixel densities 94-97
polyfills 188
progress
monitoring 254, 255
promises
about 56
reference link 58

R

RazorSQL (commercial)
reference link 237
relational storage
versus key-object storage 189-193

release build
  about 311, 312
  signing 346-348
remote debugging
  URL 260
resolution filters 103
rimraf utility 12
Root EM units
  reference link 100

S

Sass
  about 71
  calculation 73-75
  comments 73
  functions 84-86
  integrating, with Gulp 88-90
  learning 72
  mixins 84, 85
  modules 87
  nesting 82, 83
  object-oriented CSS 86
  partials 87
  stylesheets, installed via npm 90
  URL 71
  URL, for documentation 72
  variables 76-82
scale area 303
security
  concerns 257
seizures 124
server
  files, downloading from 242-246
  files, uploading to 252, 253
signed build 312, 313
signed release builds
  generating 333
simple nine-patch generator
  URL 309
simpler object definitions 47, 48
Sketch
  URL 308
Slack 294
SQLite
  reference link 221

SQLite Studio (free)
  reference link 237
SQLite utilities 236
SQL (Structured Query Language) 213
string interpolation 54, 55
Stripe Dashboard 295
substitutions
  performing 18-24
Syntactically Awesome Style
    Sheets. *See* Sass

T

tables
  creating 221-227
tap.js
  URL 277
task automation 1
test cases
  creating 177-182
TestFlight
  reference link 359
tests
  integrating, with Gulp 184-186
  writing, Chai used 146-150
test suites
  running, Mocha used 154-160
transactions 203-221
transfers
  aborting 256
Treo
  about 189
  URL 189
Tweetbot icon 294

U

UDID (Universal Device Identifier) 339
UI automation tests
  running, Appium used 182, 183
  running, Mocha used 182, 183
  writing 160, 161
uniqid
  about 251
  reference link 251
up-to-date browser support, IndexedDB
  reference link 188

V

Valentina Studio (free)
  reference link 237
values
  binding 227-231
variable arguments 49
variable existence
  testing 152
variable types
  testing 152
version numbers
  managing 31
viewport units
  reference link 100
  vh 98
  vmax 98
  vmin 98
  vw 98
visual stutters
  correcting 279
  frames-per-second beast, taming 280-282

W

WAI-ARIA
  about 126
  attributes 127
  references 128
  roles 127-131
watchdog 299

WCAG
  reference link 125
Web Accessibility Initiative 126
Web SQL Database
  about 214, 215
  reference link 214
Web Workers
  references 286
whitelist
  configuring 240, 241
  reference link 241
width filters 102
WordNet
  reference link 198

X

XPath
  references 177

Z

Zepto
  URL 277